Space-Time Colonialism

CRITICAL INDIGENEITIES

J. Kēhaulani Kauanui and Jean M. O'Brien, *series editors*

Series Advisory Board
Chris Andersen, University of Alberta
Irene Watson, University of South Australia
Emil' Keme, University of North Carolina at Chapel Hill
Kim TallBear, University of Alberta

Critical Indigeneities publishes pathbreaking scholarly books that center Indigeneity as a category of critical analysis, understand Indigenous sovereignty as ongoing and historically grounded, and attend to diverse forms of Indigenous cultural and political agency and expression. The series builds on the conceptual rigor, methodological innovation, and deep relevance that characterize the best work in the growing field of critical Indigenous studies.

JULIANA HU PEGUES

Space-Time Colonialism
Alaska's Indigenous and Asian Entanglements

The University of North Carolina Press *Chapel Hill*

© 2021 The University of North Carolina Press
All rights reserved
Set in Arno Pro by Westchester Publishing Services
Manufactured in the United States of America

The University of North Carolina Press has been a member of the Green Press Initiative since 2003.

Library of Congress Cataloging-in-Publication Data
Names: Pegues, Juliana, author.
Title: Space-time colonialism : Alaska's indigenous and Asian entanglements / Juliana Hu Pegues.
Other titles: Critical indigeneities.
Description: Chapel Hill : University of North Carolina Press, [2021] | Series: Critical indigeneities | Includes bibliographical references and index.
Identifiers: LCCN 2020051377 | ISBN 9781469656175 (cloth) | ISBN 9781469656182 (paperback) | ISBN 9781469656199 (ebook)
Subjects: LCSH: Alaska Natives—History. | Asians—Alaska—History. | Immigrants—Alaska—History. | Alaska—Colonization.
Classification: LCC E78.A3 P45 2021 | DDC 305.897/0798—dc23
LC record available at https://lccn.loc.gov/2020051377

Cover image: Crystal Worl, *Salmon Regeneration* 2020. Used by permission of the artist.

Portions of this book were previously published in a different form. Part of chapter 1 was published as "Settler Orientalism," *Verge: Studies in Global Asias* 5, no. 1 (Spring 2019): 12–17; part of chapter 4 was published as "'Picture Man': Shoki Kayamori and the Photography of Colonial Encounter in Alaska, 1912–1941," *College Literature: A Journal of Critical Literary Studies* 41, no. 3 (Winter 2014): 90–118; part of chapter 3 was published as "Rethinking Relations: Interracial Intimacies of Asian Men and Native Women in Alaskan Canneries," *Interventions: International Journal of Postcolonial Studies* 15, no. 1 (March 2013): 55–66.

In chapter 1, an excerpt from the poem, "(dis)Orient" by James Thomas Stevens, originally published in *A Bridge Dead in the Water*, is reproduced with permission of Salt Publishing through PLSclear and of the author.

In chapter 3, several excerpts are reproduced. Lyrics from the song "North by Northwest," by the Blue Scholars, from the album *Bayani* (MassLine Media/Rawkus 2007), are used with permission of George Quibuyen. An excerpt of the poem "Talking with Nora," by Ishmael Hope, originally published in *Courtesans of Flounder Hill*, is reprinted by permission of the author. Excerpts of "A Poem for Jim Nagatáak'w (Jakwteen)" and "Salmon Egg Puller—$2.15 an Hour," by Nora Marks Dauenhauer, from the book *Life Woven with Song*, are reprinted with permission from the University of Arizona Press.

for Sông

Contents

Acknowledgments xi

A Note on Terminology xv

Introduction 1

CHAPTER ONE
Settler Orientalism: The Asian Racialization of Alaska Natives 19

CHAPTER TWO
Fictions of the Last Frontier: Alaska's Gold Rush and the Legend of China Joe 50

CHAPTER THREE
Unbecoming Workers: Asian Men and Native Women in Alaska's Canneries 83

CHAPTER FOUR
Picture Man: Photographer Shoki Kayamori and Settler Militarism 118

Epilogue 155

Notes 161

Bibliography 185

Index 205

Figures and Map

FIGURES

2.1 China Joe 56
4.1 Yakutat, Alaska 119
4.2 Lon Wun Gee's café 126
4.3 Mary Thomas 127
4.4 Jack and Emma Ellis 130
4.5 Tooth-brushing lesson 133
4.6 Dance at Billy Jackson's house 136
4.7 Shoki Kayamori 153

MAP

1.1 Indigenous peoples and languages of Alaska 4

Acknowledgments

First and foremost, I would like to express my gratitude and obligation from growing up on Tlingit lands, researching and working for many years in Dakota homelands, and shifting to life and work on the lands of the Gayogo̱hó:nǫ' (Cayuga Nation). I'm excited to join new colleagues in the Department of English at Cornell University and to build with the American Indian and Indigenous Studies Program and the Asian American Studies Program.

At the University of Minnesota, I was incredibly pleased to count my first academic mentors among my colleagues. Thank you to Erika Lee, Jigna Desai, Jean O'Brien, David Chang, Yuichiro Onishi, and Kale Fajardo for your guidance over the many years. I am honored to have worked with such a generous and thoughtful group of scholars. I enjoyed an abundance of intellectual exchange through my home department of American Indian Studies, a joint appointment in the Program in Asian American Studies, and through my hire in the Race, Indigeneity, Gender, and Sexuality Studies (RIGS) Initiative. Thank you to Karen Ho, Kat Hayes, Catherine Squires, Teresa Swartz, Josephine Lee, Elliott Powell, and Kevin Murphy for your leadership and support. I also benefited from the rich interdisciplinary dialogue as a participant in the University of Minnesota's American Indian and Indigenous Studies Workshop, the Historical Injustices Reading Group, the Black Marxism Reading Group, the Bodies and Borders Research Cluster, and the Mellon Sawyer Seminar on the Politics of Land: Colony, Property, Ecology. My work was also critically supported at the University of Minnesota through a faculty fellowship at the Institute for Advanced Study and a single-semester leave from the College of Liberal Arts.

I had the good fortune of working for two excellent colleges prior to the University of Minnesota. Thank you to Jane Rhodes, Duchess Harris, Karín Aguilar-San Juan, SooJin Pate, and the Department of American Studies at Macalester College for giving me a tremendous start early in my academic career (with thanks also to the Consortium for Faculty Diversity for making my postdoctoral fellowship possible). At Smith College, my colleagues in the Department of English and the Program for the Study of Women and Gender welcomed me into a robust academic community, alongside the Five College Asian/Pacific/American Studies Program and the Five College Native

American and Indigenous Studies Program. Ambreen Hai, Kevin Rozario, Floyd Cheung, Sheri Cheung, Lisa Armstrong, Vijay Prashad, Jennifer Declue, Jennifer Guglielmo, Cornelia Pearsall, Naomi Miller, Michael Thurston, Ruth Ozeki, and David Hernández, you made me feel at home in Northampton with your warmth and generosity.

My work is strengthened because of the many scholars who engaged my project in workshops, at conferences, in conversations, and through correspondence. Thank you to Charlotte Karem Albrecht, Anjali Arondekar, Rachel Buff, Myla Vicenti Carpio, Jaskiran Dhillon, Michael Dockry, Laura Sachiko Fugikawa, Cindy Garcia, Douglas Ishii, Moon-Ho Jung, Moon-Kie Jung, Jodi Kim, Rosamond King, Paul Lai, Quynh Nhu Le, Hsiu-chuan Lee, Karen Leong, Janey Lew, Nancy Luxon, Kara Lynch, Samantha Majhor, Jodi Melamed, Scott Morgensen, Robert Nichols, Johanna Ogden, David Palumbo-Liu, Shiri Pasternak, Quynh Pham, Isabela Quintana, Mark Rifkin, Dylan Rodriguez, Shireen Roshanravan, Jennifer Row, Dean Saranillio, Sima Shakhsari, Sandra Soto, Heidi Kiiwetinepinesiik Stark, Omise'eke Natasha Tinsley, Antonio Tiongson, Anna Tsing, and Hui Niu Wilcox. That this list is long reflects the generosity of spirit from these scholars and the vibrant intellectual worlds of my three favorite academic organizations: the American Studies Association, the Association for Asian American Studies, and the Native American and Indigenous Studies Association. I'm especially thankful to scholars in the field of Alaska Native studies for their generative work and discussion: Jessica Leslie Arnett, Mique'l Icesis Dangeli, Zachary Jones, Liza Mack, Caskey Russell, Jen Rose Smith, Thomas Michael Swensen, Amy Ahnaughuq Topkok, Sean Asiqłuq Topkok, and Eve Tuck.

Thank you to Alyosha Goldstein and Manu Karuka for thinking alongside over the years, collaborating intellectually and politically, with integrity. I am immensely grateful to Iyko Day, for her deep and sustained engagement with my work through many iterations.

My research would not have been possible without the generous assistance of several institutions and individuals. The Sealaska Heritage Institute was instrumental to my research, through the William L. Paul Sr. Archives and beyond. Rosita K̲aaháni Worl, Chuck Smythe, and Emily Pastore at SHI were incredibly helpful. The archival support I received at the Alaska State Library was outstanding; hearty thanks to James Simard, Anastasia Tarmann, Freya Anderson, and the rest of the staff at the ASL. The gracious hospitality I received from Yakutat residents made researching Shoki Kayamori an absolute pleasure. Thank you to Don Bremner, George Ramos, Lorraine Adams, Bert Adams Sr., Raymond Sensmeier, Caroline Powell, Fran Latham, and Byron Mallott for their time and knowledge. My work on Shoki Kayamori was additionally strengthened by the extensive research of Margaret Thomas and Morgan Howard, particularly Margaret Thomas's donation of research documents to the Alaska State Library's Kayamori Collection. I wish to recognize and thank Edward Kunz Jr. for his time in talking to me about his mother's and his own life and experiences.

I could not have asked for better editors. My series editor Kēhaulani Kauanui has encouraged me and supported this book from the beginning and throughout. My book editor Mark Simpson-Vos has always advocated a balance of theory and story, keeping me on task in the best ways. I am honored to have the phenomenal artwork of Crystal Worl grace the book's cover, and thank you, Christy NaMee Eriksen, for helping me brainstorm the book's title, a concept that further influenced my thinking and framework.

I have been blessed by friends who have offered me their astute insights as well as a much-needed reprieve from the demands of the academy. Thank you to Bao Phi, Jasmine Kar Tang, Darren Lee, Nicola Pine, Susan Svatek, Shannon Gibney, Ricardo Levins Morales, David Mura, Emmanuel Ortiz, Erica Lee, Elisa Lee, and Eunha Jeong Wood. I am always thankful for my artistic and political communities that remind me to put my scholarship into conversation with larger social forces.

The Pegues/Hu family has supported me during long stretches of research and writing, making a home for me in Alaska. Thank you to my sister Joanne Pegues, my brother and sister-in-law, Tom and Jennifer Pegues, and my nephews Jack, Morgan, and Rylan. Thank you to the extended Pegues family for raising me to appreciate good storytelling. Two family members who have passed on deserve special mention: my uncle Bob Pegues, who shared with me his research on the Superior Cannery and Southeast Alaska, and my aunt June Aan Yax Saxeex Pegues, for her important work in Lingít language revival. Thank you to my mom, Josephine Min-Hwa Pegues, for encouraging an Asian American feminism from my youngest days, and thank you to my dad, Dick Pegues, for instilling in me his great love for Alaska. Though my father passed before I started research on this book, he is everywhere in the pages.

My greatest gratitude is for my partner and my child. To Jodi Byrd: how lucky I am to have fallen in love with you, brilliant one. Thank you for being my mountain, my ocean, my shore. To Sông Phi-Hu: you bring me the greatest joy and make me believe in messy, radiant futures.

A Note on Terminology

One of the challenging aspects of interdisciplinary work is striving to attain consistency while also respecting the intellectual autonomy and political genealogies of different peoples, communities, and academic fields. This is particularly true of my dual engagement with Native and Indigenous studies and Asian American studies. For example, I often identify Indigenous scholars by tribal affiliation, which is customary within the field of Native and Indigenous studies and stresses Native presence and expertise. I do not, however, provide ethnic identification of Asian American scholars, as such a move would erroneously conflate ethnicity and nationality and participate in the colonially overdetermined foreignness I frame as settler space. Tribal affiliation of Indigenous scholars is, on the other hand, a national identification, one that undermines U.S. settler claims to sovereignty.

For persons of Asian descent, I use both the terms "Asian American" and "Asian," the former usually when I am speaking within a larger national context, and the latter to signal that citizenship is denied to first-generation Asians in the United States and to underscore the political imperative to not assume that Alaska is unquestioningly subsumed within the United States.[1] When I use terms such as "Oriental," "Asiatic," and "Mongol(ian)," I am referring to the imperial and scientific racial discourse of the nineteenth and early twentieth centuries. I do not hyphenate "Asian American," even when this term is used as an adjective, drawing from Asian American movement history that argues against a hyphenated term as indicative of Asian American marginalization within U.S. society.

I use the term "Alaska Native," as that is the most common usage among Indigenous peoples to collectively describe the original inhabitants of the land presently known as Alaska. Alaska Native is used as both noun and adjective and is not hyphenated. I also use the terms "Native" and "Indigenous" to refer to Alaska Natives and additional first and original peoples outside of Alaska. When referring to specific Alaska Native peoples, I have tried my best to utilize ethnonyms that people use to identify themselves. For example, I do not use the word "Eskimo," which is pejorative and derived from outside the culture; instead I use "Yup'ik" (plural Yupiit when referring to people) and "Iñupiaq" (plural Iñupiat). I sometimes use Indigenous self-identification even when other terms are more commonly used, in order to highlight language and cultural revitalization but also to limit confusion due to colonial historical usage. Such is the case with the Unangax̂ people and the Sugpiat people (singular Sugpiaq) as the respective identities of "Aleut" and "Alutiit" both stem from the misidentification/conflation of the two peoples by Russian colonists. Because the plural form of Unangax̂ changes depending on regional dialect (Unangas or Unangan), I choose to keep the singular form to speak of the Unangax̂ people collectively.[2]

My use of Indigenous languages extends to other forms of self-identification, such as clan or village, and additional cultural terms and concepts. Words in Tlingit are spelled using the Revised Popular Tlingit orthography; the exception is the word "Tlingit" (not Lingít), because of its common usage and acceptance among Tlingit authors and organizations.[3] When inconsistencies in Tlingit terms arise, I have consulted the living dictionary project created by Goldbelt Heritage Foundation and the University of Alaska Southeast and edited by Indigenous language scholar X̱'unei Lance Twitchell.[4] Some variation still remains, especially concerning diacritics, which reflects diverse source material. On the subject of original sources, I apologize in advance for the racist and sexist discourse employed by various colonial authors in historical texts. Though I believe it is important to document such language as a structuring technology of imperial and colonial conquest, I acknowledge the inherent and to-this-day violence of such rhetoric.

I do not italicize any non-English terms in this book, taking my cue from Kanaka Maoli (Hawaiian) scholar Noenoe K. Silva, who intentionally does not italicize Hawaiian words, "to resist making the native tongue appear foreign."[5] Following Silva's example, I do not italicize any words in Indigenous languages, nor do I italicize any words in Asian languages, not wanting to render them foreign for other reasons, following colonialism along a different vector.[6] For consistency, I've chosen not to italicize other non-English words, even if used by colonial forces, such as Russian terms. With apologies to scholars who make a compelling and necessary critique of the use of "America" to stand in for the United States, when the Americas encompass the totality of two continents, I at times use this term when I cannot wrangle out of an awkward phrasing or when I wish to emphasize the extent of American exceptionalism. I use the term "North American" when specifying Canada and the United States collectively. Lastly, I choose to employ the terms "Filipinx" and "Latinx" as they have been taken up within queer studies to move beyond binaristic notions of gender. This intervention and distinction is especially important to me when I describe historical immigrant communities, which are considered majority male and classed as a racialized gender but must have included those who identified with more expansive or alternative expressions of gender or sexuality.

Space-Time Colonialism

Introduction

I was born in Taipei, Taiwan, and raised in my father's hometown of Juneau, Alaska, on the traditional and unceded lands of the Tlingit people. When I was growing up in Alaska, my dad often told me a story about another family from our hometown, a story that was apparently known and repeated among residents of his generation. It goes something like this: In Juneau during the 1940s, there lived a Japanese American family, part of a small yet visible Japanese American community. The parents in this immigrant family had lived in Juneau for over two decades as owners and operators of a restaurant that served those who labored in Juneau's industries—miners, longshoremen, fishermen. After the bombing of Pearl Harbor and the U.S. nation's entrance into World War II, Alaska was included in the executive order for the removal, detention, and incarceration of persons of Japanese descent living on the West Coast. The teenage son in this local Japanese American family was an excellent student and (most appealing to my father) a star basketball player, respected among his teachers and peers. In a show of solidarity, his high school scheduled a special commencement so he could graduate early and address his fellow students as valedictorian before being interned.[1]

This was a powerful anecdote to hear, and one that bolstered my father's identity as a fourth-generation Alaskan settler. The pedagogical intent of a white father telling his mixed-race Chinese American children this particular tale was not lost on me, and his desire to imagine Alaska as a place attentive to and protective from larger forces of racial oppression was understandable. At the same time, I always wondered, if my hometown was so gracious and noble, why did I not know any Japanese Americans my own age? Why was this small yet visible Japanese American community not reestablished after the war? And, perhaps more importantly, although I was offered a tale that exemplified the sympathies of an Alaskan town for its Asian American denizens, why did I not learn about the contemporaneous World War II internment of Alaska Native people until college and then only in conversation, not in the classroom? While Japanese Americans were forcibly relocated from Alaska during World War II, the Unangax̂ people from the Aleutian chain and Pribilof Islands of southwestern Alaska were forcibly relocated to my home vicinity of Southeast Alaska, the ancestral lands of the Eyak, Tlingit, and Haida peoples.

I open with this story and reflection to highlight several of my overlapping investments in writing this book. As an Asian American who grew up in Alaska, I was very aware (and often the recipient) of stories such as the one my father repeated. Asian immigrants in Alaska are understudied in both Alaskan history and Asian American studies, while, at the same time, Asian characters pepper the social imagination in both literary and popular accounts of Alaska. One impetus for the research underlying this book, therefore, pushes for deeper historical knowledge of Asian Americans in Alaska alongside a critical analysis of the longevity of certain romanticized narratives of Asian figures in Alaska and to what end they function. I am not interested simply in the historical occlusion of Asian Americans in Alaska, however, but in the interplay of absence and presence in relation to Alaska Native lands, peoples, and knowledges. In the story my father recounted, the missing aspect of Alaska Native internment is instructive. The inability to link these two events suggests a larger failure to account for interconnected colonial and racial dispossessions within Alaskan history specifically, and in the construction of the American nation more broadly.

The enduring "last frontier," Alaska, as a construction of both time and space, is crucial to apprehending the historical and ongoing form and function of American colonialism, particularly in the shift from territorial possession to national incorporation. Among the examples that express Alaska's prominence in the social and cultural imagination, one needs only to reflect on the numerous reality television shows set in the forty-ninth state—shows that convey how Alaska still represents a desire for colonial or frontier-era narratives. At the same time, very little critical scholarship on Alaska has taken stock of its engagement with structures of colonialism, settler colonialism, and racial construction. As Alaska Native studies scholar Maria Shaa Tláa Williams emphasizes, expanding scholarship in colonial and postcolonial studies has yet to account for colonial histories and legacies in Alaska.[2] In this book, I seek to address this gap by reexamining Alaska from U.S. purchase through World War II, evaluating its particular and complex role in the structure and process of American colonialism. Considering both the imperial and settler dimensions of this colonial project, I focus especially on the contingent racialization and gendering of Native and Asian peoples in Alaska.

In 1867, U.S. secretary of state William H. Seward orchestrated the sale of Alaska from Russia with neither Native permission nor participation. As the nation's first noncontiguous possession, Alaska, as Yup'ik scholar Shari Huhndorf argues, links American colonial expansion with overseas imperialism, situating America's long history of Indigenous dispossession of Indigenous lands in the transition to an incipient global economy.[3] Seward long considered Alaska a key aspect in his envisioned U.S. imperialism, an expansion that included Alaska in a conglomeration with Hawai'i, the Philippines, several Caribbean nations, and the Panama Canal. Convinced of Alaska's benefit to American imperial and economic interests, Seward negotiated the purchase of Alaska without presidential or congressional approval. Alaska remained an American territory for nearly a century, this dynamic making it an excellent site of study for the complementary and contentious relationship between empire and settler colonialism. And, until World War II, Alaska remained a territory with a majority Native population and significant Asian immigration, fueling several principal and interlocking questions. Why is the 1867 U.S. purchase of Alaska from Russia not generally viewed as the transfer from one empire to another? Why is Alaska not considered a colonial space, given the imperial ambitions of American administrators as well as the perspectives and experiences of Alaska Native peoples? Why are Asians in Alaska missing from both Alaskan and Asian American history, even when Asian immigrants historically constituted a sizable population, especially in resource extraction economies? Building from these absences, why are connections between Alaska Natives and Asians in Alaska illegible? I contend that these elisions are not simply oversight, but omissions necessary to the enterprises of the American settler state and its imperialist expansion.

Alaska is more than 590,000 square miles in area, with astounding variation in its geography, environment, flora, and fauna. Human and sociolinguistic diversity in Alaska is similarly expansive. Alaska Native peoples speak twenty Indigenous languages, in eight broadly defined cultural groups corresponding to their geographic homelands: Athabascan-speaking peoples in interior Alaska between the Brooks Mountain Range and the Kenai Peninsula; Tlingit, Haida, and Tsimshian of the Southeast Alaska coast; Siberian Yupiit of St. Lawrence Island in the Bering Sea; Yupiit/Cupiit of the southwest mainland; Iñupiat of the Arctic region in northern Alaska; Alutiit/Sugpiat of Kodiak Island, Prince William Sound, and the Alaska Peninsula in southcentral Alaska; Unangax̂ of the Aleutian Island chain, which extends from the southwest mainland; and Eyak of the Copper River Delta, between southcentral and southeastern Alaska (see map I.1).[4] This listing is, of course, a limited summary as Alaska Native nations include multiple subdivisions and dialects (for example, the eleven Athabascan peoples in Alaska are culturally related but retain distinct nationhood). Their members

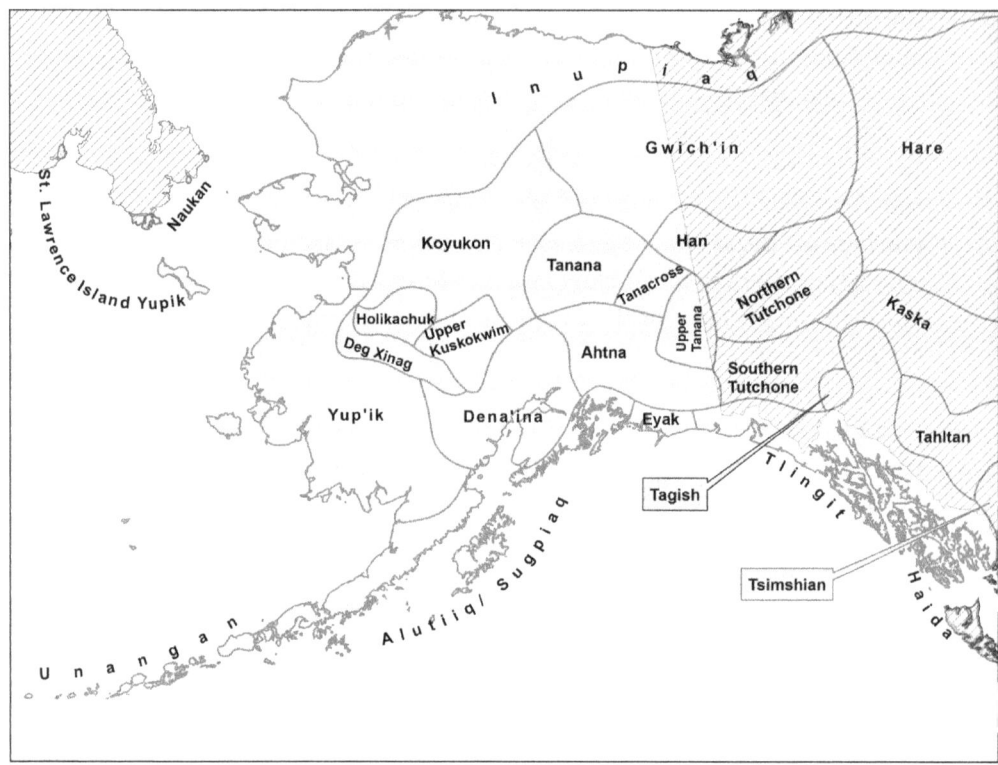

MAP I.1 Indigenous peoples and languages of Alaska. Alaska Native Language Center and Institute of Social and Economic Research. Adapted by Gary Holton and Brett Parks.

may live within traditional territories or outside them, and Alaska Native peoples enjoy a long history of intermarriage and other forms of political and kinship relationships.

I foreground this multiplicity because this book is grounded in Alaska Native studies, an emergent field that has produced a growing body of creative and scholarly texts on Alaska Native peoples, cultures, and politics, in conversation with national and global Indigenous studies, history, anthropology, social theory, and environmental studies.[5] The inception of Alaska Native studies as a distinct subfield responds, in part, to Alaska's anomalous treatment within American Indian studies scholarship. Of the more than 570 federally recognized tribes in the United States, nearly half are in Alaska, yet little attention has been given to the confusing and often contradictory legal and political status of Alaska Natives.

Alaska came into American possession a few years before the formal end to the American policy of treaty making with Indigenous nations, and no treaties were signed between the United States and Alaska Native peoples.[6] Instead, Alaska Native people occupy an ambiguous legal status marked historically by a racialized discourse of civilization. In Article III of the 1867 Treaty of Cession between Russia and the United States, a distinction was made between the "uncivilized native tribes" and other "inhabitants of the ceded territory," and only the second group (the not-uncivilized) was designated to obtain rights to be admitted as citizens of the United States.[7] Legal and political rights, therefore, hinged not on nation-to-nation negotiations but on individualized citizenship, and qualifications for citizenship, in turn, depended on demonstration and performance of being "civilized." This meant that until the Citizenship Act of 1924, citizenship was granted through adoption of white, heteropatriarchal social norms such as dress, language, employment, habitation in nuclear families, and Christian religious practice, alongside a renunciation of Indigenous cultural practices.[8] By heteropatriarchal I mean the social ordering in which heterosexuality, binaristic gender, and patriarchy are viewed as natural, normal, and desirable, and where the male-led nuclear family serves as the model and elementary unit for social relations and institutions of the nation-state. The discourse of civilization enunciated in Alaska's purchase is relevant for several reasons. It serves as a precursor and acts to substantiate what will become national policy under the assimilation era, serving as the basis and justification for land dispossession via assimilation policies. Citizenship relied on white settler norms of gender, sexuality, and family, underscoring the importance of Native feminist theorizing of the assimilation era. The explicit reliance of legal claims on the ideas and the legibility of who was civilized or, alternately, uncivilized also highlights the importance of examining racial discourse in the example of Alaska, and how colonialism operates through racialized and gendered technologies.

Another unique attribute of American colonialism was the racialization of Alaska Native peoples as Asian. Following U.S. purchase, government officials, tourists, missionaries, and ethnographers all contributed to an imperial narrative that racialized Alaska Natives as "Orientals," to distinguish Alaska Natives from other Indigenous peoples of the Americas. Such conceptions had enormous consequences in limiting Alaska Native peoples' political negotiations. In 1872, Commissioner of Indian Affairs Francis A. Walker, using the logic that Alaska Natives were not Indian but of Asian ancestry, argued that the Office of Indian Affairs' jurisdiction should not be "extended unnecessarily to races of a questionable ethnical type."[9] Walker's administrative refusal located the rights, and therefore political strategies, of Alaska Natives as distinct from those of other Indigenous people in the United States, which further hindered sovereignty and facilitated land dispossession. This is an omitted yet crucial aspect of the historic and contemporary political and legal distinction between Alaska Native and American Indian, a separation constituted through Asian racialization. Reading the dual orientalist and primitivist discourses that racialized Alaska Native peoples is a means of reading the overlapping and contingent imperial and settler colonial desires of the nation-state, serving as one answer to Maria Shaa Tláa Williams's call for colonial and postcolonial studies to address histories and legacies of colonialism in Alaska.

The racialization of Alaska Native peoples as Asian was superseded by the arrival and establishment of Asian immigrant laborers in the territory. Although early historical records reveal that Asians traveled to Alaska during the Russian colonial period, large numbers of predominantly male Asian laborers arrived in Alaska within the first twenty years of the American colonial period.[10] Successive waves of Chinese, Japanese, and Filipinx migrants followed the American colonial expansion of land expropriation and labor industrialization in Alaska, coming from the Pacific Northwest and British Columbia and working as highly exploited, mobile, and temporary workers in resource extractive economies such as canning, logging, and mining. Some of these workers settled and formed small ethnic enclaves, most without Asian female partners, while others joined Alaska Native communities, usually through forming relationships with Native women.

This history of Asian migrants and settlers in Alaska remains obscure and undertheorized, even though Asians constituted a sizable population during the territorial period, far outnumbering white settlers. In the rare instances when they are mentioned, Asian Americans are discussed as absentee or foreign elements, which disavows their labor and residency.[11] This historical gloss is also common in Asian American studies, with Alaska operating as the northernmost point on a migratory route, subsumed into the literature on West Coast Asian American labor. While other points in this itinerant cycle have been further explored, Alaska is overshadowed by the larger contiguous motions of workers throughout British Columbia, Washington, Oregon, and California.[12] In this way, Asian American studies implicitly reinforces the elisions within Alaskan history by accepting the overdetermination of Asian migrant laborers who traveled seasonally but never permanently settled in Alaska. Further, such historical oversight minimizes the important connections Asian migrants may have made with Indigenous peoples, regardless of the length of their stay in Alaska.

This project engages Asian American studies scholarship that theorizes imperialism and migration, viewing the United States as an imperial project.[13] This book extends the insistence within Asian American studies to make legible both American empire and the U.S. nation-state's concomitant renunciation of imperial identity. Asian American studies scholarship has underscored Asian immigration as essential to understanding racialization in the United States and the co-constitutional development of American capitalism.[14] Alaska emerges as a key site for this transformation, because of its dependence on Asian labor as well as its status as one of the last two states to be incorporated into the nation. At the same time, the primacy of labor as the vehicle for understanding Asian American oppression, contribution, and resistance is shortsighted. Transient labor may be placed in opposition to settlement, but the Indigenous genocide and land theft that precondition and make possible ongoing settlement are rendered invisible. Settler colonialism is a political, economic, and social formation in which colonizers act as settlers, with the primary purpose of claiming land as their own by attempting to eliminate, materially and discursively, the original Indigenous inhabitants. One of the inherent challenges in studying settler colonialism is that, by its very nature, it is a process that cloaks its own colonial operation, through exceptional and celebratory narratives. Spotlighting labor and labor exploitation as the dominant mode through which to register colonial power, Asian American studies risks obfuscating the colonial expropriation of Indigenous land and life within its configuration of empire and migrant labor. I therefore insist that settler colonialism is not simply a productive optic but a necessary and foundational framework through which to understand America's historical formation, that in order to truly understand Asian experiences in Alaska, we must understand that Asian America is always conditioned by and through settler colonialism.[15]

Colonial and Racial Entanglements

To consider Alaska's colonial and imperial dimensions, particularly colonial development through the overlay and interdependence of Indigenous dispossession and Asian labor exploitation, I turn to the instructive examples of Canada and Hawai'i, places where scholars and activists have extensively studied and elaborated on indigeneity and Asian racialization within colonial structures. First Nation studies and Asian Canadian studies scholars critically engage histories of Indigenous dispossession through the interlocking complexities of extraction, settlement, and migration, to understand Canada as a place, where, in Renisa Mawani's words, "Europeans, aboriginal peoples, and racial migrants came into frequent contact, a conceptual and material geography... of locally configured and globally inflected modalities of colonial power."[16] More pointedly, Bonita Lawrence (Mi'kmaw) and Enakshi Dua argue that postcolonial and antiracist analyses in the Canadian context further the settler state when such theorizations fail to address the foundational and ongoing colonization of Native peoples and lands, and the corresponding presence and resistance of Indigenous peoples.[17] Without a reckoning of enduring colonial violence, non-Native people of color deflect away from their own investments and benefits in settler legal, economic, and political infrastructures. Given the geographic and historical ties between Alaska and Canada, particularly in Canada's western provinces and among Indigenous nations that straddle the imposed settler-national border, such as Athabaskan and Inuit peoples, it is all the more surprising that Alaska's history has not similarly been analyzed with attention to settler colonialism and racial construction, a void that suggests the lasting power of romanticized narratives that sanitize American conquest and colonialism in Alaska.

Existing scholarship on Alaska lacks a sustained engagement with theories and frameworks on colonialism, whereas Hawai'i is almost always seen within a colonial lens. There are important distinctions to be made between the colonial processes and structures enacted and fortified in these two places. Hawai'i is a single sovereign nation, the islands in Hawai'i having been consolidated in 1810 by King Kamehameha I, and was widely recognized by European powers before being illegally occupied and overthrown by the United States. Alaska, on the other hand, is a landmass comprising numerous Native nations, none of which were politically or juridically recognized by imperial nation-states in the nineteenth century, the territory's coherence formed out of the Russian imperial quest for furs and solidified in the sale to the United States. Even with these differences, however, Alaska and Hawai'i share a colonial history, caught in the late-eighteenth-century imperial rush for territorial expansion and capitalist extraction. It was, after all, on his third expedition in 1778, en route to the North Pacific in search of the fabled Northwest Passage, that James Cook accidentally arrived at the Hawaiian Islands, an event that foisted predatory imperial contestations for economic, military, and political power onto Hawaiian lands and people. It would be on his return trip to Hawai'i, after traveling to the Pacific Northwest and Russian Alaska, that Cook attempted to take a Hawaiian king hostage and was killed in the ensuing conflict. When the two ships on the expedition continued without Cook to Macao and sold the sea otter pelts they had obtained on their voyage, the furs sold for 1,800 percent profit, catalyzing England's entrance into the maritime fur trade. Nearly two hundred years later, Alaska and Hawai'i were again brought into the same ambit, this time by the statehood movements of settler boosters, and were the last two territories admitted into the U.S. nation-state, in 1959.[18]

Hawaiian studies scholarship is critically important in understanding Alaska, therefore, not through settler colonial narratives of liberal and benevolent incorporation, but through analyses of imperialism, colonialism, and racial capitalism as overlapping projects and modes of power. Hawaiian and settler ally scholars and activists such as Haunani-Kay Trask, ku'ualoha ho'omanawanui, Candace Fujikane, Jonathan Okamura, and Dean Saranillio theorize what Fujikane and Okamura have termed "Asian settler colonialism," to name the history and process whereby Asians in Hawai'i, from early settlers to the present, have invested bids for inclusion and rights within settler colonial discourses that erase Kanaka Maoli (Native Hawaiian) presence and deny Hawaiian sovereignty.[19] As Fujikane stresses, it is not individual intent or action "that defines the status of Asians as settlers but rather the historical context of U.S. colonialism of which they unknowingly became a part."[20] Locating and specifying the distinct structural formation of Asian settler colonialism in Hawai'i as simultaneously a tool and a component nested within U.S. settler colonialism exposes and refutes the liberal multicultural construction of the "local" resident in Hawai'i as a specific strategy and desire among Asian settlers to conflate the racial with colonial, thereby positioning the independence and freedom of Hawaiian lands and people as either redundant or irrational.

To analyze Alaska in conversation with the formulation of Asian settler colonialism, as well as Lawrence and Dua's similar conception of "settlers of color," I return to the statehood movements of Alaska and Hawai'i, in particular a comparative examination of the sustained discourse among proponents and detractors. Among those opposed to statehood in Hawai'i, including government officials and popular-press authors, the primary impediment to statehood was expressed as an anxiety over a territory with a white minority—most prominently, antagonism to the Japanese American demographic majority on the island.[21] Conversely, Alaska was viewed as a "land without people," a literal terra nullius.[22] Both narratives, of course, effaced Native presence and attempted to render sovereignty illegible. In Hawai'i, the Asian settler colonial mobilization of a civil rights narrative and strategy, particularly within the post–World War II ascendance of an East Asian American electoral and economic power bloc, was instrumental in gaining statehood while propagating a multicultural myth of democratic freedom.[23] In Alaska, the image of uninhabited land could not be similarly rectified with a peripatetic Asian workforce, and instead Alaska's supposed vacancy was ameliorated after World War II military development finally achieved a settled white majority. In both Alaska and Hawai'i, Indigenous homelands were colonized through a development and restructuring that depended on imported Asian labor, though the plantation economy in Hawai'i encouraged settlement, and, in Alaska, resource extraction economies relied on a mobile and disposable labor force. This resulted in respective hypervisible and invisible Asian populations, and corresponding colonial racializations. In Hawai'i, settler colonialism was (and is) promulgated through Asians as Indigenous/Indigenous-adjacent through the articulation of Asian-in-place as local. In Alaska, dispossession occurred through the inverse: Alaska Native peoples were racialized as Asian/Asian-adjacent. The juxtaposition of historical processes in Alaska and Hawai'i underscores the distinct formation of Asian settler colonialism in Hawai'i, and also suggests that Alaska might be more closely aligned with the U.S. West, functioning more as exemplar than exception, in terms of both economic formation and colonial racialization.

In order to disentangle the relationships among colonialism, racial capitalism, and settlement, I shift to Jodi Byrd's analytical framework of arrivant colonialism, a formation imbricated with settler colonialism but not completely subsumed within it, theorized from the term "arrivants" in the poetry of African Caribbean writer Kamau Brathwaite to "signify those people forced into the Americas through the violence of European and Anglo-American colonialism and imperialism around the globe."[24] Allowing for the distinct articulation of arrivant colonialism is key to Byrd's method of analyzing power within a cacophony of colonial and imperial vectors, a reading strategy emanating from the Chickasaw and Choctaw concept of haksuba, the variant and simultaneously destructive and generative force of chaos. As Byrd elaborates, "In geographical localities of the Americas, where histories of settlers and arrivants map themselves into and on top of indigenous peoples, understanding colonialism as a cacophony of contradictorily hegemonic and horizontal struggles offers an alternative way of formulating and addressing the dynamics that continue to affect peoples as they move and are made to move within empire."[25] In this way, Byrd's formulation of arrivant colonialism foregrounds the incommensurate and asymmetric power relations of conquest, dispossession, enslavement, and exploitation without collapsing colonization into racialization, especially within the liberal remediation of redress or inclusion within the nation-state, so-called solutions incapable of addressing Native sovereignty or land reclamation. Byrd's is a necessary parsing, for in Alaska, colonialism initially functions not by remaking white settlers or Asian migrants into Indigenous inheritors but, rather, dispossession occurs through the attempt to make Indigenous peoples into arrivants.

Similar to considering arrivant colonialism as neither model nor identity category, but as an investigative strategy, I also take up Lisa Lowe's use of intimacy as a reading practice in her project of the intimacies of four continents, a critical genealogy of late-eighteenth- and early-nineteenth-century European liberalism through the imbrication of settler colonialism in the Americas, the transatlantic African slave trade, and Asian contract labor. Lowe deploys intimacy as a heuristic, to contemplate across archives and beyond discrete academic fields. In a turn away from intimacy as the romantic and private realm of the possessive liberal individual, Lowe instead focuses on "the range of laboring contacts that are necessary for the production of bourgeois domesticity; they are also the intimacies of captured workers existing together, the proximity and affinity that gave rise to political, sexual, intellectual connections, including subaltern revolts and uprisings."[26] I borrow from Lowe's multivalent definition of intimacy to denote not only romantic or familial relations, but more so the political economies (colonial and Indigenous) produced from proximities and affinities, and the myriad contestational possibilities derived from a lived intersection of differential colonization, racialization, and gendering, what Lowe shorthands as the "volatile contacts of colonized peoples."[27]

Fundamental to Lowe's analysis is an understanding of racial difference forged within and intrinsic to capitalist development. Racialization is not born simply from capitalist endeavors, not a tactical device to create division among workers but, instead, racialization is a constituent and constituting process within capitalism, and racial capitalism, as originally conceptualized by Cedric Robinson, is produced and furthered through historic and ongoing colonial processes.[28] Racial capitalism in North America, as Iyko Day argues, originates from settler colonial capitalism, an economic, political, and social formation that produces and expands white property through Indigenous land dispossession and racialized labor exploitation.[29] To account for these constitutive processes, Day moves beyond a binary opposition of Native versus settler to theorize settler colonialism through a triangulation of Native, settler, and alien. Day is careful to emphasize that this expanded model is not in service to what Eve Tuck (Unangax̂) and K. Wayne Yang caution as a settler "move to innocence" but, rather, emerges from the imperative to understand racial capitalism within the settler colonial context of North America, that collapsing racialized laborers within a generalized settler subject position "constrains our ability to understand how their racialized vulnerability and disposability supports a settler colonial project."[30] Noting the common feature of Asian racialization within settler colonial sites of the Anglo imperium (United States, Canada, Australia, New Zealand), Day posits the racialized alien as a particular attribute of settler colonialism. The settler capital triangulation into Native, settler, and alien subject positions does not exempt those racialized as alien from actively or involuntarily participating in or benefiting from settler colonial domination over and against Indigenous peoples and lands; moreover, "the distinctions between alien and settler are by no means stable or fixed but are meant to emphasize the role of territorial entitlement that distinguish[es] them."[31] What I wish to highlight, and certainly in the example of Alaska, is the additional mutability between Native and alien, an inconstant and permeable borderline that serves to dislocate Native peoples from Indigenous lands and refute claims to indigeneity through either nearness to or descendance from alien origins. Sharing their insistence on the indivisibility of white supremacy and colonialism, I utilize Byrd's, Lowe's, and Day's frameworks in analyzing Indigenous and Asian intersections in Alaska, especially in discussions of arrivant colonialism as a means to understand manifold circuits of imperialism in conversation with settler colonialism, and alien capital in relation to capitalist expansion and Indigenous dispossession under American colonialism, especially the transition from mercantilist to industrial forms of extraction in Alaska.

Space-Time Colonialism

Indigenous studies scholars have long examined and elaborated on discourses of time. As Dakota philosopher Vine Deloria Jr. has theorized, European American identity is premised on "the assumption that time proceeds in a linear fashion." In this context, American hegemony privileges history as an absolute, a progressive teleology that "assumes that at a particular point in the unraveling of this sequence, the peoples of Western Europe became the guardians of the world."[32] This temporal strategy, which differs fundamentally from Indigenous epistemologies and ontologies based on land and emplacement, situates white Americans as the privileged subjects of history, resulting in a vicious binary of "modern" versus "traditional," an overarching dichotomy that Kevin Bruyneel terms "colonial time." Colonial time, according to Bruyneel, encompasses the economic, cultural, and political narratives of the settler state that "place temporal boundaries between an 'advancing' people and a 'static' people, locating the latter out of time."[33] By this logic, Indigenous peoples are caught in a no-win configuration—they are either relegated to the past or exist inauthentically in the present. Of course, Native peoples have participated in modernity, materially and discursively, making their own meanings and choices when confronted with the disciplining binary of authentic versus inauthentic, traditional versus modern.[34] Such actions and experiences remain invisible within settler colonial temporality, however. Formulated as outside time itself, Native peoples, as historian Jean O'Brien (White Earth Ojibwe) summarizes from her study of nineteenth-century New England, "can never be modern."[35]

While Indigenous studies scholars have focused critically on time and colonialism, those in Asian American studies have been more centrally concerned with colonialism's spatial dynamics or, perhaps more pointedly, U.S. racial exclusion and exploitation articulated in spatial form. Within this framework, the Asian body's physical presence in space is the sign of that which is unassimilable, an external threat to the settler state and its economic, political, and societal success. Sylvia Shin Huey Chong characterizes the orientalist character of American racism in its "denial of Asian American assimilation or hybridity . . . , casting Asians as 'forever foreigners' indelibly marked with their racial origins elsewhere."[36] A refusal of Asian being-in-place within American territory, such logics fortify ongoing spatial exclusion, the perpetual "where are you *really* from?"

This evaluation of colonialism's spatial and temporal dimensions is not particularly revelatory or innovative—these short synopses will certainly be recognizable to scholars in the respective fields of Indigenous studies and Asian American studies. But I want to juxtapose these two overriding analyses of colonialism, one temporal and one spatial, in order to suggest the generative potential of thinking about them alongside, relationally. The particular circumstances and conditions of Alaska invite us to consider in conversation the forever foreign and the never modern. This is the first way that I posit space-time colonialism, to draw attention to the fact that space and time are constructed and relative (opposed to natural, unitary, or universal) and that multiplicities of space and time are constructed in relation to one another—in this case, spatial and temporal logics deployed in the service of the settler colonial state. Both Native and Asian are meant to be disappeared (disappearance not accidental, but a willful and intentional action) in the trajectory toward colonial horizons, though these horizons are respectively and differentially spatial and temporal. That is, Native vanishment is the condition of settler time, that Native peoples and cultures must disappear under the developmental push toward the modern. Conversely, Asian hypervisibility affronts settler space, and banishment is the spatial solution, the ongoing social and juridical exclusion from national belonging.

Considering thusly these space-time dimensions, I argue that the ideas of foreclosure and failure in terms of colonialism's proper subject fueled colonialism in Alaska while simultaneously masking its function. Government administrators and popular-press authors alike racialized Alaska Natives as Asian, concomitant to the American acquisition and early industrial development of Alaska, an imperial discourse that sought to distinguish Alaska Natives from other Indigenous peoples of the Americas. This racialization (an important and overlooked aspect in the genealogy of the Bering Land Bridge theory) was supplanted with the arrival and establishment of Asian laborers in extractive economies. In the shifting discourse, Asian migrants were considered modern laboring subjects yet could not properly inhabit settler space. Gendered racialization is a critical aspect for understanding this conundrum: the almost exclusively male population of Asian migrant workers provided necessary labor for the territory yet forestalled the futurity of a white settler state. They were therefore materially expulsed or epistemologically rendered failed subjects. Indigenous Alaskans, on the other hand, were considered inhabitants of Alaskan space yet failed to be modern subjects, were seen to be outside of settler time. Within this pernicious construction, the violence required to occupy land already inhabited was not located within colonial ambitions but blamed on notions of so-called primitive Native culture fundamentally at odds with modernity. These two relational logics, of settler colonial time and space, worked in tandem to simultaneously conceal and authorize the land dispossession and labor exploitation essential to the settler colonial project. Not only relational but also differential, these discourses made incoherent the connections between the very people being colonized and racialized. Relationships remain unrecognizable when Asians can never be "here" and Natives can never be "now." Once associated through an imperial discourse of racialization, Asian and Native peoples in the territory were narratively separated under settler colonial machinations, even as they lived and labored in close proximity.

A second way that I deploy the analytic of space-time colonialism is to consider the messy and overlapping spaces and times of imperial conquest and colonial governance, troubling the discrete classifications of imperialism, colonialism, and settler colonialism.[37] The American purchase of Alaska in 1867 presaged the official age of American overseas imperialism beginning in 1898. Alaska's prolonged territorial liminality not only challenges our chronologies of origin for American empire; it also complicates a clear break between the development of the American nation-state and the inauguration of its imperial ventures. Here I am in conversation with Byrd's adoption of the term "settler imperialism" to note the imperial designs born out of settler colonialism; and, more specific to Alaska, historian Jessica Leslie Arnett uses the same terminology to refer to a distinct legal formation that conditions how imperial and settler colonial policies and practices merged in Alaska.[38] Alaska also confounds spatial demarcations for how we think of empire in this period. It reminds us that the American westward march of manifest destiny collided and converged with an east-moving Russian empire. We might also consider Manu Karuka's refutation of U.S. national cohesion: that, from the perspective of Indigenous nations, "there is no 'national' territory of the United States. There are only colonized territories. There is no 'national' U.S. political economy, only an imperial one, which continues to be maintained, not through the rule of law, contract, or competition, but through the renewal of colonial occupation."[39] In the distinction between Karuka's continental imperialism and the outset of overseas empire (as Huhndorf argues, Alaska the hinge between), Alaska functions as neither and both, the overlay of American territory and saltwater colony.

The separation of colonialism from settler colonialism may be too exacting, certainly in the example of Alaska. The Russian occupation of Alaska, treated in the historiography as a colonial possession within the larger sphere of Russian imperialism, is not a framework historians typically transfer to the United States in the handoff of 1867. In material history, however, American Alaska does not appear very different from Russian Alaska—very little changes when colonial overseers change places, the United States inheriting Russian military forts as well as colonial economic ventures, such as the Unangax̂ fur seal harvest on the Pribilof Islands. Although resource extraction enterprises grew rapidly in Alaska from the late nineteenth century and into the twentieth century, a settled white majority would not be achieved until World War II. All the same, discourses that naturalized and anticipated colonial territorialization and white settlement predominated, which is why I term the contrasting racialization of Alaska Natives and Asian immigrants as the logics of *settler time and space*.

Space-time colonialism is, of course, a play on words, and the evocation of the space-time continuum establishes the third way in which I use the term, in its aspirational and futuristic connotations. Beyond the general thematic of relativity, I am less concerned with the scientific expression of the space-time continuum and more attuned to science fiction. Think *Star Trek* rather than string theory, because "space, the final frontier" shares a certain colonial longing, an anticipatory geography, an enunciated propinquity with "Alaska, the last frontier."[40] Despite Frederick Jackson Turner's assurance otherwise, the frontier might not be closed after all, but stuck in a time loop of its own telling—in the case of Alaska, an enduring quest, a recursive avidity for acquisition, a rebounding discovery narrative animated by the compound voracity of conquest and settlement. In gesturing toward space-time colonialism as speculative and fictional, I am not attempting to discover the "truth" or the "real" as a corrective, but rather, I read history discursively, principally concerned with the racialized and gendered constructions that conditioned and forestalled subjectivity, in conversation with the cultural production of Alaska Native and Asian immigrant authors and artists to demonstrate that Native and Asian peoples created alternate modes of meaning and belonging in excess of settler colonial logics.

SPACE-TIME COLONIALISM reevaluates four historical periods in Alaska: purchase, the gold rush, incorporated territorial status, and World War II, through an expansive archive of texts, including government documents, newspapers, travelogues, literature, oral histories, interviews, and photography. Each chapter examines a specific narrative crafted about each of these historical eras, and, though generally chronological, these chapters are not meant to provide a comprehensive history or even a progressive narrative. My primary aim in studying these four periods is not about filling a particular historic gap in knowledge but, rather, about focusing on several different moments of Native and Asian entanglement when racialized and gendered narratives are formed or shift. I selected these moments because they highlight Asian and Native connection in some way, as well as traces of disavowed violence. The chapters are also organized around a specific economy, each with both historical and present-day significance: tourism, gold mining, salmon canning, and the military. The historical scope of the book begins with the U.S. purchase of Alaska from Russia and ends with World War II, as World War II is typically viewed as a turning point after military development provides the modern infrastructure needed for statehood, achieved in 1959. By placing Indigenous subjects and racialized immigrants into conversation, however, the narrative of Alaska shifts from that of the last frontier's developmental achievement in modern statehood to an imperial project of a settler colonial nation.

Following the U.S. purchase of Alaska in 1867, government officials, tourists, missionaries, and ethnographers all contributed to an imperial discourse that racialized Alaska Natives as "Orientals." I examine this phenomenon of *settler orientalism* in chapter 1, a racial distinction for Alaska Natives that exoticized conquest and rationalized land dispossession. Tourists normalized this racial narrative to a popular audience, and women tourists in particular located the success of the territory on the promise of gendered domestication for Alaska Natives through orientalist tropes. In contrast to government documents and travelogues of the late nineteenth century, Tlingit author Ernestine Hayes's memoir *Blonde Indian* provides a twentieth-century Indigenous feminist account of working in the tourist industry. Close analysis of Hayes's text demonstrates the importance of Alaska Native epistemology, a reading practice that continues throughout the book.

The gold rush era transformed Alaska, both in terms of economic development and of ushering in the first major wave of settlers, and stories of the gold rush are most often associated with Alaska and its identification as the "last frontier." In chapter 2, I focus on the folklore figure China Joe, who appears in two tales, widely reiterated from the late 1800s to the present: in his generous role as a baker who sustains starving prospectors during a winter freeze, and also as the only Chinese who is allowed to stay in Alaska when the Chinese working in a nearby mine are driven out. I mine and undermine the tale of China Joe's exceptional benevolence by reading the driving out of Chinese in juxtaposition to the lynching of three Tlingit men—the two events taking place within three years of each other in the same Alaskan mining town.

By the 1910s, salmon canneries emerge as a predominant industry of the Alaskan economy, dependent on the racialized and gendered labor of migrant Asian men and resident Native women. In chapter 3, I excavate the traces of a labor union by examining two repeating figures, the Asian male sex worker and the promiscuous Native woman, to ask how unproductive workers elucidate contingent understandings of labor and land. Cannery documents and other archival sources form the first half of the chapter; the second half examines the narratives of cannery work expressed in the poetry of Tlingit author Nora Marks Dauenhauer and in Filipino writer Carlos Bulosan's novel *America Is in the Heart* in order to ruminate on queer affinities within settler colonial racial capitalism.

Chapter 4 focuses on the life and photographs of Shoki Kayamori, a Japanese cannery worker who settled in Yakutat, Alaska, in the 1910s. For three decades, he photographed the everyday activities of the town's Native, Asian, and white residents, but, as World War II escalated, Kayamori committed suicide as rumors circulated that he was a spy. Based on more than seven hundred recovered photographs and interviews with Yakutat residents, Kayamori's oeuvre captures Asian immigrants within the Native place of Alaska as well as the complex sovereignty strategies of mid-twentieth-century Alaska Natives, approaches that exceeded settler temporality.

In the epilogue, I conclude with a return to my opening story, with a discussion of a recent public memorial on interned Japanese American residents of Alaska. I ask after the still-to-be-memorialized experience of Unangax̂ internment to remark on the limits of recognition or redress under the logics of settler time and space. Cautioning against celebratory narratives of multicultural inclusion, I stress the importance of examining the messy, contingent, and incommensurate violences enacted against Indigenous and Asian peoples in the colonial constructions of the settler state. As I endeavor to show in this book, counter to space-time colonialism, Native and Asian peoples created their own forms of identity, relationship, and affinity through their literature, photography, political organizing, and sociality.

Readers will note that chapters 1 and 3 include counterhegemonic literary productions by Alaska Native and Asian American authors, while chapters 2 and 4 center on historical figures, China Joe and Shoki Kayamori, neither of whom authored a written history. I therefore include speculative, creative interludes for these chapters, to speak to either the absurdity of the colonial archive (in China Joe's case) or multivalent possibilities (for Kayamori). Because I open these two chapters with creative ruminations, I opt not to include epigraphs as I do for chapters 1 and 3. This book is not comprehensive, as I hew closely to coastal communities, particularly in Southeast Alaska. Part of the reason is historical, as the greatest number of Asian and Indigenous interactions occurred in the archipelago of Southeast Alaska. I was also drawn to specific stories that I grew up with or encountered while doing research, and, in this way, the book may be considered as my attempt to make sense of one's hometown violences, even if I am implicated in such structures. Rather than a project that argues for historical revision or incorporation, *Space-Time Colonialism* demonstrates how Native and Asian contingencies, discursive and material, are crucial to understanding both the function and concealment of imperial and settler colonial statecraft. The parsing of settler logics into distinct yet relational spatial and temporal modalities underscores the need for deep and sustained analysis on the differential effects of and responses to settler and imperial governance, as well as the conjoined stakes for Asian American studies and Native and Indigenous studies.

CHAPTER ONE

Settler Orientalism
The Asian Racialization of Alaska Natives

I have always been glad that good luck gave me Mr. Young as a companion, for he brought me into confiding contact with the Thlinket tribes. . . . It was easy to see that they differed greatly from the typical American Indian of the interior of this continent. They were doubtless derived from the Mongol stock. Their down-slanting oval eyes, wide cheek-bones, and rather thick, outstanding upper lips at once suggest their connection with the Chinese or Japanese.

— John Muir, *Travels in Alaska*

The imaginative examination of things Oriental was based more or less exclusively upon a sovereign Western consciousness out of whose unchallenged centrality an Oriental world emerged, first according to general ideas about who or what was an Oriental, then according to a detailed logic governed not simply by empirical reality but by a battery of desires, repressions, investments, and projections.

— Edward Said, *Orientalism*

The landbridge will not be forced
to function
by what you find familiar
                on either side.

— James Thomas Stevens, "(dis)Orient"

In 1890, South Carolina author Septima Collis published her travel narrative *A Woman's Trip to Alaska*. Collis's account of her Alaskan trip culminated in a stop to the territorial capital Sitka where she encountered "the most interesting experience of my whole trip,—certainly one that has made an everlasting impression on my mind."[1] Invited by missionaries, she and other tourists first stopped at the Tlingit village on the outskirts of town, known by non-Native people as the Ranch or Rancherie. Walking into Tlingit people's homes unannounced, tourists bore witness to their colonial notions of the primitive other, what Collis categorized as "savage" and "uncivilized ignorance." From there, tourists proceeded to the Sitka Industrial and Training School, a boarding school run by the Presbyterian mission, where they were treated to gendered demonstrations of industrial education that evoked, in Collis's mind, "deportment" and "domestic felicity."[2] Rehearsing a civilizational narrative of the late nineteenth century, Collis employed the vernacular of her time, naming the boys she saw at the school "Siwash," a denigrating term from the colonial trade language known as Chinook jargon used to refer to Native men, thought to derive from the French "sauvage," or savage.[3] But Collis also invoked and enmeshed a different racialized construction when she praised the intelligence of the students' "Mongolian faces," adopting the social Darwinist term to denote those from Asia, a racial taxonomy that included Mongoloid, Caucasoid, Negroid.

Collis's invocation of a Mongolian racialization was neither unique nor coincidental, but a contribution to a larger discourse of Asian origins for Alaska Native peoples concomitant with Alaska's purchase and incorporation into the U.S. nation-state. The formulation of this linkage is an important facet in the genealogy of the Bering Land Bridge theory and, more broadly, elucidates the colonial articulations of the related racial and gendered constructions of Alaska Natives and Asian Americans. This chapter is not a scientific study of the Bering Land Bridge, recognizing that the theory is both supported and contended within a variety of fields such as anthropology and geology.[4] Similarly, within Alaska, different Native peoples hold origin stories that alternately coincide with or contradict anthropological hypotheses about the first peoples of the Americas.[5] Rather, I seek to understand the widespread desires by non-Natives in the late nineteenth century in their imagining Native origins in Asia, and the particular place Alaska holds in that imaginative construction. In articulating this settler orientalism located in the U.S. acquisition of Alaska, government officials constructed a kinship between Alaska Native peoples and their perceived Asian ancestors. This conceptualized familial and biological linkage is conjured by the collective colonial imaginary of a variety of government actors and colonial proponents. In examining the work that such an imagined relationship produces and enables, I am building off the contributions of American Indian studies scholars who demonstrate that the discourse of Asian origins discounted (and continues to discount) Native claims to land and territory, while Native epistemological claims that locate alternative origins are dismissed as falling outside of accepted history or science.[6] In the case of Alaska, a conglomeration of government officials, tourists, missionaries, and ethnographers repeatedly constructed Alaska Native peoples' ancestry as, to use the parlance of the time, "Asiatic," "Mongolian," or "Oriental," to justify fluid and overlapping imperial and settler colonial ambitions for Alaska as a territory and future state.

Reading postcolonial and Indigenous critique in conversation is important to examining the overriding discourse of Alaska Natives as independent from American Indian peoples within what would become the contiguous United States, while also placing them as inferior to and innately separate from white Americans, a double move made through a constructed racial intimacy with Asian peoples. If Edward Said's foundational postcolonial scholarship argued that the construction of the Oriental revealed little about the actual lives of people in the Arab and Asian world and instead represented the logics and desires of European colonialism, how does the formulation of the Alaska Native in relation to a different notion of Oriental inform the contours and intent of American colonialism?[7] How are racialized and gendered constructions central to the colonial and settler colonial project in Alaska? Conversely, how are Western knowledge and the construction of race and gender informed by the historical demands of empire and settler colonialism? This chapter attempts to think alongside Chickasaw scholar Jodi Byrd's formulation of transit of empire, wherein Indianness functions as an imperial sign that facilitates colonial incorporation while simultaneously reiterating the "lamentable but ungrievable" figure of the Indian.[8] In the case of Alaska, however, Indianness is, at some times, overlaid with and, at others, oppositionally juxtaposed to an abstract and signifying Asianness. This is not to refute Byrd's theorization, as I remain firmly invested in her locating the origin of U.S. empire with the birth of the nation-state and its prior and continuing colonization of Indigenous peoples, lands, and knowledges. Likewise, Byrd compellingly demonstrates that U.S. overseas empire from the 1890s to the present transfers a paradigmatic Indianness onto the colonized to justify and naturalize a notion of colonial benevolence over the constructed backward and uncivilized "Natives." In conversation with Byrd's scholarship, I'm interested in the U.S. imperial project in Alaska as another dense transfer point that complicates and deepens the interplay between primitivist and orientalist discourses, between notions of internal and external consolidation, and, ultimately, witnesses the deferral and disavowal of Alaska Native peoples' claims to indigeneity through a temporal and spatial separation enabled through the sign of the Asian other.

During and following the acquisition of America's first noncontiguous territory, Alaska was alternately configured as either an imperial or a settler colonial space through the emphasis on Alaska Natives peoples as distinct and exceptional, racial notions that hinged on Asian lineage. Government officials proffered racial categorization, albeit shifting and uneven, of Alaska Native peoples as Asian in arguing the case for Alaska's purchase. This fictive kinship was extended to Indian affairs, setting a precedent for Alaska Native exceptionalism that rendered illegible nation-to-nation status in favor of limited rights gained through assimilated individualism. The colonial imaginary that linked Asians and Alaska Native peoples through a racialized intimacy was fortified and extended through a broad compendium to the state archive, authored by a diverse group of informal actors including missionaries, ethnographers, and tourists. The commencement of Alaskan tourism in the 1880s cemented this racial construction within popular culture. Thousands of wealthy passengers made the journey each year, and by 1890, 5,000 tourists visited Alaska during the summer season.[9] The profuse publication of travel guides, memoirs, and adventure narratives brought Alaska into the national imaginary and configured Asian ancestry for Alaska Natives as common sense to a broader American audience.[10]

Women tourists in particular highlighted the missionary project of assimilation and gendered domestication within the racial and colonial logics of American empire, as women touring Alaska located the success of the recently acquired territory upon the premise and promise of normative race and gender. Septima Collis and writers like her highlighted that colonialism is always a racial, gendered, and sexualized project, specifically one that must repeatedly bolster white supremacy, heteronormativity, and heteropatriarchy in order to assert the sovereign claims of settlers. As Nez Perce literary scholar Beth Piatote's study of the assimilation period demonstrates, the coercion needed to enforce boarding school attendance reveals not a break between removal and assimilation policies but, rather, a continuation of military violence marked by the withholding of food and rations and the threat of imprisonment. Removal from national space shifts to removal of Native children from their families, facilitated by what Piatote, in engagement with postcolonial feminism, terms "foreign domesticity," or how assimilation policies strive for the elimination of Indigenous sovereignty through legal and discursive ideology dependent on notions of Native family and kinship as childlike, aberrant, and nonnormative.[11]

In connecting the removal and assimilation federal policy eras, Piatote is detailing the functioning of what settler colonial studies scholar Patrick Wolfe has termed the "logic of elimination."[12] Wolfe argues that an eliminatory logic fundamental to settler colonialism remains consistent within this historic shift, that once U.S. territorial acquisition reached the Pacific Ocean, the repeated westward removal of Native people from their homelands gave way to internal national projects that extolled the assimilative possibilities of interrupting Native identities and polities. Wolfe's highlighting of an assimilative process within the territorial bounds of the United States indexes the rise of temporal discourses over spatial rationalizations; that is, as U.S. policy shifted away from an enunciation of removal outside of national boundaries, assimilationist agendas required a temporal insistence that a generational usurpation of culture and identity ostensibly assured an Indigenous-free future. To be clear, Indigenous territory was taken and collective governance of land was opposed under assimilation-era policies (as seen by the two-thirds decrease in Indigenous-held land from the 1880s to 1930s), but the overriding narratives that justified and facilitated this expropriation increasingly relied on temporal, not spatial, civilizational discourse.[13] Wolfe marks the first major indication of this transition with the U.S. end to treaty making with Native nations in 1871, a policy shift that was enacted four years after the U.S. purchase of Alaska but was presaged by the Treaty of Cession with Russia and the marked absence of negotiation with Alaska Native peoples or polities. As previously discussed, the treaty with Russia addressed Native peoples through a lens of negation, conferring citizenship only to the not-uncivilized. In this way, U.S. possessory claims to Alaska can be seen as marking this shift in federal Indian policy wherein the absence of formal national recognition via treaty making is replaced by a civilizational discourse. Lacking a prior precedent of U.S. removal or Indian treaty making, Alaska Native peoples were especially affected by the assimilation era of boarding schools: Alaska Native children attended day schools and state boarding schools, and some were sent out of state, most often to the Chemawa Indian School in Oregon. As Alaska purchase and U.S. occupation coincided with the shift to assimilation policies, the spatial horizon of colonial acquisition became rationalized and naturalized through an overriding temporal discourse, articulated and fortified especially by women's travel literature, a corpus of texts that enmeshed primitivist and orientalist discourses.

To close this chapter, I juxtapose the gendered and racial pedagogies expressed by Collis and her cohort with the work of Tlingit author Ernestine Hayes and her memoir *Blonde Indian*, published in 2006 and the winner of the 2007 American Book Award.[14] While this is an anachronistic choice of texts, I have purposely chosen an Alaska Native author published more than a century after early tourists to Alaska to disrupt the assimilative promise of colonialist desires, to highlight what Anishinaabe scholar and author Gerald Vizenor terms Native "survivance," Native endurance that refutes civilizational discourses of Native declension and disappearance.[15] As a Tlingit woman writing about her life in the latter half of the twentieth century, Hayes intervenes in ideas of settler orientalist kinship, to show that Asian and Alaska

Native peoples were not connected through colonial notions of relation but, rather, share space and time in their materially grounded living conditions under racial and economic oppression. Further, she specifically unsediments the colonial violence of boarding school benevolence, highlighting the gendered and intergenerational trauma that results from forced and reiterative coercion. Hayes makes an especially astute interlocutor for the tourist writers that visited Alaska more than a century ago, as her adult return and reconnection to Alaska is facilitated, in part, by working in the tourist industry. A close analysis of Hayes's text demonstrates the importance of Alaska Native epistemology generally and Indigenous feminism specifically, a reading practice that continues throughout the book. Hayes refuses colonialist teleology through open and cyclical Tlingit worldviews of time and place, demonstrating that it is not Native people who are arrested in their development; instead, Hayes indicts American colonialism for its inability to account for capacious notions of Indigenous kinship and belonging.

Classification of the State: Colonialization and Emancipation

Although the hypothesis that Asian immigration populated the Americas had been in circulation since the Spanish Jesuit José de Acosta proposed it in 1590, based on his missionary work in Peru and Mexico, the specific idea of Alaska Native peoples' racialization through Asian origins became prominent through the latter half of the nineteenth century.[16] By that time, Europe and its settler societies had shifted from religious and national origin formations of race to the post-Enlightenment idea of scientific racial difference. Linnaeus's *Systema Naturae*, published in 1735, was pivotal in making this shift, providing a single taxonomy for scientific identification and classification of difference. Formulating what Michel Foucault has termed a "science of order," eighteenth- and nineteenth-century scholars created a body of scientific racism, wherein totalizing logics naturalized racial hierarchies on a global scale, an intellectual project that worked to explain and justify imperial expansion and exploitation.[17] With the 1859 publication of Charles Darwin's *On the Origin of Species*, scientific notions of difference were placed within a unified progressive teleology as social evolutionists rejected biblical time for a secular and all-encompassing notion of natural history. Linnaeus's idea of a totalizing classificatory schema was now applicable to culture and history. As anthropologist Johannes Fabian has argued, evolutionary and social progress were linked through this temporal conceptualization, particularly in the ways imperial superiority was deployed through a spatialized time, in which civilization emerged through developmental stages (with white Anglo-Saxon culture as its pinnacle) that, while progressive, were not conceived of as a line but mapped as a tree.[18] The emergent disciplines of history and anthropology naturalized time and progression within a patrimonial racial taxonomy, the "family of man." The linkage between Asian and Native peoples that materialized alongside the U.S. colonization of Alaska was an important node in the development of racial thought within this shift in western epistemology.

Less than a decade after Darwin's publication, in 1867, Massachusetts senator Charles Sumner presented a three-hour speech in favor of ratifying the U.S. purchase of Alaska from Russia, devoting considerable time to describing and classifying Indigenous Alaskans.[19] He introduced his discussion on Alaska's populace emphasizing that previous population estimates had been greatly exaggerated, and invoked the idea of terra nullius when quoting his recent correspondence with geologist and paleontologist Louis Agassiz, who related, "To me the fact that there is as yet hardly any population would have great weight as this secures the settlement to our race."[20] Agassiz was a leading scholar in the study of natural history and, as his quote suggests, a contributor to the ideas of scientific racialism. Agassiz believed in polygenism, or the idea that human races were so different and distinct that they came from separate (and divine) origin. Though Agassiz's ideas and sentiments would become eclipsed by a growing social and scientific acceptance of Darwinism, Sumner's use of Agassiz in his speech signals that the racialization of Alaska and its Indigenous inhabitants was located within larger national and transnational discourses on racial construction and white supremacist thinking.[21]

In addition to citing Agassiz's expertise in order to authorize the colonial project of white settlement, Sumner alluded to the nascent field of ethnography to classify Alaska Native peoples. As he elaborated, "If we look at them [Alaska Natives] ethnographically we shall find two principal groups or races, the first scientifically known as Esquimaux, and the second as Indians. By another nomenclature, which has the sanction of authority and of usage, they are divided into Esquimaux, Aleutians, Kenaians, and Koloschians.... The Esquimaux and Aleutians are said to be Mongolian in origin..... The Kenaians and Koloschians are Indians, belonging to known American races."[22] The racial taxonomy that Sumner provided illustrates the imperial logics that were circulating even before the purchase of Alaska, and as the territory was enfolded into the American system of colonial expansion, these discourses were reiterated, argued against, and expanded. In general, however, the idea of distinguishing some or all of Alaska Native people from other Indigenous peoples in the United States became an overriding preoccupation in official and popular discourses, and that distinction was based time and again on perceived Asian origins. In his speech, Sumner almost immediately contradicted the stability of his taxonomy in describing the "Esquimaux" of Kodiak: "Although by various intermixture they already approach the Indians of the coast, losing the Asiatic type, their speech remains as a distinctive sign of their race."[23] Both the desire to fix racial categories and the concomitant impossibility of doing so resulted in recurring anxieties and ambiguities for officials.

It was not just physical resemblance that motivated Sumner's characterization of Alaska Native peoples' uniqueness, however, but a set of attributes tied to both colonial pasts and futures. As Sumner explained, "There are general influences more or less applicable to all these races [of Alaska Natives]. . . . There is something in their nature which does not altogether reject the improvements of civilization. Unlike our Indians, they are willing to learn."[24] Sumner's paternalism of American Indians notwithstanding, Indigenous Alaskans' propensity for civilizational achievement is particularly marked through indices of colonial economies. Of the "Koloschians" of the southeast Alaskan coast, Sumner described them thus: "Some are thrifty, and show a sense of property. Some have developed an aptitude for trade unknown to their northern neighbors or to the Indians of the United States, and will work for wages, whether in tilling the ground or other employment."[25] The proclivity Sumner describes is underwritten by the history of the colonial fur trade, an economic experience that conditioned the Indigenous peoples of Southeast Alaska (presumably Tlingit and Haida, the Tsimshian relocating from British Columbia in 1887) for their incorporation as wage laborers into a settler colonial America. Sumner not only invoked Alaska Natives as a laboring class but also underlined their respect for "property," an important prerequisite for white settlement.

At the same time, Sumner created hierarchy and progression between Russian colonial resource extraction and American settler colonial ventures. Though he cautioned that "Koloschians" from Southeast Alaska were notoriously bellicose to other Native peoples and imperial occupants, compared to the Aleutians' "peaceful even to cowardice" demeanor, the Tlingit people's assimilative potential out of a perceived fierce and backward culture is prescribed by their participation in American commerce: "And yet this fighting race is not entirely indocile, if we may credit recent report, that its warriors are changing to traders."[26] Sumner is claiming that the Unangax̂ and/or Sugpiat (those he identifies as Aleut), whose colonial relationship with Russians resulted in huge cultural changes due to forced hunting, relocation, intermarriage, and Russian Orthodox conversation, were emasculated through that process. The gendered subtext reveals the sedimented knowledge that the Russian fur trade in Alaska was not actually trade but a coercive system that forced Unangax̂ and Sugpiaq men to hunt for sea otters in order to ensure the safety and release of female and child hostages, a practice that Gwenn Miller refers to as an "economy of confiscation."[27] In contrast, Tlingit who traded with imperial forces (Russian as well as British, Spanish, and American), and who attacked Russian forts at Sitka and Yakutat, were positioned with a militant virility well suited to American economic ventures. This depiction of Tlingit traders articulated the masculine image of the frontier and served as antecedent for the image of the Alaskan state that develops, situated within the shift from a resource extractive colonialism to settler colonial industrialism, a process that is based repeatedly on racialized and heroic masculinity.

Although Sumner was a steadfast proponent of Alaska's acquisition, it was Secretary of State William H. Seward who accomplished the sale. Seward presumed Alaska as a central component in the imperial expansion he conceived for the United States, a project that included not just Alaska but also Hawai'i, the Philippines, and several Caribbean islands. Confident of Alaska's benefit to American economic interests, he negotiated the purchase of Alaska with the Russian minister to the United States, Eduard de Stoeckl, with neither presidential nor congressional approval. Sumner's congressional speech was, in part, to ensure the ratification of the treaty Seward arranged with de Stoeckl, which passed the Senate only to have the appropriation of funds for the purchase opposed by the House of Representatives. The U.S. Treasury would not approve funding until 1868. The purchase of Alaska occurred two years after the close of the Civil War and was supported and orchestrated by the same Northern leaders who opposed the institution of slavery, such as Sumner and Republican politician and newspaper publisher Thurlow Weed. This cohort of officials envisioned Alaska as part of an American imperial project in Asia and the Pacific to ensure national prosperity once a plantation economy based on enslaved Black labor had officially ended. As the prime architect of the Alaska purchase, William Seward's commitment to abolition was long-standing. When he was a young lawyer, the cause of abolition drew him to his future wife, Frances Miller, and, after marrying, the couple moved into her father's Auburn, New York, home, which was an active stop on the Underground Railroad. As a politician, Seward established himself as an abolitionist first as New York senator, and then as New York governor and U.S. senator, and, finally, as Abraham Lincoln's secretary of state. Additionally, the

Sewards were financial backers of Frederick Douglass's *North Star* newspaper and, of their abolitionist efforts, are perhaps most well known for their support and patronage of Harriet Tubman, providing a home (and home base) for her in Auburn.[28]

Just as Seward's abolitionist convictions were formed well in advance of the Civil War, so too were his commitments to an imperial future for the United States. For Seward, imperialism and abolition were conjoined projects. In an 1854 address, he argued that "no ignoble race can enlarge or even retain empire," that the continuation of slavery forestalled and even made impossible the project of U.S. imperialism.[29] Conversely, two years later, in a speech delivered in New York to oppose slavery's extension, Seward conceded that "our commercial and political systems must be extended somewhere, or else the growth of the cities and towns of Western New York must be arrested." Expansion was possible, Seward argued, only if "new and distant regions" were made "tributary to them for manufactures and for commerce."[30] Thus, for Seward, American imperialism and the abolition of slavery were mutually supporting projects, a vision realized with the post–Civil War purchase of Alaska in 1867. Here we see the construction of U.S. exceptionalism, wherein what is clearly colonial expansion, the transfer from the Russian empire to the American, and the first American acquisition of noncontiguous territory, is configured as a necessary and desirable outcome of the United States' putative emancipatory break from a slave-based economy.

Seward also claimed an Asian origin for Alaska Native peoples. He retired as secretary of state in March 1869 after serving two terms, and, although almost seventy years old and not in good health, he traveled on the just-completed transcontinental railroad, continuing up the West Coast and into Alaska. There he delivered a speech in the newly named territorial capital of Sitka (changed from the capital of Russian America, Novo Archangelsk, or New Archangel); the speech was subsequently published for a national audience.[31] Diverging from Sumner's classificatory system, Seward marshaled every Alaska Native group into a common provenance: "All of them are manifestly of Mongol origin. Although they have preserved no common traditions, all alike indulge in tastes, wear a physiognomy, and are imbued with sentiments peculiarly noticed in Japan and China."[32] What these specific peculiarities are, Seward does not elaborate. The differences in Seward's and Sumner's respective racial taxonomies highlight the shifting ambiguities of racial construction, all under the overarching discourse of Asian ancestry. An Asian racialization allowed Seward to reconfigure Alaska Natives not as Indigenous to the Americas but, by asserting an Asian ancestry and appearance, as part of his vision of American imperial hegemony. By temporal linkage to an Asian past, he situated Alaska outside of national boundaries, intrinsically as (acceptable) colonial space.

"Races of a Questionable Ethnical Type"

Government attention to Alaska extended beyond the support of purchase and into Indian affairs, where Asian racialization had significant repercussions in circumscribing Alaska Native peoples' political claims. In 1869, the same year that Seward traveled to Alaska, Vincent Colyer, the secretary of the newly formed Board of Indian Commissioners, produced a survey of Alaska Natives based on his own observations, previous official reports, and the statements of more than a dozen officials and non-Native residents of Alaska.[33] He perpetuated the general confusion as to the racial classification of Alaska Native peoples, as his informants debated which of Alaska's Indigenous peoples were or were not Indian, and which were "a distinct race of people, purely Mongolian in origin."[34]

Not only did Colyer reiterate Alaska Natives' exceptionalism via a speculated Asian origin, but he also repeated the distinct characteristics of Alaska Native peoples, claiming a general consensus that they were more intelligent and industrious than other Native North Americans. For example, the Unangax̂ were praised for their schools and churches (products of Russian colonialism), seen by Colyer and his informants to have resulted in high literacy rates and general levels of education.[35] It was the Tlingit and Haida of the southeast Alaskan coast, however, who elicited the greatest praise. Colyer quoted the former customs agent and mayor of Sitka as saying, "For half a century educated into traders by the Russian American and Hudson's Bay Company, . . . they have become keen, sharp-witted, and drive as hard and close a bargain as their white brothers."[36] While Unangax̂ were complimented for their book learning, it was the Tlingit and Haida "education" in colonial commerce that was more highly regarded under U.S. occupation. Here, again, we see the comparison between different relationships under Russian and British colonial rule ordering the hierarchies for the transition to U.S. colonialism. As the post trader of Sitka described the local Tlingit, "They are industrious and ingenious, being able to imitate admirably almost anything placed before them."[37] This mimetic quality, as a trait sought by industrial capitalism, becomes a distinctive feature describing the Alaska Native, and especially seen as an Asian trait. If, as Homi Bhabha reminds us, "colonial mimicry is the desire for a reformed, recognized Other, as a subject of a difference that is almost the same, but not quite," Asianness functions as the site through which both Alaska Natives' proximity to whiteness and difference from whiteness is determined.[38] The authority created in Colyer's report had huge effects related to Alaska Natives and Indian policy. Although Colyer supported Native claims to lands and financial compensation, and recommended reservations as well as funding for Indian agents, schools, and health services, Congress failed to implement Colyer's suggestions.[39] Instead, the influence of Colyer's report derived from its detailed discussions of Alaska Native origins and racial consignment, scrutinization that would influence governmental policy for the next decade and longer.

In 1872, the commissioner of Indian Affairs, Francis A. Walker, relied on Colyer's report to argue that Alaska Natives were not Indian and, therefore, fell outside of the purview of the Office of Indian Affairs (OIA) and the Interior Department that housed the office. Walker's argument depended on an Asian racialization:

> I have never believed that the natives of Alaska were Indians, . . . any more than are Esquimaux or Kanakas, and I am disposed to avoid entirely the use of the word Indians as applied to them. The balance of probabilities seems to me to incline toward an Asiatic origin, at least so far as the inhabitants of the coast and of the islands are concerned. The inference from their geographic position, strong as it may be, is hardly so strong as the inference from their singular mimetic gifts and the high degree of mechanical dexterity which they are capable of attaining. These are qualities characteristic of the Oriental, and they are precisely the qualities in which the North American Indian is most deficient.[40]

Walker was not only repeating the prevailing racial discourse of Asian origins, he was also fusing previous official reports on Alaska Native adaptability to industrial labor with those origins. In doing so, he masked the colonial genealogy provided by previous governmental officials through a naturalized hierarchy that postulated a racially exploitable labor class preferred by capital. In Walker's model, the spectrum of Native responses to colonial and settler colonial dictates, from accommodation in colonial economies to resistance to more than a century of colonialist violence, were reduced to essentialized notions of capitalist competency and deficiency, all defined in relation to Asianness.

Given this racial distinction, Walker contended that the Office of Indian Affairs' administration should not be "extended unnecessarily to races of a questionable ethnical type, and occupying a position practically distinct and apart from the range of the undoubted Indian tribes of the continent."[41] In rejecting and rendering discrete Alaska Native peoples, Walker limited the political rights of Alaska Natives to organize as Indigenous peoples. He articulated that it was in the interests of Alaska Natives to be regarded separately because identifying with American Indians could result in, "constitutional disqualification for citizenship."[42] Nation-to-nation negotiations between Indian tribes and the OIA were being eschewed for the assimilative promise of Native petitions to citizenship as individuals, and this political inducement was based on the colonial history of Alaska Native peoples. Echoing the ambiguity of the Treaty of Cession's figuration of citizenship based on not belonging to an "uncivilized native tribe," Walker's reasoning resuscitated the logics of Russian imperial rule, within a new matrix of racialization based on perceived Asian lineage. Ironically, Asian origins yielded the possibility of citizenship for Indigenous subjects while Asian origins for immigrant workers during the same period foreclosed such possibilities.

What Walker's rationale both conceals and reveals, however, is that by refusing Alaska Natives status as Indians, he limited the capacity of Alaska Native peoples to make land claims as nations of people. Instead of viewing Alaska Natives as the Indigenous inhabitants of Alaska, Walker and other government officials viewed them as having origins elsewhere, which placed them on a trajectory from those Asiatic beginnings to an American settler future, while everything in between was transitory. Land is being lost here, figuratively and materially. Jodi Byrd cogently argues that the figure of the Indian functions as a transit, a transferable paradigm through which U.S. empire acquires lands and territories, while simultaneously disavowing the attendant violence enacted on Indigenous peoples. This process is being rehearsed through Walker's reasoning, but unlike Byrd's supposition that this transit pivots on a production of Indianness, in this instance Indigenous dispossession is orchestrated through Asianness. Rather than articulate this as a break, even as American boosters of Alaska were wont to do, we might view the recursive nature of this exceptionalism, evident throughout and a key feature in the longue durée of American colonialism, with (mis)recognition in the originary moment of Christopher Columbus's hailing of the Indio. If, within Byrd's formulation, "ideas of 'Indianness' have created conditions of possibility for U.S. empire to manifest its intent," indigeneity and orientalism have consistently been enfolded within settler and imperial ambitions and machinations, and Alaska, rather than acting as the precursor to the post-1890 age of American overseas empire, makes impossible sequential or causational conclusions.[43] The figure of the Indian is always already an attempt at dispossession through Asian belonging, and ironically, the categorization of "Alaska Native" separate from "American Indian," an alterity born from this moment of racialization within the Office of Indian Affairs, reiterates four hundred years of settler imperial violence and dominion wrought through orientalist logics.

The Tourist Gaze

Travel writing in the mid- and late nineteenth century served a central role in representing the other to an imperial audience, acting as a vanguard of empire's interests shaped by and also reshaping a colonial project of knowing the world.[44] In Alaska, tourists' first-person observations expanded the American grammar of colonialism, naturalizing racial discourses of ambiguity and exception for Alaska Natives, all undergirded by notions of Asianness. The completion of the transcontinental railroads in the latter half of the nineteenth century marked an expanded national economy that included the emergence of tourism by upper-class Americans eager to view both sublime landscapes and putatively authentic Indigenous peoples.[45] In the 1880s, both the construction of the Northern Pacific Railway and regular steamship travel to and from Southeast Alaska facilitated a new tourist destination in Alaska, similarly fueled by demands to experience pristine wilderness and the Alaska Native indigene. Visible are the tourist demands that fueled this emergent tourist economy; less apparent is the Asian labor that intersected with these tourist routes. Chinese laborers were integral to the construction of the Northern Pacific Railway and, likewise, Chinese labor contracted by Alaskan canneries constituted a major factor that compelled regular steamship travel along Alaska's Inside Passage. Starting in a U.S. port such as San Francisco, Portland, Tacoma, or Seattle, the main stops would include Fort Wrangel, the mining town of Juneau, and the Alaskan capital Sitka, with visits to Native villages such as the Haida village of Kasaan. Some trips included nature-related sites such as Glacier Bay before returning south. Stops were brief, and the entire journey usually lasted two weeks or less.

The orientalizing of Alaska Natives was ubiquitous among tourist travelers to Alaska in the late nineteenth century and early twentieth century. Of the roughly two dozen most popular Alaska travelogues published during this period, all remark on Asian attributes or origins for Alaska Native peoples. Tourists traveling to Alaska reinforced and expanded the prevailing racial discourse of Alaska Natives' descendance from Asians, frequently asserting their personal observations of physical resemblance. As tourist destinations were predominantly to coastal communities, the Tlingit, Haida, Tsimshian, Sugpiat, and Unangax̂ were all observed to have Asian facial features, coloring, or physical stature. Similar to the government officials of the previous decade, tourists debated which tribes, or whether perhaps all of Alaska's Indigenous peoples, were of Asian origin. Within this shifting terrain of Asian interpellation, late-nineteenth-century tourists debated Asian specificities, whether certain tribes were Chinese or Japanese, or if all were generally "Mongolian." Upon visiting the Haida village Kasaan on Prince of Wales Island, traveler Abby Johnson Woodman remarked, "They look much like the Japanese, and possess many of their characteristics."[46] Physical traits were emphasized, as when Henry T. Finck reported, "It is impossible to look at these Indians and not come to the conclusion that they are descended from the Japanese. The whole cast of the face is Japanese: the cheeks, the small, sparkling black eyes, with their scant lashes and brows, and the complexion, are unmistakably so."[47] This closely scrutinizing objectification was also articulated by the most widely read traveler to Alaska, naturalist John Muir, who opined, "It was easy to see that [the Tlingit] differed greatly from the typical American Indian of the interior of this continent. They were doubtless derived from the Mongol stock. Their down-slanting oval eyes, wide cheek-bones, and rather thick, outstanding upper lips at once suggest their connection with the Chinese or Japanese."[48] What Muir and other tourists underscored was their personal witness to physical attributes. As Finck stressed above, given such intimate observations, it was simply not possible to come to another conclusion regarding the origin of Alaska Natives.

Tourists bolstered their perceptions with the official reports that preceded their entry into Alaska, yet their first-person observations surpassed governmental classifications and naturalized an Asian-Native racial connection for a popular audience. The level to which empiricism authorized claims is evidenced by missionary Livingston Jones's critique of naturalist William Healy Dall, who asserted that he could see no connection between Alaska Natives and Chinese or Japanese.[49] Jones argued, "This is surprising, coming as it does from a man of his intelligence and research. Even tourists and transients passing through Alaska have observed the striking resemblance of native Alaskans to Japanese. The Thlingets, especially, seem so closely related to the people of the east coast of Asia, that a European traveller who had been around the world once remarked to a missionary, 'How many Japanese you have in Wrangell!' At the time there was not a Japanese in the place. The people he saw were native Alaskans."[50] The hierarchy of knowledge production that Jones provides is telling. Though acknowledging Dall's authority as a scientist, he stressed that *even* a tourist or transient, using a word that highlights the lower-class character of a prospector or laborer, can see what Dall cannot. The erudite scholar failed to comprehend what was obvious and common sense to those visiting and living in Alaska. For Jones, a European tourist indexed a global empirical knowledge while a missionary represented local expertise. Passages such as these highlight how empiricism undergirded a spatial and temporal authority, an epistemological superiority dependent on racialized difference. Tourists understood Alaska as outside of the national bounds and viewed their spatial travel to a distant and unfamiliar locale as representing a reverse trajectory, typifying the spatialization of modernity's temporal protocols. As Johannes Fabian elaborates, tourists embodied the notion of secularized or spatialized time; that is, through their movement across topos, they served as witness to more "backward" peoples.[51] It was not only space and time that were metaphorically linked but, as Qadri Ismail argues in his postcolonial critique, the empiricist "will make generalizations about *all* of the natives, about their personality and character, based on *some* of them, based, indeed, on his 'experience' . . . of some of them."[52] Tourists, endowed with empiricist logics, not only contributed to and furthered racial constructions, but simultaneously produced themselves, precisely as outsiders to the spatiotemporal world they were observing, as experts not only on Asian racialization but, perhaps more insidiously, as adjudicators of Indigenous authenticity.

The manner in which tourists engaged in and furthered racial discourses within popular culture illustrates what Raymond Williams terms "structures of feeling," or, perhaps more accurately, his expanded notion of "structures of experience." Working from Antonio Gramsci's concept of hegemony as the co-constitution of coercion and consent, Williams explains that hegemony "is a lived system of meanings and values . . . which as they are experienced as practices appear as reciprocally confirming. . . . It is, that is to say, in the strongest sense a 'culture,' but a culture which has also to be seen as the lived dominance and subordination of particular classes."[53] As examples of "practical consciousness" (as opposed to "official consciousness"), structures of feeling are "concerned with meanings and values as they are actively lived and felt"—in this case, the travel experiences of tourists were shaped by and, in turn, shaped the discourses of racialization, empire, and capitalism.[54] Tourists naturalized the imperial and settler colonial categorization of Alaska Natives as Asian and, through their firsthand accounts, posited that naturalization as what Antonio Gramsci termed "common sense" for their readers. Or, following Gramsci, Mark Rifkin has formulated "settler common sense" to encompass the affective and quotidian ways settler society forms and reforms Indigenous dispossession as natural and normal.[55]

The notion of visiting and viewing distant and distinct Indigenous peoples tied in to larger national and transnational imperial discourses of the exotic and foreign. As Julie Cruikshank and Robert Campbell have each detailed, Alaska and Africa were brought into a shared constellation through the adventures of numerous explorers, those who traveled to both destinations, such as young Edward James Glave, as well as those who narrated their Alaskan adventure through a vocabulary of African exploration.[56] Tourists similarly emphasized foreign difference of Alaska Natives through Asian associations. Tourists described Native religious practice as Asian idolatry, such as one tourist's assertion, "Shamanism is a religion of awful superstition which prevails in Northern Asia, consisting in a belief in evil spirits, and in the necessity of averting their malign influence by magic spells and horrid rites. The prevalence of this religion among the Alaska Indians is one of the many evidences of their Asiatic origins."[57] As this passage demonstrates, tourists often felt compelled to describe and comment on what they found objectionable or repulsive. Additional aspects of Native culture, on the other hand, met with praise. This was true of Native material culture, particularly craftwork, as evidenced in one tourist's praise for the Haida, who "excel in their stone carvings. We saw some beautiful dark stone vases, very antique and oriental in shapes."[58] In both flattery and denunciation, the tourist discourse of the other depended on a foreign and exotic Asianness. Even though American tourists patriotically incorporated Alaska into a larger sense of national belonging, such incorporation was always premised on a future settlement, an envisioning of the white settler nation to come. In terms of their present-moment desires, however, tourist fascination was held by their ideas of a pure and pristine landscape, unsullied by development, a sublime expanse inhabited by a noble and primitive other. Even as industrial and modern futures were touted and expressed, this forthcoming vision contradicted imperial wishes to dwell in an imagined past, timeless and remote. Such tensions underscore the ambivalence inherent in settler orientalism, as Asian racialization indexed both imperial and settler inclinations, projects tethered by colonial claims to space produced through sentiments of otherness but diverging in vexed transcendent and industrial visions. This contradiction can be apprehended in part through historian John Kuo Wei Tchen's study of American orientalism in the period before Chinese exclusion. As Tchen elaborates, early American patrician orientalism that conveyed bourgeois social status, distinct from European wealth, through Chinese objects and curios, shifted to a commercial orientalism fascinated with Chinese wealth even as China was seen to be a waning culture marked by despotism and effeminate excess and "by the middle of the nineteenth century a commodifying culture had arisen that was both adoring and hostile."[59] Settler orientalism held this discordance, a colonial yearning and dread marked and overlaid by American concerns for expansion and inclusion indexed by the figure of the Alaska Native, simultaneously Indigenous and foreign.

"Half a Mile from Savage . . . to . . . All Human Happiness"

The Sitka stop on the Southeast Alaska tourist route highlighted the missionaries' achievements at the Sitka Industrial and Training School. Unlike incipient towns in Alaska tied to extractive economies such as mining and timber, the territorial capital occupied the site of the former Russian colonial capital. Outside of administrative and military employment, Sitka's emerging settler society depended on two conjoined enterprises: tourism and the missionary school system. Presbyterian missionaries founded the Sitka Mission School in 1878, which became a boarding school for boys in 1881 with the conscription of a former Russian hospital. By 1888 it was known as the Sitka Industrial and Training School, and included female students.[60] Although not technically travelogues, missionary writings were also part of the larger body of tourist literature, as missionaries published widely read articles and books, and were also known to correspond to those interested in Alaskan history and culture, including tourists. Additionally, many missionaries served as contributors to the state archive through their flexible transformation into government officials, such as missionary John G. Brady, appointed as Alaska's territorial governor for three terms (1897–1906), and Presbyterian minister Sheldon Jackson, the general agent of education for Alaska. Like African American industrial schools and American Indian boarding schools throughout the United States, the mission school was premised on an uncivilized versus civilized dichotomy in which "heathen" youth could be rehabilitated into modern Christian citizens. Tourists visiting Sitka were invited to witness this wondrous transformation by first visiting the Tlingit village, known by the West Coast colonial terminology of "Ranche" or "Rancherie," followed by a tour of the mission school and its neighboring cottages, Victorian houses where graduates resided.[61]

As the first major group of white women in Alaska, women tourists performed a particular disciplining function for Alaskan empire in their travel narratives, and women tourists were especially conducive to the missionaries' civilizing project, often describing the Sitka "tour" in great detail. As Septima Collis depicted the mission school, "I saw perhaps twenty dark-skinned Siwash Indian boys, whose Mongolian faces and almond-shaped eyes had assumed an expression of intelligence, so different from the stupid, bleary-eyed appearance of the same age and race whom I had seen in the rancherie, that it was difficult to realize that they could possibly be twigs of the same tree."[62] In this instance, Collis invokes the social Darwinist tree of man, indexing Asianness as the realization of assimilationist promises, juxtaposing almond eyes to bleary eyes in a nonlinear leap in racializing assimilated Natives as Asian kin, skipping over the unassimilated boys in the Tlingit village. Here space and time become unlinked, and the asynchronous progression that Collis proffers suggests the contradictory racializations of settler orientalization—a settler nation's imperial aspirations manifest as always also the shadow of its imperial origins. Collis continued, "Those ladies and gentlemen who accompanied me through the rancherie and the schools at Sitka can vouch for the fact that it is only half a mile from savage, uncivilized ignorance, superstition, filth, and immorality to education, deportment, thrift, domestic felicity, and all human happiness."[63] Similar to the staging of the progressive teleology performed at world fairs, travel from the Ranche to the mission school not only held the civilizing promise for Natives, but also reinforced what Beth Piatote has termed the "performative taxonomy of citizenship," noting that assimilation was performed through dress, comportment, and vocation, and these "bodily submissions" served as classificatory competency for future national incorporation.[64] Indeed, Collis's only detailed proof that all human happiness had been attained was her description of the schoolboys solving an arithmetic problem while the girls mastered sewing skills. Looking at the doubled meanings of "domestic," of nation and home, Amy Kaplan argues that domesticity in the latter half of the nineteenth century operated as a "mobile and often unstable discourse that can expand or contract the boundaries of home and nation, and that their interdependency relies on racialized conceptions of the foreign."[65]

As Collis praised the mission's cottages that demonstrated how "pupils live when they marry and go to housekeeping," she enfolded the racialized and gendered domestic promise of the Sitka Industrial and Training School into the larger imperial vision to shape and mold Alaska Natives into civilized and heteronormative members of American society. That the family modeled the nation was essential to settler colonialism; enticing married graduates into nuclear living arrangements in the Victorian houses bordering the school was an attempt to destroy the matrilineal clan-based Tlingit society.

Historian Paige Raibmon demonstrates that Tlingit families contradicted missionary expectations of the cottages in manifold ways, as when extended families resided in cottages intended for nuclear families. As part of these extended and intergenerational living arrangements, bilingualism was the norm, with family members conversing in Tlingit and English, with some speaking only Tlingit. Householders continued to work outside the economies prescribed by missionary schooling and also refuted the goal of settlement, instead engaging in seasonal practices of both colonial and Indigenous economies including salmon fishing, cannery work, carpentry, lumbering, hunting, trapping, and berry picking. Tlingit customary practices and kinship ties were strengthened by such activities, as well as by frequent and regular socializing between the village and cottages. The unidirectional project of the cottages was further repudiated when cottage residents left to build homes in the Ranche.[66] Such complexities were lost on tourists however, as Collis and women travelers like her amplified notions of Asian ancestry for Alaska Native peoples to a popular audience, cementing romanticized colonial racializations to an assimilative and heteronormative futurity.

The Anxiety of Laboring Bodies

Similar to Indian Commissioner Francis Walker's racialization, tourists fused the idea of Asian origins and industrial aptitudes, attributing a particular imitative ability as an essential trait of Asians and, by extension, Alaska Natives. As one tourist remarked, "The natives . . . are different from the red men of the United States in appearance, habits, and customs. They seem to have had a Japanese origin, have a Mongolian cast of features, and, unlike our Indians, are naturally intelligent, with industrious habits, keen in trade, good mechanical ideas, quick to learn."[67] More than situating Alaska Natives within the popular white supremacist ideology of the time, this relation additionally configures Alaska Native's assimilability precisely at the moment that Asian laborers are entering wage labor in Alaska's resource extraction economies, a material relationship that cannot be overlooked. Travel writer Charles Hallock made this connection when he wrote, "As a whole, the Indians of Alaska . . . [are] industrious to a degree unknown elsewhere among the aborigines of America. . . . There is assuredly a strong facial resemblance between the Chinese coolies now living on the coast and some of the native Indians. They seem to affiliate naturally."[68] Alaska Natives were constructed in relation to Asians even as tourists observed them working together in waged labor. As one tourist observed at a salmon cannery with Chinese and

Native workers, "We saw nineteen Chinamen and some twenty Indians working at the same long table. But for the dress and pigtail, we could not tell the Chinese from the Alaska Indians, so close was the resemblance of features, and the color was exactly the same. Upon inquiry we found that several Chinamen had intermarried with squaws, that they seemed to have a ready understanding of each other, and could communicate through their language with greater facility than the whites. I imagine that they must have sprung from the same original stock."[69] In this passage, Asians and Natives are understood to share origins because they are phenotypically indistinguishable to white tourists as they work together on the cannery line, and imagined origins take on an industrial futurity made possible by intermarriage and a "ready understanding." The racial kinship outlined by colonial intimacy was realized though interracial relations in Alaska's nascent industrialization. This linkage between Alaska Natives' singularity and their participation in wage economy was bluntly articulated by territorial governor Alfred P. Swineford, who claimed that Alaska Native peoples "have not a drop of Indian blood in their veins," and that regarding the Tlingit and Haida specifically, "there is not a more independent, prosperous, and contended 'lower class' in any country on earth than the native population of southeastern Alaska."[70] As an Alaska booster, Swineford understood that to picture white settlement as inevitable depended on transforming a majority Native populace into an exploitable and segregated laboring class.

Not all tourists viewed Chinese immigrant labor as a positive example, however. Tourist adventures that started in San Francisco were replete with descriptions of Chinatown's cramped quarters, malodorous smells, opium dens, gambling, and prostitution.[71] Tourists appeared unable to connect these descriptions to similar understandings of Native villages and Native quarters in boomtowns as debased and culturally othered sites. Instead, several tourists disconnected these negative visions of capitalist expansion by locating Alaska Native origins as specifically Japanese. Here, we see the first fissures in the Asian-Native racialization, that the imperial promise of an assimilable other is contradicted by the racialized class composition of settler colonial capitalism. A paradox is presented: while the civilizing project was dependent on racially separating Alaska Natives from other Indigenous peoples in the Americas through a discourse of Asianness, Asian immigrant workers were also being racialized as improper and other during this period. Although the racial distinctions of Alaska Natives were forged to prevent primitivist interpellation, those who were shaping this discourse had to attend to orientalist configurations of the Asian migrant worker as well. The contrast between these two constructions is evident in the fact that missionaries in Alaska never showed the slightest interest in converting Chinese workers or any of the successive waves of Asian immigrant workers to follow. Several tourists skirted this contradiction by racializing Alaska Natives as Japanese in looks and character.[72]

Chinese labor in Alaska revealed both the dream and nightmare for settler colonialism, a reminder that an exploitable racial class provided the material base for settlement but also limited the white future of that settlement. For John Muir, this contradiction proved that the civilizing enterprise was unneeded and unwanted. Muir bemoaned what he viewed as the decline and eventual disappearance of Native culture and saw industrialism as a particularly horrific aspect of this declension narrative. On the Harriman Alaska expedition in 1899, he described, "a fearful smell, a big greasy cannery, and unutterably dirty, frowsy Chinamen. Men in the business are themselves canned."[73] To Muir, the promise of a civilized Native working alongside the Asian laborer was a dystopic vision. Homi Bhabha reminds us that "mimicry is . . . the sign of a double articulation; a complex strategy of reform, regulation and discipline, which 'appropriates' the Other as it visualizes power. Mimicry is also the sign of the inappropriate, however, a difference or recalcitrance which coheres the dominant strategic function of colonial power, intensifies surveillance, and poses an immanent threat to both 'normalized' knowledges and disciplining powers."[74] In Alaska, the lauded mimetic abilities of the orientalized Native revealed how "mimicry is at once resemblance and menace," representing the redemptive mission of "civilizing" the Alaska Native, on one hand, and the improper labor of the Chinese worker, on the other.[75] The imperial advantages of distinguishing Alaska Natives through an Asian racialization were straining under settler colonial development.

Bering Land Bridge as Travel Narrative

Ethnographers, as part of the nascent discipline of anthropology, also participated in the Asian racialization of Native peoples, at once reifying similarities as scientifically based while also, paradoxically, extending the discourse of Asian origins outside of Alaska to include other Indigenous Americans. Anthropologist Franz Boas, whose research included fieldwork in Alaska and British Columbia, connected the popular discourse at the time to scholarly theories. In a report following his research trips to British Columbia in the 1880s, he described the large numbers of Native peoples living and working in urban Victoria: "These are squat figures whom we meet here; the color of their skin is very light; they have prominent cheekbones, straight, shortcut hair, and dark eyes. They remind us so strongly of the east Asiatic peoples that throughout British Columbia there is the indisputable opinion that they are descendants of Japanese sailors."[76] This passage is remarkably similar to tourist depictions, echoing the personal observations of tourist authors that are dehumanizingly detailed in physical description. And, just like the tourists traveling to Alaska during the same period, Boas utilized empirically based knowledge to assert claims of Asian origins, though in Boas's case, his reputation as a man of science lent additional credence to this "indisputable opinion." His reported observations and their resonance with popular racial discourse on Asian and Native connections is also notable when one considers that this early fieldwork in British Columbia is where Boas developed what would become the branch of anthropology known as cultural anthropology, known for its methodological fusing of empirical observation and field research. Boas's diaries further reveal the moment he personally "discovered" the Asian-Native connection, during an 1888 research trip while consulting with a Haida informant in Victoria, British Columbia, and also while collecting skulls in a region northeast of the city. In the middle of writing up notes, "it suddenly occurred to me that Haida and Tlingit did not have the structure of Indian languages, but that of the Asiatic. You can imagine that this thought caused me a great deal of excitement because that would be an important discovery." After musing that this revelation occurred auspiciously on his birthday, he was compelled to extend his stay, "to find a basis for this idea."[77]

Boas was not only engaging with the popular origin narratives of the period but also extending the common racial discourse of the day into scientific discussions of Indigenous origins. Based on his early research in the Pacific Northwest, as well as his fieldwork on the Inuit on Baffin Island in the early 1880s, Boas came to believe that the Americas had been peopled by a migration of early settlers that crossed the Bering Strait, at ice age intervals that would have lowered sea levels and made the strait into a land bridge. Other theories were advanced at this time, including an Atlantic land bridge and the hypothesis that American Indians were the lost tribes of Israel.[78] By the turn of the century, however, the scientific community had reached a general consensus that the Americas were peopled by Asian ancestors who had migrated east. This understanding was solidified by the Jesup North Pacific Expedition (1897–1902), a collaborative ethnographic venture to establish the origins of America's Indigenous peoples by examining the biological and cultural similarities between the Native peoples of Asia and the Americas. Franz Boas, then the assistant curator of the American Museum of Natural History's department of anthropology, organized and coordinated the expedition.

The fact that Boas, regarded as the founding "father" of American anthropology, is a key contributor to the intellectual history of the Asia to America migration theory stands as a powerful marker of this discourse. Boas also helps us understand the shift from Alaska Native exceptionalism configured through Asianness, to locating all of Indigenous Americans through Asian origins and an Alaskan migration. How and why does the exception become the rule? His report and diary entries based on Pacific Northwest fieldwork in the late 1880s echo the sentiments of Alaskan tourists during the same time period, even down to the specificity of objectifying physical characteristics, and, in this way, we might consider how the Bering Strait theory functions as part of the larger genre of tourist or travel narratives. This suggests that the two theories—Alaska Natives as distinct from other Indigenous Americans because of Asian origins and all Indigenous Americans as descendants of Asians—are actually built on the same racialized and orientalist discourse, the conclusions having been changed to serve different ends.

Instructive in marking this change are the anxieties surrounding industrialized racial labor in Alaska, as noted in the section above. To explore this idea further, I return to the idea of an Asian interpellation to facilitate Alaska Native future industrial incorporation into the national body politic. The same steamships that carried tourists throughout Alaska's waterways are also transporting Chinese migrant workers to labor in the territory's nascent salmon canning economy (the Chinese will be followed by successive waves of Japanese and Filipinx workers and smaller numbers of South Asians). Tourist Abby Johnson Woodman explicitly described on her 1888 voyage, "Dr. Sheldon Jackson, U.S. School Commissioner in Alaska, came on board at Tongas Cannery, bringing with him thirty-seven bright Indian boys. . . . We have already on shipboard one hundred and fifty Chinamen, about sixty cabin passengers, miners, adventurers, etc., besides Mrs. Willard and ourselves."[79] Woodman revealed the entangled economies that the steamships depended on: tourism, salmon canning, and mining. In doing so, however, she drew several distinctions. The cabin passengers were separate from laborers, "miners" and "adventurers" were further separated from the racialized Chinese cannery workers, and the Native young men that Jackson intended to educate were separate from the Chinese cannery workers as well. Outside of Woodman's and a few other authors' fleeting remarks on cannery workers, however, there is no sustained engagement with the Asian workers arriving in the territory, certainly no connection between the assimilative promise of Asian racialized Natives and the presence of Asian laboring bodies, even as they traveled on the same ships as tourists. Evident here is one of the strongest articulations of what I call settler colonial space: even while Asian racial figurations signaled modernity, especially for Alaska Natives, and even while Asian laborers were essential to the economic foundation of the territory, Asian immigrants were disregarded as part of territorial space and written out of its history. This paradox was constituted through gendered racialization; even though the majority-male population of Asian immigrant workers furnished labor necessary for the territory and its extractive wealth, they blocked the progression toward an eventual goal of a white settler state. The Asian migrant men who labored in Alaska could not reproduce settler colonialism racially or biologically. Therefore, even as missionaries such as S. Hall Young praised Alaska Natives' capacity for Christian assimilation based on perceived Asian cultural traits, no effort was made by missionaries to interact with Asian migrant laborers. Seen as already failed subjects of a heteropatriarchal settler futurity, they were simply ignored.[80]

Understanding the relational race and gender logics of settler colonial space, in turn, elucidates the discourse of foreclosed modernity for Alaska Natives, or what can be considered settler colonial time. In putting the industrialized promise of an Asian interpellation in conversation with the simultaneous yet unrecognized Asian labor occurring in Alaska, we see that the industrial and domestic activities of the young men and women at the Sitka school have less to do with their future economic lives and more to do with the function their vision serves as a corrective to the Indian Rancherie. If we look closely, we see that the transformation being staged in "half a mile from savage . . . to . . . human happiness" is nothing more than that—a staged performance, not meant to have an actual future in the territory. Orientalism holds the promise of a non-Native future, a future that cannot include either Asian or Native bodies. Redressed in soldier suits and white dresses, acting out shoe cobbling or needlework, the gendered images of Native girls and boys function as a disappearing act, a maneuver meant to vanish the Native people in the Rancherie. As Asian origins become less useful for selling the settler colonial future of Alaska, the overriding fascination with an Indigenous Asianness becomes conveniently tied to justifying settler colonial pasts, that is, the settlement of North America. Indigeneity rendered through an Asian lens makes immigrants out of Natives, disappearing settler violence along with Indigenous claims.

Beyond the Tourist Gaze: Ernestine Hayes's *Blonde Indian*

To offer an alternative reflection on colonial space and time, I juxtapose the gendered and racial pedagogies expressed by Collis and her cohort with the work of Tlingit author Ernestine Hayes, focusing on her first book, *Blonde Indian: An Alaska Native Memoir*.[81] As a Tlingit woman, Hayes makes an excellent interlocutor for the tourist writers that visited Alaska more than a century ago, particularly in her challenges to settler colonial space and time. The daughter of a white man and Tlingit woman, Hayes, a member of the Kaagwaantaan or Wolf clan, spent her early childhood in the Indian village on the outskirts of Juneau, Alaska, in the 1940s. Hayes chronicles being raised by her maternal grandmother and aunt while her mother recovered in a tuberculosis sanatorium, and then her memoir transitions to turbulent teen years marked by juvenile detention, boarding schools, and alcoholism. After moving with her mother to what Alaskans call the "Lower 48," Hayes struggled with addiction, homelessness, and abusive relationships before returning to Alaska as a middle-aged adult. This is not a story of individual triumph, however. Instead, Hayes provides a multivocal cast of characters, interspersing her own narrative with that of her mother and grandmother, Tlingit oral histories, Kaagwaantaan clan histories, a mother bear, and even a good story a friend tells her over beers at the Arctic Bar. Several reviewers have critiqued Hayes's unorthodox aesthetic, uncomfortable with what they view as her "jarring" writing style, with "isolated passages that seem to float in the text with no chronological grounding."[82] This misses the crucial point, however: Hayes intentionally refuses the progressive teleology of assimilation; her return to Alaska rejects the bildungsroman arc of personal self-discovery for a cyclical journey inhabited by multiple community actors, human and nonhuman, across time. The spiral nature of her work is underscored when Hayes utilizes the Tlingit storytelling technique of repetition, repeating some passages word for word.

Eschewing abstract orientalist origins for Alaska Natives, Hayes locates Asian people, raced and classed within the space of Alaska. She recounts walking from the Native village to school as a young girl, climbing stairs, "behind rattletrap apartments and past Native and Filipino houses perched here and there along the hillside."[83] Contradicting notions that Asian immigrants were temporary workers in Alaska, Hayes's description locates Filipinx settlers living in homes contrasted to the rickety and precarious apartments. Readers might surmise that the Native and Filipinx occupants of these homes were in a better financial position than apartment renters or residents, such as

Hayes and her grandmother, of the Native village on the tidal flats. As Hayes traces her journey to the school in the white section of town, however, we understand that these Native and Filipinx house dwellers were also situated on the hillside segregated from the white denizens of Juneau. In another passage, Hayes describes the wintertime job of Suzie, a young Tlingit woman, in a local café "that allowed Native men and women to work as staff and even welcomed Natives and Filipino people as customers."[84] Hayes is most likely referring to the City Café, a Japanese American–owned restaurant that served Native and Filipinx customers during a period when numerous Alaskan businesses upheld discriminatory practices. Rather than connecting Alaska Natives to imagined Asian ancestry, Hayes connects Native and Asian people in their shared experiences of racial exclusion.

Another way Hayes confronts the dominant narrative of settler colonialism is in "the story of Tom's tale"—threaded throughout her memoir. Tom is a contemporary of Hayes's generation, whose name was changed from Tawnewaysh to Tom when he was taken to a boarding school at the age of ten. His transition is descriptively marked by gendered, non-Native garments when, "a white lady dressed in a shiny gray skirt and an unfriendly jacket," comes to take him away, and he is made to "dress in a buttoned shirt and stiff pants."[85] Here, the sartorially encoded formation touted by the missionaries to symbolize civilized accomplishment is seen as suspicious and unwelcoming. And rather than believe in the redemptive promise of industrial education, Tom realizes that, at the Sheldon Jackson School, "all the jobs they were offered had to do with being a servant."[86] Continuing Tom's story of depression and alcoholism after graduation, and his eventual estrangement from his son, who is also taken away to boarding school at the age of ten, also by "a white lady dressed in a shiny gray skirt and an unfriendly jacket," Hayes locates the cause not within Tom's failure to assimilate into settler modernity but within the reiterative physical and spiritual violence of compulsory missionary schooling.[87] In juxtaposition to the aspirational achievements extolled in the tourist-witnessed movement from Native village to mission school, Tom and Young Tom's experiences highlight the disruptive and cyclical nature of coercive colonial education.

Hayes intervenes explicitly in colonial logics by locating Asian Americans in Alaska's segregated spaces and by disputing missionary benevolence, but her description of experiences working in the tourist industry are where she most strongly provides an alternative paradigm of space and time, grounded in Tlingit epistemology and ontology. Upon her return to Alaska, Hayes worked summers on tour boats, both as a guide for a small cruise ship and as a deckhand on two-hour whale-watching tours. In a series of nine successive sections, Hayes provides alternate accountings of the journeys she takes with the tourists, starting and restarting in different parts of these tours, and locating land in different registers of past and present. She positions her own personal history into the tours, such as, "We steamed south on Gastineau Channel. I pointed out the ruins of the Alaska-Juneau gold mine, where I had climbed and run as a child."[88] Or, in one section describing the journey by colonial landmarks, and, in the next, "We are leaving Aak'w territory and entering Chilkoot territory, going past Berner's Bay, Daxanáak. . . . Daxanáak lies within the ancestral territory of the Auk Kwan. It is still remembered for the richness of its fish and the abundance of its berries."[89] She displaces colonial mapping through Tlingit place-names, reinforcing Tlingit occupancy through memory and land use. The 1882 navy bombardment and burning of the Tlingit village Angoon is the subject of one section, placed within a colonial timeline, enacted through masculinist negotiation: "Fifteen years after United States men at Sitka negotiated a transaction with Russian men that resulted in the loss of millions of acres of ancient occupied lands, and only six years after the famous military engagement at Little Bighorn."[90] In contrast to the logics of settler space and time, which attempted to separate Alaska Natives from other Indigenous peoples of North America, Hayes formulates time and place to highlight the consistency of American colonial violence while also resisting U.S. hegemony by alluding to Custer and the Seventh Cavalry Regiment's defeat. In these passages, Hayes presents a dense and overwhelming sense of space-time: repeated place-names, in English and Tlingit, stories of violence, histories of resistance, childhood memories, and humorous descriptions of feeding tourists bagels and juice pouches all collectively underscore the failure of the progressive narrative, instead rendering history as open and unfinished. Importantly, this occurs through connection to land, exactly what the settler colonial project desires to dispossess from the first peoples of Alaska. Hayes is enacting what Mishuana Goeman describes as a (re)mapping, wherein Native women's literary production metaphorically and materially generates new understandings in response to the colonial imaginary.[91] By emphasizing Native presence, both land and bodies, imbricated within colonial knowledge yet also prior and outside of non-Native epistemology, Hayes highlights that however much settler logics seek to naturalize Indigenous elimination, they can never truly do so, and must instead continually repeat possessory claims in the face of such incompleteness.

Not only does Hayes point to settler colonialism's failure to account for Indigenous place and time, she does it in an Indigenous feminist fashion. For if the heteropatriarchal project of settler colonialism was (and is) to override the capacious familial connections of the Tlingit in favor of a male-dominated nuclear family, Hayes provides a different model of kinship that is illegible to the tourists and settlers of Alaska. Consider the following passage, where she narrates her tour alongside tourist reaction:

> "On the port side in the far distance is Admiralty Island," I continued. "The original name for that Island is Xutsnoowú, which means 'Fortress of the Brown Bear.' That's a good name for it, because the brown bear population on that large island is thought to be one bear per square mile. At sixteen hundred square miles, it's the largest concentration of brown bear in the world." Another pause while I held up my hands to show my silver bracelets. "The Native people of this area associate themselves with different animals that we then take as our crests. My clan—the Wolf clan—considers itself related to the brown bear, so I'm always careful to point it out to you when we go by!" For some reason, this never failed to make them laugh.[92]

Similar to the tourist gaze of the late nineteenth century, the laughter of those on the whale-watching tour reveals their consumptive practice, viewing Hayes's racial and gendered body (and jewelry) as object but not as subject or producer of knowledge. Hayes continues, "When I was a girl, my grandmother used to tell me we don't eat brown bear meat, because to do so would be just like eating our own cousin!"[93] Not only is the brown bear recognized as a family member, but also, the knowledge is passed on by a matriarch, the grandmother who raised her as a young girl. The tourist audience cannot comprehend that Hayes is telling an actual, factual history, from her matrilineal Kaagwaantaan clan. To the tourists who view the world through settler heteropatriarchy's logic, Hayes's detailed and complex knowledge appears absurd. This incomprehension is shared by her white boss: "The captain had been surprised when he realized that I still considered the brown bear my cousin, the Taku Wind my grandfather, the spider my neighbor. After being brought the truths of virgin birth, resurrection, and walking on water, why would I now persist in believing a myth?"[94] Hayes asserts her Tlingit knowledge of familial relations and spirituality, sarcastically juxtaposing Christian "truths" next to her cosmology. How Hayes ends this passage is telling: "But I let the passengers laugh, the captain preach, the jet engines clog. Every day is the same, every passenger is the same. Every captain is the same. Every moment is unique."[95] Hayes turns the tourist narrative on end. Instead of the Native person surveilled, gendered and nameless, engaged in rote activities, industrial or domestic, it is the passengers and captain, the tourists and settlers, who become a unified, predictable mass. It is settler colonialism and heteropatriarchy that are trapped by their narrow social order, while Ernestine Hayes's multivalent and expansive history and worldview allow for possibility, for an Indigenous space and time that encompasses past, present, *and* future.

Conclusion: Every Moment Is Unique

Alaska Natives were racialized as Asian from the start of the U.S. colonial period in Alaska, a ubiquitous but previously overlooked aspect of the imperial desires and deployment of a settler nation. Government officials who argued for the acquisition of the Alaskan territory configured Alaska Natives as separate from other Indigenous Americans through a lens of Asianness, a distinction that romanticized imperial conquest alongside the promise of a settler colonial future. This racialization had a long-lasting effect on the relationship between Alaska Natives and the federal government, constructing claims based not on a nation-to-nation status but instead instituted through racialized and gendered notions of citizenship. Government officials, tourists, missionaries, and ethnographers all configured kinship between Alaska Natives and Asian ancestors, an abstracted intimacy based on imperially informed empiricism. Through widely read travel literature, tourists visiting Alaska cemented the perceived Asian origins of Alaska Natives, naturalizing American colonial ambitions in Alaska as common sense.

Women tourists in particular elucidated the heteropatriarchal disciplining inherent in the prescribed assimilation of Alaska Natives, relying on both orientalism and primitivism. Placing these discourses into conversation exposes how Asians and Natives are differentially connected through notions of settler colonial space and time, a contingency that configures them as failing to be modern. In contrast to tourist depictions, Ernestine Hayes in her memoir *Blonde Indian* exposes settler colonialism's failure to account for a complex and multilayered understanding of colonial, racial, and gendered history. Ernestine Hayes reminds us that settler colonialism and heteropatriarchy are not (and never were) total or guaranteed, that Indigenous feminist epistemology provides us with future, past, and present possibilities, that every moment is unique.

By the close of the nineteenth century, the colonial imaginary connecting Asians and Alaska Natives had begun to fracture, driven by anxieties produced by the arrival of Chinese immigrant workers in Alaska. Concurrent to the development of racialized colonial discourse, anthropologists were instrumental in shifting Alaska Native exceptionalism (via Asian origins) from other Indigenous in the Americas to a larger narrative of Asian origins for all Indigenous peoples in the Americas. Though Alaska Native racialization as Asian would be superseded by other discourses, the idea of indigeneity through Asianness would find a lasting articulation in the Bering Land Bridge theory. As early tourist literature in Alaska made way for the white male heroics of gold rush narratives, the discursive gulf between Alaska Natives and Asian migrant workers would further widen within Alaska's narrative development as the "Last Frontier." Chapter 2 examines these new forms of racialization during the gold rush era, as colonial constructions shifted to frontier notions of kinship and belonging. Centered on romantic ideals of white male triumph over land and labor, gold rush narratives furthered the gulf between legible Asian and Native connections. Chapter 2 focuses on the folktale of Alaska's popular figure China Joe to illustrate disavowed violence, racial antagonisms, and possibilities for affinity.

CHAPTER TWO

Fictions of the Last Frontier
Alaska's Gold Rush and the Legend of China Joe

Day had broken cold and gray, exceedingly cold and gray, and the Cassiar miners knew they were facing famine. A bitter winter and the Stikine River had frozen early—the last steamboat of the season would never arrive. The miners could not remember the year, their bodies so frozen they could no longer discern the passing of time. How long ago was it that prospectors struck gold in the calm creek that fed into Dease Lake? The rush was on then, and swarms of men stampeded the Cassiar Mountains, traveling up the Stikine from Fort Wrangel in American Alaska. The overwintering sourdoughs had gambled on sitting out the cold and gray days for an early start on spring prospecting, and they had lost. To be sure, without the last steamship, no one had enough food and supplies to last through the winter. No one, that is, except China Joe, the Chinese baker who cooked for prospectors in the mining camp. Swindlers arrived at his tent, with schemes to buy his flour to resell for a hefty profit. Joe refused and the crooks doubled down. They waved their guns and threatened Joe, but he would not be swayed. Instead, China Joe shared his provisions with everyone that winter, saving the miners from their starvation, and their despair. He asked for nothing in return.

A few years later, Joe moved downriver to Fort Wrangel, the old Russian fort where the Stikine meets the Pacific, by then a boomtown outfitting miners on their way to the gold fields. Always ingenious, China Joe set up a restaurant and bakery in the hull of the lilting Hope, *a beached sternwheeler. The miners never forgot the freezing winter on the Cassiar and the generosity of their friend, and China Joe never lacked for customers.*[1]

The tale of China Joe, a gold rush story from the mid-1870s repeated in Alaska for well over a century, is presented here, a condensed and composite version replete with the sentimental and superlative affectation often employed in the telling. China Joe's story is integral to stories of the gold rush period of Alaska, and makes an additional appearance in the occasional tourist travelogue.[2] Within Alaskan history generally and local histories of Juneau specifically, the China Joe tale appears frequently and with surprising longevity, resurfacing over the years as a central part of Juneau's origin story.[3] Newspapers highlight Joe's prominence as a local figure, during his life and after, and his legacy includes a former mayor donating a memorial plaque in the 1960s for his gravesite and, in more recent years, a pair of Juneau residents penning a play about his life.[4] China Joe also surfaces within Asian American literature and history, most notably in Maxine Hong Kingston's biomythographical novel, *China Men*.[5] This chapter focuses on the China Joe folktale, heavily repeated in Alaskan press and popular histories from the late nineteenth century to the present, to comment on the construction of white settler masculinity and, more pointedly, the multiple yet divergent registers of racial violence that make such heroic narratives possible.

Gold rushes in Alaska fueled two crucial developments: economic growth and non-Native settlement, the trends together signaling a shift from colonial extraction to an incipient settler colonialism. Starting in the 1870s, Alaska became a preferred route for accessing the gold country in British Columbia and the Yukon. Traveling on steamship routes established by the tourist trade, tens of thousands of argonauts disembarked in Southeast Alaska to make the trek up rivers and mountain passes to the streams and riverbeds that promised gold. The quest for gold brought not only prospectors but also entrepreneurs who flocked to nascent boomtowns to outfit and entertain the gold seekers and Alaska Native and First Nation peoples from various nations and villages, as well as non-Natives from points south. In 1880, prospectors struck paydirt in Alaska proper, and soon after, industrial mines were established in three towns along the Gastineau Channel—Juneau, Treadwell, and Douglas—turning Southeast Alaska into the hard rock mining capital of the world. Alaska was permanently transformed, its non-Native population surging from fewer than 500 in 1880 to more than 30,000 in 1900; with the Klondike stampede that started in 1897, 100,000 prospectors would endeavor to reach the Yukon gold fields, the vast majority traveling through Alaska.[6]

Stories of Alaska's gold rushes built on the tourist narratives of colonial adventure, and, moreover, they became synonymous with Alaska itself, exemplifying Alaska's identification as the "Last Frontier." Gold rush stories reinforced notions of white masculinity and triumph over economic and environmental adversity, exalting white working-class notions of manliness, for in the grand narrative of gold seekers, even well-to-do miners had to physically labor and dirty their hands. The idea of Alaska being the final space for such classed, raced, and gendered adventure is undergirded by Alaska as the setting for the "last" great gold rush, the Klondike stampede of 1897–99.[7] The Klondike Gold Rush took place during a global depression; in the midst of bread lines, the Klondike was popularly known as the "poor man's gold rush," especially appealing for its promise of sudden wealth. The Alaska gold rushes, occurring at the turn from the nineteenth to the twentieth century, promulgated alternatives to the drudgery of industrial wage labor, positing the image of the independent prospector succeeding through hard work and perseverance as synonymous with Alaska even as gold extraction became dominated by wage labor in mines.

China Joe's story and its ongoing re-formation demonstrate the composition of folklore, a familiar yet informal tale that is reinforced through its ongoing reiteration within an archive of public memory constructed from a conglomeration of local and regional histories, popular-press reports, memoir, and literature that highlight China Joe's legend and its importance within the gold rush narratives of Alaskan colonialism. These records construct, repeat, and disseminate the legend of China Joe, necessarily including that which is often deemed trivial or anecdotal. Based on speculation and repetition, folklore is particularly well suited to narrate the colonial space of gold mining. In July 1897, when the steamship *Portland* arrived in Seattle, just three days after the *Excelsior* docked in San Francisco—both ships bringing prospectors from the Klondike—5,000 people greeted the ship, shouting, "Show us the gold!"[8] Disheveled miners disembarked, carrying jars and bundles collectively filled with two tons of gold. The Klondike rush was on, and within days, thousands had booked their passage north.[9] To catch gold fever was not a rational condition but a high-risk outlook dependent, to a large degree, on word-of-mouth information. As one author on the Klondike described, "Once in the atmosphere of the gold country one hears constantly of newly found placers which are reported to be vastly richer than anything yet discovered."[10] Poet Robert Service revealed that, "the Arctic trails have their secret tales"; and what was the ill fate of Jack London's protagonist in "To Build a Fire"? As London surmised, "The trouble with him was that he was without imagination."[11] The hunt for gold was nothing if not the experimental belief in one's future wealth. It is the speculative nature of gold rush narratives, and the archive of China Joe's tale specifically, that I highlight in this chapter.

Popular fiction of the gold rush period, such as the short stories of Jack London, the poetry of Robert Service, and the novels of Rex Beach, highlighted the white masculine individualism that was ostensibly needed not only to survive but also to succeed in the Great North.[12] At the outset, the story of China Joe appears to contrast the rugged individualism common to Alaska's mythic past: the opposite of the "every man for himself" dictum, China Joe's actions are communitarian and highlight his seeming selflessness. Alongside his oft-repeated tale, he is described as "the only man in Alaska without an enemy," "a friend to everyone," and "he lived by the golden rule."[13]

In the mining communities of colonial Alaska, a male-dominated world that quickly assembled in boomtowns and gold fields, a homosocial community developed that was essential to creating a sense of kinship. The tale of China Joe, therefore, incorporates him as a character in the gold rush narrative as a racialized and feminized, yet exceptional, member of the frontier family. In this way, settler colonial folklore incorporates China Joe into a frontier intimacy with white male prospectors, and his racialized difference, which is also always read as a gendered difference, works to highlight white masculinity and heroism. What initially appears as exception ultimately reproduces intrepid white masculinity. Chapters 1 and 2 both examine figures produced through colonial imaginaries, chapter 1 focusing on the orientalized Alaska Native that animates the imperial ambitions of a settler nation-state while chapter 2 looks at China Joe as cipher, an opaque blankness that serves to both valorize settler masculinity and excuse its normative violence. The racialized connection forged in settler orientalism is severed within the ascent of industrial capitalism, China Joe's legend juxtaposed to contrasting modes of brutal management for Native and Asian peoples. Because frontier intimacy is constructed through the speculative, networks of affinity and intimacy conditioned by but outside of the logics of settler colonialism can also be addressed through speculation. Within China Joe's mythological story, this requires questioning his asserted exceptionalism, to speculate on his knowledge and being within a larger Chinese migrant community as well as to comment on his proximity to Native peoples.

To use gold rush metaphor, I hope to mine and undermine China Joe's narrative, reexamining the tale of China Joe's exceptional benevolence through several registers of disavowed violence. What happens when we reenvision Joe as part of a larger Chinese immigrant community, connected to the circle of workers who were driven out of the Cassiar initially, then allowed back in to work the tailings of white miners. Similarly, I confront the idea of empty land settled through the mining activities of white prospectors, looking at the Stikine River as a Tlingit place, as a way to reread the starving winter of the mid-1870s. Rereading for violence is not a particularly difficult exercise when China Joe's role as a generous baker who sustains starving prospectors makes up only half of his reiterated tale. Several years after the freezing winter, China Joe is reportedly the only Chinese person allowed to stay in the mining town of Juneau when Chinese laborers at a nearby mine are driven out. He is protected from the incited mob by old time "sourdoughs," prospectors who remember his magnanimousness in the Cassiar gold fields. Seen through a colonial lens, however, this is not simply a tale of prospectors repaying China

Joe's good will but proffers a pedagogical judgement in the shift to settler colonialism, the romanticization of the colonial extraction period winning out over the base values and violence of industrialized settler capitalism. China Joe is allowed to remain not solely because of his previous acts of kindness, but because his racialized placement in the economy is tied to an older model of colonialism that allows him, unlike Asian industrial workers, to participate in the (homo)social milieu as a supportive, and nonthreatening, helper. As a singular Chinese migrant, rather than a class of racialized workers, his gendered feminization within the homosocial space of Alaska resource extraction can be understood as upstanding rather than improper.

I expand my reading for disavowed violence by studying the driving-out of Chinese miners in juxtaposition to the lynching of three Tlingit men, the two events taking place within a few years of each other in the same Alaskan mining town. If the driving-out of Chinese is the response of settler colonial volatility, how does the lynching of Alaska Native men signal a different register of violent control? How do Native and Asian peoples operate as internal and external threats to the colonial and social order of Alaska, exposing the unstable and contradictory process of American settler development known as the "frontier"? The differential violence and disciplinary techniques of control directed at Asian migrants and Indigenous peoples highlight another manifestation of space-time colonialism, in this case the spatiotemporal dimensions of living under the threat of terror formations, a subjection that Achille Mbembe conceptualizes as necropower. I close this chapter with a final reading of China Joe and his social and political affinity with Native residents, an affective reading that allows for possible alliance outside of settler logics and in solidarity against disciplinary terror.

Myth Multiplied: The Making of China Joe

After the decline of the Cassiar gold rush, and after Wrangell faded as a boomtown, similar to the prospectors he is credited with saving, China Joe followed the subsequent mining rush to Juneau. In 1880 the discovery of gold in the Silver Bow Basin in Southeast Alaska was attributed to Joe Juneau and Dick Harris, two prospectors grubstaked by mining engineer George Pilz. Juneau and Harris were veterans of the Cassiar rush, and it is quite probable that they knew Joe and possibly were recipients of his generosity during the freezing winter of the 1870s. Certainly, they were aware of the China Joe tale. It is reported that Joe Juneau's last request, on his deathbed in Dawson City in the Yukon, was to be buried in Juneau with China Joe as one of his pallbearers.[14]

Credit for the city of Juneau's gold rush, however, should be given to K̲awa.ée (alternately Kowee, Koweeh, Cow-eeh, Cowee), a leader of the Áak'w K̲wáan Tlingit, k̲wáan referring to the social geography group of the winter village. K̲awa.ée both brought ore samples to Pilz in Sitka and guided Juneau and Harris, not once, but twice, to the mountain valley two and a half miles up what is now known as Gold Creek. The first expedition failed because Juneau and Harris spent their grubstake on liquor and spent almost a month on a drunken binge, never making it past the mouth of Gold Creek.[15] The Áak'w K̲wáan's territory included what would become named Gold Creek, Silver Bow Basin, and the Gastineau Channel, and K̲awa.ée's actions mirrored those of many Tlingit leaders in Southeast Alaska who, under overwhelming colonial pressure, sought to incorporate their people into the cash economy of gold. Tlingit sources also introduce multiplicity into this story: that it was perhaps a Tlingit man named Geinax Éesh who led the white men up Gold Creek and that it was a woman known as Sheep Creek Mary who found the gold nugget that enticed Pilz.[16] These revisions or additions underscore the collective contribution of the Áak'w K̲wáan Tlingit in this endeavor, as well as the relationships among clans and between clan members and leaders. Within a year of the second and successful gold exploration, the boomtown of Juneau was established, along with the towns of Douglas and Treadwell across a saltwater channel on a nearby island. Tlingit settlements formed along the beach on the outskirts of Juneau, and between Douglas and Treadwell.

China Joe followed this wave of miners to the area and purchased a half lot in Juneau in the summer of 1881, where he built a log cabin bakery with room for his personal lodging in back, residing there until his death in 1917. The early years in Juneau are not well recorded; the first Juneau newspaper did not start publishing until 1887. Because of this, neither the bakery's establishment nor the driving-out of Chinese in 1886 was reported in local presses when they occurred.[17] Juneau's printed press was established in the late 1880s, flourishing in the 1890s concomitant to the Gastineau Channel's (Juneau, Douglas, and Treadwell) development in industrial gold mining, and China Joe's story proliferates in tandem with Juneau's political importance within Alaska. With the passage of the Alaska Act in 1900, Alaska's seat of government was moved from Sitka to Juneau, a transfer that was completed in 1906. This shift reflected the change from Alaska's colonial past, with Sitka representing the former capital of Russian America, to Alaska's settler colonial future in the gold economy of Juneau, American Alaska's first founded town. Benedict Anderson charts this phenomenon as "print-capitalism," to describe the powerful concatenation of industrial capitalism and print culture

FIGURE 2.1 Photograph of the baker known as "China Joe." The brothers Joseph Nicoll and Henry John Harrison operated a photography studio, Harrison Brothers, in Juneau, Alaska, circa 1888–1900, which most likely sold this card to tourists. In a style common among cartes de visite of this period, China Joe in this studio portrait holds several items meant to signify his singularity or curiosity to viewers. Several items in the photograph—his fan, opium pipe, and quilted jacket—emphasize China Joe's foreignness, while a brimmed hat conceals his queue and a pocket watch spotlights a modern temporality. Alaska State Library, Early Prints of Alaska Collection, ca. 1870–1920, photo by Harrison Brothers, ASL-P297-118.

that facilitates the discursive development of a shared community and destiny.[18] China Joe's frequent press appearance is not simply a folktale of Alaska's gold rush but also a gold rush narrative constructed through, and in service to, Alaska's settler colonial ambitions. As Patrick Wolfe has elaborated on Anderson's now classic work, the "imagined community," within a settler colonial national formation, simultaneous to a collective memorializing, must also enact a forgetting of the "criminal legacy of genocidal theft."[19] It is the process of forgetting this complex legacy, with its attendant racial and colonial violence, that concerns us in the following sections.

China Joe's first newspaper appearance was in the *Alaska Journal* in 1893, which reported his registration with the U.S. commissioner in accordance with the Geary Act.[20] In 1892, the Geary Act renewed the 1882 Chinese Exclusion Act for an additional decade and made proof of legal entry and residence compulsory for all Chinese in the United States. Chinese laborers were required to register with the government and carry identification cards.[21] Having lived in Juneau for twelve years by this time, he was described as "our 'Joe.'" The paternalist intimacy extended to "our Joe" in this moment is underscored by governmental surveillance, as his belonging is simultaneously marked as racialized and conditional. China Joe begins to make a regular appearance in the local press in the late 1890s, and particularly in the early twentieth century, both as a colorful local character and within the reiteration of his Cassiar and Treadwell tales. In several human-interest stories, Joe is alternately duped by a magician, makes weather predictions, and repeatedly hosts his Chinese New Year celebrations.[22] At the same time that these supposedly entertaining stories do little more than tell a localized event, the repeated language in these articles assert China Joe as foundational to Juneau's gold rush origins and stress his singularity. He is repeatedly described as a settler and pioneer, typically modified as the only Chinese settler or pioneer. For example, in one of the articles describing Joe's Chinese New Year festivities, he is identified as "'Chinese Joe,' the pioneer Chinaman of Juneau, and the only Celestial in the city." In this way, his status as a pioneer is tied to his exceptional Chinese status in the Alaskan frontier. As with the "our Joe" in his first press appearance, belonging and paternalism coalesce in a frontier intimacy that, at once, incorporates China Joe while maintaining racialized boundaries.

Several aspects of these earliest written accounts deserve examination. For one, when China Joe's background is mentioned, it always includes both his saving prospectors from starvation and, in turn, the protection that the old-time miners provide for him during the driving-out of other Chinese. Though his generosity toward miners may have been known as oral knowledge prior to 1886, the fact that the first printed accounts of China Joe's life occur after the driving-out means that the two parts of the story are always told together. Joe's beneficence is rewarded by his protection, while the white miners redeem their heroism through virile and militant defense. These early stories also tie in to the larger literature of the gold rush, in both dramatic and humorous ways. Take, for example, Joe being fooled by a magician to break all his eggs, and his disappointment that there were no gold coins to be found inside.[23] "'Him one debbil,' said the mystified old Chinaman," echoes the French-Canadian who says of the protagonist sled dog in Jack London's *Call of the Wild*, "Dat Buck two devils."[24] It's not surprising that the immigrant vernacular in the China Joe story is similar to London's writing, given that *Call of the Wild* was arguably the most popular literary depiction of Alaska in the early 1900s, having been serialized in the *Saturday Evening Post* before being published as a novella in 1903. Even when an accent is not ascribed to him in these early Alaska press accounts, Joe is asked about all manner of prosaic, everyday matters: the weather, how long he has lived in Juneau, and so on. What he is never questioned about, however, is either his saving the freezing miners in the Cassiar or the Treadwell driving-out of Chinese. China Joe's linked generosity and exceptional status as conferred by the first generation of prospecting pioneers narrates the gold rush as a specific rationalization for colonial and racial violence, underscored by the fact that China Joe, as conduit, never offers his own perspective on the founding narratives in which he features.

This is especially evident in longer pieces devoted to the history of the driving-out, such as a 1911 article titled, "When the Chinese Were Driven Out," printed in the *Alaska Sourdough*, a Douglas newspaper published by socialist Arthur B. Callaham.[25] The article begins, "There was at least one man in Alaska in 1886 who was not in sympathy with the anti-Chinese uprising which occurred in that year." That person, however, was not China Joe, but Alaska's territorial governor Alfred P. Swineford. The article proceeds with Swineford's opposition to the mob agitation and expulsion of Chinese miners and his unsuccessful attempts to enforce the law, marked by the resignation of the deputy sheriff and the refusal of the navy commander to return the Chinese to Treadwell. An official report by Swineford is quoted extensively. The last paragraph in the article opens very similarly to the first: "However unanimous the general feeling . . . against the Chinese on the Gastineau Channel . . . may have been, there was one Chinaman in Juneau who was not affected by it. That was 'Old Joe,' the one chinaman who lives on the channel today." Joe's generosity to the old-time prospectors is repeated, and the article ends with his protection by Juneau's pioneers. The juxtaposition of Swineford and Joe is telling: Swineford is the exemplary "man," while Joe can only be the "one chinaman." Swineford is quoted extensively, but Joe remains silent on his rescue. Swineford and the prospecting pioneers share an aversion to the mob violence of industrial wage laborers and seek to protect the innocent and seemingly powerless Chinese. In this way, Alaska's government, not the local deputy or the federal navy but the person emblematic of Alaska as territory and future state, is read as the same as the pioneering generation of gold rush heroes. The voiceless figure of China Joe makes this linkage possible.

The pedagogical function of China Joe's character is featured in 1910, when Juneau's school principal, Emma Sarepta Yule, penned an essay simply titled, "China Joe," for the regional magazine *Pacific Monthly*, published in Portland, Oregon.[26] Frequent contributors included Sinclair Lewis and Jack London. Though Yule admits that she has never met China Joe or visited his bakery, she imagines his "Buddha smile" and wonders what thoughts lie behind "that placid celestial mask." Fascinated by his story, she relies on "his best friend 'Mr. Jack'" to detail Joe's history in Alaska gold rush lore—his role as cook in the Cassiar, as proprietor of the Fort Wrangel hotel on the *Hope*, and his generosity to prospectors during a time of famine. After his protection during the 1886 driving-out, Yule reports that he cared for the sick and tended the graves of the old-timers. In contrast to the pioneering heroes in the *Alaska Sourdough* article, Yule's essay paints a picture of a completely saintly and selfless individual. At the same time, his magnanimity is always racialized, as when Joe is attributed to saying, "Boy never payee me. No, no—that allee right." As with Joe's response to the magician, such accented language reinforces the mythological character of Joe—in this case fusing his selflessness to his racialized immigrant status. Yule's piece also highlights the gendered aspects of this racialization, as China Joe's caretaking of the prospectors is rendered as feminine and matronly, from initially cooking for prospectors during a time of hardship to housing them, caring for them when sick, and, finally, devotedly tending their graves after they have passed. Although the focus of the two longer pieces in the *Pacific Monthly* and the *Alaska Sourdough* feature different protagonists, I argue that they are interwoven—white male heroism and racialized, feminized, immigrant selflessness are mutually interdependent foundations to Alaska's gold rush mythology; together, they neutralize the very racial and gendered violence of Alaska's gold rush economy.

Taken as a whole—both the anecdotal news items and the longer exposés—the early-twentieth-century telling and retelling of the China Joe story formed a particularly powerful gold rush narrative in Alaska's nascent settler colonialism. The tale of China Joe has enjoyed a pronounced longevity to the present. Joe's story was emphasized with his death in 1917, and has reappeared periodically within histories of Alaska and of gold mining.[27] Emphasizing Anderson's thesis on the creation of common discourse within national formation, China Joe's story is recollected during historical commemorative periods, such as in the 1980s with the celebration of Juneau's centennial.[28] Local recuperation of the China Joe tale has included a play written by a pair of Juneau authors, a photo exhibit of the "five Joes" in the Juneau senior housing Fireweed Place, and a woodcut of China Joe by the Alaska-based printmaker and illustrator Dale DeArmond.[29] As a story that gets carried across different genres, China Joe becomes an established part of public and cultural memory. In recent years, China Joe's story has enjoyed an especially marked comeback, China Joe appearing in nearly a dozen newspaper stories since 2000, as well as mentions in books on Alaska.[30] With this abundant retelling, the details of the story remain essentially the same from the early 1900s.

Given the consistency of the China Joe story and the gold rush narrative facilitated through his "placid, celestial mask," the identity of the figure known as "China Joe" remains surprisingly speculative. There is a general consensus as to certain historical aspects, including his immigration from China to Victoria, British Columbia, in 1864, and his subsequent travel to the gold mining area of Boise, Idaho. In 1874 he followed the rush into the Cassiar. Although China Joe is universally recognized in Alaskan history through his racialized nickname or, alternately, as "Joe the Baker," many different versions of his Chinese name exist. He is listed as Hi Ching on an 1880 U.S. Navy census, as As Hie in 1881 in Juneau documents, and as Hi Chung on the 1910 U.S. census and on his charter to the Juneau Pioneers Association.[31] China Joe registered in 1893 under the Geary Bill as Ting Tu Wee, and he has additionally been identified as Ching Thui, Chong Thui, and Lee Hing.[32] Though some of these names appear to be Anglicized variations of the same name (Ting Tu Wee, Chung Thui, Chong Thui), enough differentiation exists within the entire list to prevent an exact pronouncement. Given these discrepancies, how can we be certain that the legendary China Joe is one person and not a composite of several Chinese immigrants? Alternately, could the different names signal something about China Joe's past and his desires for reinvention? Or, more simply, do the variations reflect the myriad complexities and politics of translation?

The desire for a historical notion of absolute "truth," however, persists. The probate records for China Joe reveal that his file was initially labeled under "Tui Ting Chu," but upon discovering his written will, the file was changed to "Chong Thui," so that the heading read, "In the Matter of the Estate of TUI TING CHU whose American name was China Joe but whose true name was CHONG THUI, deceased."[33] In the well-intentioned quest for "true" names, it didn't occur to anyone to notice the similarity between "Tui Ting" and "Chong Thui," slight variations of the same words in reverse order. Looking at China Joe's signature on his will, which contains three characters, the family name he writes is Chu (Yao in Cantonese), so the original name on the file is perhaps the most accurate.[34] This example highlights the absurdity of defining a sole or single truth in the face of such contradiction and multiplicity. As researcher and scholarly interlocutor, I am tempted to accurately locate his "true" name, if only to avoid referring to him through the racialized moniker "China Joe," uncomfortably close to an epithet. At the same time, the variance in his name corresponds to the multiplicity in his story.

In addition to the perplexity surrounding his given name, other embellishments and divergences surface in the standard story of China Joe and his generosity toward white prospectors. In at least two instances, the Cassiar gold fields are changed to the territorial capital of Sitka, where Joe is said to have opened a bakery in 1880. In this alternate tale, a steamer carrying provisions is lost, and Joe solves the food shortage out of his stores.[35] Similarly, in some stories his bakery in the Cassiar morphs into a grocery store; in others, his bakery in Juneau transforms into a laundry. What remains constant is his beneficence, at times magnified beyond the winter of an early freeze, so selfless that payment is not required for his services at any point, and he operates his business as a charity for white miners. In this way, China Joe's historical archival existence, outside of and independent from his folktale, is an impossibility. The myth is larger than the person, and as a fiction his name can only be China Joe. A cipher, he can exist only as an indefinite character of the gold rush or, as Chinese American author Maxine Hong Kingston concludes, "Perhaps any China Man was China Joe."[36]

The Absent Presence of Chinese Miners

The tale of China Joe and the starving miners in the Cassiar naturalizes white prospectors as the only community of adventurers, the tale scripted to highlight white male struggles for survival with the aid of the lone Chinese baker. Chinese were in the Cassiar, however, both before and at the start of the Cassiar Gold Rush, having moved north from previous Canadian gold rushes, but were pushed out once the stampede was on. Additional Chinese followed the Stikine to the Cassiar Mountains alongside other miners. As the rush took hold, white miners forced the Chinese out, but no details are given as to how this was accomplished, an archival absence that suggests disavowed racial violence.[37] China Joe was among these early Chinese in the Cassiar, and when the Chinese were driven out, he was allowed to stay.[38] This information brings to light other possible motivations for China Joe's action as a baker in the Cassiar. As the only Chinese allowed to remain when other Chinese were driven out, Joe must have clearly understood the white hegemony that undergirded gold rush social economy. The essential service that he provided as a baker kept him in the area even as racial exclusion was being enforced. At the same time, he must have understood that his exceptional standing in the community was based on his role in service occupation rather than as economic competition. He would have also understood the inherent risks of being Chinese in the Cassiar, with the tacit agreement that he could never pursue his own gold claims. Discerning a longer continuum of driving-out from Cassiar to Juneau, the legend of China Joe serves as a bridge between demonstrations of this settler methodology, both enabling and erasing this spectacular and reiterative violence.

Chinese also returned to the Cassiar as the rush petered out, picking over former miners' claims. They were recorded in the area starting in 1879, right around the time China Joe moved to Fort Wrangel. From 1879 to 1883, approximately thirty mining claims were issued in the Cassiar District to Chinese miners, some given to individual miners but most to Chinese mining companies, which worked the claims with crews of multiple Chinese miners. They mined during warmer weather and wintered in Cassiar boomtowns such as Telegraph Creek or Laketon, or went downriver to Wrangell or Juneau. The practice of the Chinese miners following after a gold rush boom was over, to mine claims already worked, was a practice well established in the American West since the 1849 rush in California, and gave rise to the term "Chinaman's wages."[39] Although technically prospectors, the Chinese were essentially wage laborers, contracted by Chinese companies to work over the land in large numbers for low yet guaranteed pay. This contrasted with the image of the high-risk, high-reward frontier prospector and reinforced the idea of Chinese workers as feminized and racialized others compared to the idealized, individual, and heroic white male miner.[40] The British explorer Warburton Pike, known for his travels and writings on British Columbia and the Canadian Arctic, observed the Chinese miners in the Cassiar in the late 1880s, "being of a persevering nature, satisfied with small returns for their labor."[41]

Taking into account these two larger contexts of Chinese in the Cassiar—being driven out at the start of the rush and being allowed back in to pick over white miners' claims in groups organized by Chinese companies—China Joe's story of wintertime beneficence serves multiple disciplinary functions. Though Joe is the ostensible protagonist in this story, it is not his heroism that is ultimately conveyed, but that of the gold miners who embody white male masculinity, who risk the elements and starvation. The knowledge that Joe is allowed to stay when the Chinese who are deemed competitors are chased out further undermines Joe's primacy in his gold rush tale. He is rendered exceptional not just through his racialization as the sole Chinese but is singular also as the only feminine figure in this narrative. Relegated to the feminized role of cooking for the prospecting men, his resourcefulness and generosity serve to restore their colonial adventure and quest for wealth. In the kinship created by the frontier community, Joe must play the solitary feminine role in an otherwise homosocial fraternity. His racialized and gendered status cohere in his exceptionalism—he serves and saves the starving miners simultaneously as the only Chinese and only feminized caretaker in the Cassiar.

The Stikine as a Native Place

It is not only Asian workers who are effaced in gold rush tales; such stories of white male fortitude also depend on an absenting of Native peoples and places. Alaskan gold rush adventures often depicted the hardship of traversing dense forests, tempestuous rivers, and steep mountain ranges to get to the gold fields of British Columbia or the Yukon, reinforcing white male heroism and capitalist adventurism. Through perseverance and determination, these stories narrated, even the most humble white man could attain fortune and fame. Such triumphalist narratives of white masculine success obfuscated not only Chinese labor in the gold fields but also the labors of Alaska Native and Canadian First Nation peoples who worked as guides and packers and who staffed the stores, hotels, saloons, and dance halls of gold rush boomtowns. In May 1879, Captain George Bailey visited Fort Wrangel as part of the U.S. Revenue Marine and reported, "The permanent population (white) is seventy-five persons, although in the winter it is increased by two hundred and fifty or three hundred miners.... The Indians belonging at this place (the Stickeens) number about two hundred and fifty. At the same time, there are upwards of two thousand about the place, consisting of Chilkats, Tahkos, Sundowns, Kakes, and Hydas, during the summer and fall, employed in transporting goods and stores up the Stikeen river to the gold mines."⁴² The Alaska Native people that Bailey describes are most likely Tlingit from the villages of the Stikine (Shtax'héen K̲wáan), Chilkat (Jilk̲áat K̲wáan), Taku (T'aak̲ú K̲wáan), Sumdum (S'awdáan K̲wáan), and Kake (K̲éex' K̲wáan). The Haida (Hydas) are a separate nation whose historic and ancestral territory is south of Tlingit homelands, existing in present-day Alaska and British Columbia. Bailey's quote divulges the immense Native presence and labor necessary to support the heroic white male enterprise of gold prospecting as well as the Native mobile labor catalyzed by gold economy.

Viewing the Alaska gold rush through the narrow lens of white male adventure and triumph obfuscates the historical land ownership of Native peoples and the dispossession that occurred in the clamor for gold. All the gold rush routes from Alaska into Canada passed through land historically controlled by Tlingit, such as the thirty-two-mile Chilkoot Pass through Chilkoot Tlingit (Lk̲óot K̲wáan) land or the Chilkat and White Passes in the domain of the Chilkat River Tlingit (Jilk̲áat K̲wáan). The Stikine River, the route to the Cassiar gold fields, is another such place. Tlingit of the present-day Wrangell area trace their origins to the Stikine River, their ancestors having moved from the interior and down the Stikine River to the Southeast Alaska coast many thousands of years ago.⁴³ This history is expressed in the Tlingit territorial name of the Wrangell area, Shtax'héen K̲wáan, Shtax'héen the word that Stikine is derived from, thought to mean, "river of bitter, unwholesome water," or "river of water so silty it must be chewed," both referring to the river's murky water.⁴⁴ As anthropologist Thomas Thornton explains, Tlingit place names are synesthetic, describing not only the visual but also sounds, smells, and tastes as signature attributes. Colonizers, in contrast, focused simply on the visual and often named places for people. The process is rare in Tlingit culture, and even opposite, when people are named for places, highlighting Indigenous place-based ontologies and cosmologies.⁴⁵

The Shtax'héen territory is large, covering a sizable part of the coast mainland as well as several islands and parts of islands. Their inland territory extends a lengthy distance up the Stikine River, far into present-day Canada, just beyond the town of Telegraph in British Columbia. Different clans in the Shtax'héen K̲wáan established and retained ownership of summer camps along the river, where they hunted mountain goat, beaver, and porcupine, fished for salmon, and harvested berries and root vegetables. The large size of Shtax'héen territory is partly due to the unification of several smaller villages under the first Chief Shakes (Shéiyksh), a consolidation that occurred prior to American occupation.⁴⁶ Among the Tlingit, the Shtax'héen K̲wáan are known as a powerful and wealthy group of clans, particularly because they controlled trade with interior aboriginal groups through access to the Stikine River. Whether their consolidation and growth was a result of this trade arrangement or, conversely, was organized to monopolize this exchange, is not recorded in written colonial histories. That the two events are related is fairly certain.

The Shtax'héen colonial encounter commenced under Russian colonial rule when the Russians established the stockade Redoubt St. Dionysius in 1834 at the mouth of the Stikine and named the nearby island Wrangel after Baron Ferdinand Von Wrangel, the governor of Russian America at that time. The Russians had depleted most of the Pacific sea otter by overhunting, and the new fort was part of an effort to obtain land mammal furs from interior tribes. Throughout Southeast Alaska, Tlingit tribes held a monopoly on this trade, acting as middlemen between European traders and interior Native nations. In 1839 or 1840, Hudson's Bay Company leased the fort from the Russians, renaming it Fort Stikine. The Shtax'héen fought with British traders for control of the river, and lost some of their dominance, mostly because of illness and death brought on by smallpox epidemics in 1836 and again in 1840. It was the American colonial period, however, that posed the greatest challenge for Tlingit control of the Stikine River. The stockade was refortified by the U.S. military in 1868 and renamed Fort Wrangel. Military occupation conditioned and disciplined the daily lives of Tlingit people, with severe consequences, the most extreme example being the 1869 bombardment of the Tlingit village of Khaachxhan.áak'w, just south of the fort.[47] Even in the face of disease epidemics and armed military violence, however, the Tlingit control of the Stikine was finally wrested away with the travel of tens of thousands of prospectors traveling upriver, all looking for gold. Under the sheer number of newcomers, the landscape was changed—marking the connection and distinction between colonial conquest and resource extraction.

Understanding the Stikine as a Tlingit place (and the Cassiar gold fields as Tahltan Athabascan land) denaturalizes white settler claims to the land, a region poet Robert Service described as "where the mountains are nameless, / And the rivers all run God knows where."[48] In contrast, in Tlingit-based knowledge, the mountains had names, and the direction and path of the Stikine River was known through complex clan ownership claims to land use and trading rights. Returning to China Joe's story in the Cassiar, Native knowledges are located in the shadow of this tale. Even as settler colonial imaginaries desired to overdetermine a land as inhospitable, endured and overcome by white men and their sidekick Chinese cook, other connections threaten to emerge. Alaska Native and First Nation peoples lived in and traveled through this region; Haida, Tlingit, and Tsimshian coastal peoples moved up mountainous rivers in social and economic relations with inland Athabascan. Did Indigenous peoples experience the bitter winter in China Joe's story as unusually cold? What were Native knowledges of winter food sources, or, alternately, how had hunting, fishing, and gathering fared in the preceding seasons? How did reliance on steamboat provisions curtail Native trade, including food items? Did the Cassiar miners understand themselves to be on and moving through Native land, and did that ease or heighten anxieties as food stores ran low? The tale of China Joe saving white prospectors in the freezing winter in the Cassiar reinforced settler ideas of the land as empty and unrecognizable rather than the historical and customary knowledge and abundance of the Tahltan Athabascan and Shtax'héen Tlingit.

The Driving-Out, China Joe as Exception

Until the 1880s, the gold mined in Alaska and Canada was placer—the dust, flakes, and nuggets washed down from quartz veins in the mountains and found in the sand and gravel beds of streams. The Treadwell mine was Alaska's first industrial mine, built in 1882, a stamp mill with 900-pound pistons slamming repeatedly onto large chunks of ore mined from the mountain, then washed in a sulfur and mercury bath, the gold amalgamating with the mercury. By 1899, the Treadwell was the largest mine of its kind in the world, wreaking enormous change on the surrounding environment.[49] The Gastineau Channel shook with the incessant thunder of the stamps, twenty-four hours a day, seven days a week. Smoke spewed in the air and sulfur burned all the surrounding foliage, chemicals washing down the beach and into the ocean.

In the shift from placer to lode mining, from prospecting to wage labor, Treadwell managers complained about both the white prospectors and Tlingit who sought employment at the mine. Content to wage labor through the winter, both groups were apt to abruptly quit work during warmer months for more attractive pursuits, prospectors to try their luck on their individual gold claims while Tlingit miners left to participate in Native economies of fishing, hunting, and trapping. Mine superintendent John Treadwell hired Chinese miners in 1885, citing the need for year-round labor, but the economic advantages were also evident when Chinese miners were paid no more than two-thirds the standard wages for white or Native miners. In some accounts Treadwell recruited the workers from outside Juneau; in others, the

Chinese were seasoned miners who migrated to Juneau, many coming from the Cassiar rush.[50] The latter case holds particular resonance, given what transpired within the next year. White animosity and resentment was swift, and Chinese quarters were dynamited in June 1885. Another bombing took place in January 1886; no one was injured, but several buildings in the heart of Juneau were damaged. In August, a citizens committee met with Treadwell to demand the ousting of the Chinese. Treadwell refused, and on August 6, more than one hundred armed white men rounded up eighty-six Chinese men in Juneau and Douglas and packed them into two small schooners. With no room to lie down, the Chinese made the journey standing up to Fort Wrangel in eight days.[51]

One Chinese was not forced out. China Joe, the sequel:

> *When the incited mob, a bit drunk and bristling with weapons, arrived at China Joe's bakery, they found a rope snaked on the ground in front of his cabin, warning them to go no further. A grizzled old-timer from the Cassiar Gold Rush stepped out from the shadows. Rubbing his gray beard, he relayed Joe's generosity in the Cassiar, concluding in no uncertain terms, "You are not taking him because he is one of us." To emphasize this proclamation, riflemen appeared from every vantage point—doorways, windows, behind logs and stumps, each ready to lay down his life in defense of China Joe. No Treadwell miner dared cross that line, and China Joe lived out his days, the only Chinese person to remain in Alaska's gold country.*[52]

On the surface, this tale appears to mirror the Cassiar winter story, Joe's generosity recognized and repaid by the old-timers from the Cassiar rush. The pedagogical intent is to invoke a sense of fairness and closure, revealing the white prospectors to be as honorable in nature as Joe. By reading for disavowed raced, gendered, and classed dynamics, however, this tale is shown to reinforce and exacerbate similar dynamics. In this story, the veteran prospectors known as sourdoughs are the overt heroes, their masculinity magnified through the standoff with Treadwell miners, guns cocked. In contrast, China Joe's sense of agency is nonexistent. While this event is an essential part of his folktale, he doesn't actually appear in the story, remaining inside his cabin. His racialized femininity expands in the telling of his rescue by the old-timers, transformed from the feminized domestic cook to the heroine the prospectors protect. The story of Alaska being performed engages competing narratives of colony and settler colony. The sourdoughs are defending not only China Joe but also their adventures on the Cassiar gold fields as the rightful gold rush narrative, against the industrialized and debased mob mentality of wage laborers. Although the prospectors' frontier justice trumps that of the Treadwell miners' as the most authentic, it also makes acceptable the ousting of the Chinese who don't share Joe's exceptional racialized and gendered status. Ultimately, the tale functions as settler colonial myth wherein the prospectors become originary, the rightful primogenitors of Alaska, displacing Native provenance.

The saving of China Joe from the driving-out also marks a turning point in which his racialized exceptionality becomes marked by an honorary whiteness. As part of his fabled protection on the day of the driving-out, the prospectors declared that China Joe was "just as good as a white man."[53] Alternately, the miners' mob was questioned about why they didn't have "the Chink" when they returned to Treadwell. "'There's no Chink over there,' the leader answered. 'But there's a man they call China Joe, and he's the whitest man God ever let breathe.'"[54] Whether or not such terms were uttered, China Joe's honorary whiteness was embedded into his legend and propagated in reiterations such as an 1897 article that proclaimed that China Joe, "though his skin is yellow, has a heart all white."[55] Honorary whiteness was officially conferred on China Joe when his old-time associates declared him "a white man" in order for his induction as a charter member of the Alaska Pioneer Association in 1887.[56] That his whiteness is gendered as masculine in the above descriptions is ironic given that his titular racial status is feminized, as we see in his legendary rescue by prospectors. The kinship and belonging that the prospectors extend to him at once renders him honorary white and honorary female, as China Joe stands in the role of the moral and proper white woman who must be protected from the compromised masculinity of industrial workers by the valiant and stouthearted pioneers. His frontier intimacy is predicated on his status shifting from Chinese to white, which is in turn predicated on a shift from masculine to feminine. Though in this legend China Joe's homosocial intimacy to white prospectors is presumably chaste, it is still implicitly sexual as the frontier relationship is reproduced in a linked yet contrasting manner: from matronly cook to damsel in distress. And back again to matron and caregiver in the passing years—as Joe looks after and tends to the prospectors in their old age, he is repeatedly described as "kind," "dignified," and "gentle."[57]

Joe's exceptionality provides justification for the exclusionary and violent driving-out. The fact that not all the Chinese are driven out, that the heroes in this tale are the old-timers and the villains are the industrialized mine workers, maintains settler status quo without complaint. Joe's story is repeated as one that proves the kindness of human nature, while the driving-out taking place in the background contradicts this theme. Joe's singularity is repeatedly emphasized in stories throughout his life: "He was the only Chinese that, for twenty years, was permitted to live in the town";[58] there was "no one with whom he could speak his mother tongue"[59]; and "Joe died alone."[60] Such proclamations amplified the tragic and romanticized idea that no other Chinese ever resided in Juneau from that moment on, reinforcing Juneau as a white settler space, even if it wasn't true. For example, when Joe registered under the Geary Act in 1893 (seven years after the driving-out), a Chinese cook named An Gee also registered.[61] Similarly, by the 1910s, Joe socialized with other Chinese in Juneau, and while he may have died by himself in his own bed, the night before his death he entertained several Chinese friends late into the evening.[62] The fact that these details are ignored as the story is reproduced over the years demonstrates the discursive power of settler colonial public memory to order its own system of racial and gendered logics, and to define legible and illegible forms of intimacy.

The Necropolitics of Settler Colonialism

The enduring attention and foundational significance bestowed on the China Joe tale not only serve to justify masculinist xenophobia but also elide other forms of contingent violence, most notably, methods of terror and control enacted on Alaska Native peoples. In 1883, three Tlingit men were arrested in Juneau for the murder of a white man, and, before the arrival of the navy, all three men died as a result of "miners' justice," two of the men by hanging. This is a difficult story, to elaborate on the telling of this violence, yet important to acknowledge both as historic erasure of Native life and death and as a precursor to the driving-out, evincing that the settler terror directed three years later at the Chinese miners was neither singular nor unprecedented. Understanding that the Native men killed were working as packers, hauling materials for prospectors over the two-and-a-half-mile stretch from the mining town to the gold fields, the story of their deaths provides an additional or alternate gold rush account, one that, unlike the unending reiteration of China Joe's tale, forcefully produces white settler subjectivity while remaining unspeakable as a foundational narrative. Reading lynchings and drivings-out together reveals the structural terror that undergirded miners' law and, rather than collapsing lynchings and drivings-out into a flattened equivalence, their shared appearance within a few short years provides a way to read these actions not only as linked together in their similarity, but also as incommensurate yet differential violence. What was considered frontier justice was known to be harsh, racist even, but was often viewed as rash and indiscriminate. What the broader picture of lynchings and drivings-out—the violence enacted against the differently colonized and racialized bodies of Native and Asian people—exposed was the necropolitical function of settler colonialism.[63]

If Michel Foucault's theorization of biopower, the management of life through the connected processes of disciplining bodies and regulating populations, is, as Achille Mbembe argues, insufficient to analyze colonial terror, Mbembe's shift of focus from life-worlds to death-worlds proves instructive to the relational examination of drivings-out and lynchings.[64] Instead of attending to the white heteronormative settler subject produced in the disposability of racialized others, a necropolitical frame parses the messy and uneven violent management of multiple populations targeted for violence and the specific precarities intended for those who are differentially racialized and colonized. Though Mbembe's formulation of the necropolitical was developed to account for the formation of late-modern colonial war and terror, critical Indigenous studies scholar Scott Morgensen challenges the idea of a historical break between early and modern colonialism, that such a genealogy naturalizes settler colonialism, and "theories of the biopolitical state, regimes of global governance, and the war on terror will be insufficient unless they critically theorize settler colonialism as a historical and *present* condition and method of all such power."[65] I build on Morgensen's assertion that settler modernity is constituted through a biopolitical imperative of both genocidal and assimilative governance of Indigenous peoples, to argue that an imbricated incorporative disposability of immigrant populations works simultaneously to cohere the space and time of that modernity.

The lynching finds its way into popular press of the time because of the coincidental arrival of a steamship, its passengers witnessing the moment immediately following the lynching, a Tlingit man hanging from a makeshift scaffold, his limp body over the beach at low tide. The tourists onboard included the former U.S. Attorney General Edwards Pierrepont and his son Edward. As the younger Pierrepont recounted, "Even as we touched the wharf, we noticed something unusual in the scene—no bustle, no merriment, no noise; all quiet, men pale.... As our eyes wandered along the shore, searching for a cause, there, standing out plainly defined against the dark background, we saw a newly erected gallows under which an Indian's body slowly swayed to and fro."[66] Sixty to seventy white miners had assembled for the hanging, and to assume collective responsibility (and avoid individual punishment), all had pulled on the hanging rope. Pierrepont's account runs counter to the travel adventure reenactment of discovery, by negating the celebration of arrival: "no bustle, no merriment, no noise." What interrupts and refutes this narrative, the "cause," is the lynched Native body. I offer this reading not to expand or prolong the sensationalism of the scene but to unflinchingly witness the colonial violence that ruptures the celebratory tourist narrative, even as colonial justice tries to suture settler sociality back together through the unified action of the white miners and their juridical documentarian, son of the former eminent law enforcement officer in the nation. This scene is at once biopolitical and necropolitical portrait, the consolidation of white male subjectivity and its sovereign right to kill, over and against the abject and criminalized Native body.

According to Pierrepont and other published sources, the man executed on the beach was one of several Tlingit caught in a disagreement between two rum sellers on the trail from the mouth of Gold Creek to the mining field at Silver Bow Basin.[67] Bootlegging establishments were supposedly for white miners, but in actuality did business primarily with Alaska Native customers. In the altercation, British immigrant Dick Rennie came after a group of Tlingit with a bung-starter (the wooden mallet used to loosen the cork on a cask) and was clubbed by two Tlingit men, known by settlers as Cut Nose Jim and Charley Green. The two Native men reported that during their fight, Rennie's competitor, a Frenchman named Martin, looked on without intervening. After Rennie died, Jim and Charley were arrested along with a Tlingit man known as Boxer who protested or intervened in some fashion. The three Tlingit were jailed to await Navy Commander E. C. Merriman, the highest-ranking military officer in Alaska at that time. The Native prisoners escaped by killing both their jailor and another white settler who tried to stop them, running into the woods. The first man caught was hung after a night session of the miners' court determined his guilt. While the steamship remained in port, another of the men was found in the woods and shot. The third was turned over by a rival Tlingit clan and was hung as the steamship departed.

Black studies scholars have long elucidated the role of lynching as a particularly horrific performance of white racial terror.[68] Lynching in U.S. regions outside of the South has been less studied, and lynchings directed as racial violence against communities other than Black are occluded from national consciousness.[69] In Philip Dray's social history of the lynching of Black Americans, he offers up his preconceived notions as, "I was aware that lynching had been an aberrational form of racial violence in the Deep South, and a means by which cattle rustlers and card cheats had sometimes received rough frontier justice."[70] Though Dray's study critiques his first assumption, demonstrating the lynching of Black people to be less sporadic and far more systemic and structural than he had originally postulated, he leaves his second premise of "frontier justice" unchallenged. As Ken Gonzales-Day argues, in his study of lynching in California, the prevalent myth of the frontier elides the racial dynamics of lynching in the West.[71] As his work reveals, the majority of lynching victims in California from the mid-nineteenth to early twentieth century were people of color and Indigenous peoples.[72]

The lynchings in Juneau in 1883 reinforce Gonzales-Day's argument, wherein the miners' vigilante actions are narrated by notions of frontier justice yet constantly reveal underlying racial violence toward Native peoples (a contradiction that is repeated three years later with the driving-out of Chinese). Though the lynchings in Juneau elicited sadness in Edward Pierrepont over the "violence and lawless death," he rationalized such instances of violence as serving a necessary purpose, because "the whites have no protection from the United States.... Miners' rights have sometimes to be contested with the rifle: murderers and desperadoes have to be hanged by lynch-law."[73] The spectrum of killing of Alaska Natives (lynchings as well as shootings) meted by both settlers and the government outlines a broad system of violent treatment. To be sure, the Army bombardment of the village of Khaachxhan.áak'w and three K̲éex̲' Kwáan villages in 1869, as well as the 1882 navy destruction of the village of Angoon (under Merriman, the same navy commander who was en route to Juneau when miners hung and shot the three Tlingit), contradict the idea that white settlement and the creation of the Alaskan state was a natural or inevitable process; instead, an extraordinary level of violence was necessary to construct territory on land already inhabited by its original occupants.[74] As Pierrepont articulated, "From all sources we learned that fear was the great force that controlled the Indians," confirming that violence was indeed intended to produce terror.[75] Terrorism, as performed in Southeast Alaska, was not indiscriminate about who would be targeted in its violent grasp—it was only unpredictable in varying and rampant violence enacted against Native people. A white settler in Juneau further underscored the lynching as terrorist practice when he explained that the gallows were constructed in view of the Native village "in order that it might be a lesson to them." The white settlers continued their education in colonial horror by leaving the lynched men in hanging suspense. "When they had hung long enough, their bodies were cut down.... It had an excellent effect on the natives afterwards. They were quite civil to the whites."[76] Here is the specter of the Treaty of Cession, with its civilized/uncivilized dichotomy, but instead of renounced primitivism as a precondition for citizenship rights, we see that execution and terror undergird settler civilization. Assimilation and extermination are intertwined, as settler biopower constitutes itself through what Heidi Kiiwetinepinesiik Stark has termed "criminal empire," wherein, "the imposition of colonial law, facilitated by casting Indigenous men and women as savage peoples in need of civilization and composing Indigenous lands as lawless spaces absent legal order, made it possible for the United States and Canada to shift and expand the boundaries of both settler law and the nation itself by juridically proclaiming their own criminal behaviors as lawful."[77]

Looking at the 1883 lynching of Tlingit in connection with the driving-out of Chinese that takes place three years later in the same mining town exposes the limits of framing frontier justice as simply a precursor to a legal system or a justifiable governing body that acts in the absence of an official court. The 1884 Organic Act established civil government in Alaska, with a federally appointed territorial governor and district court.[78] This ostensibly provided the very mechanism that the miners' committee sought in their argument that lynching was necessary without government protection. However, instead of disbanding once the Organic Act was established, the miners' court was still very much organized and active when they orchestrated the driving-out of Chinese workers in 1886. Conversely, the miners' earlier actions in lynching Tlingit belied the notion that the driving-out was simply class-based competition but, rather, elucidated part of a larger system in which measures of frontier justice enforced levels of white racial control and discipline. With this expanded reading, China Joe's story tells the tale of neither an immigrant's generosity nor the benevolence of white prospectors; instead, his life and livelihood can be placed within a larger register of racial terror and dominance.

Both the 1883 lynchings and the 1886 driving-out were spectacles—large public events that performed white racial dominance and superiority.[79] They also rehearsed the symbolic power provided by white male protectors. Because of these reasons, we might think of lynchings and drivings-out as inherently part of the larger gold rush narrative. For white spectators, the messages of the two events cohered and complemented one another. As spectacles of racial terror, however, the two events had very different audiences. Prescriptions for violent and terroristic control appeared very separate for Native and Asian (specifically, Tlingit and Chinese) people during the gold rush era of southeast Alaska and, I suggest, in the history of the American West. As elaborated in chapter 1, Asian immigrants could be conceived as modern laboring subjects yet could not properly inhabit settler colonial space. Conversely, the overarching logics of settler colonial time meant that threats to Alaska Native life and livelihood was explained through a discourse of failed engagement with modernity. Nayan Shah outlines the difference in his discussion of the driving-out of South Asian migrant workers in the North American West:

> There was a difference between lynch mobs and driving-out mobs in the outcome of their rage. On the Pacific Coast, South Asians, like the Chinese before them, were numerous enough to be perceived as a threat, but not a sufficiently widespread presence to nullify the belief that they could be expelled and erased. Their presence was fleeting, a temporary nuisance that could be permanently eradicated, and the driving-out mobs underlined the transience. . . . The driving-out mobs asserted male authority and policed contact, but they were seeking to eradicate their targets, not to impose deference and servitude by force. Unlike in the case of the Native Americans whose land, resources, and claim to place white settlers had usurped, the desire to humiliate and deter any return outstripped the desire to kill.[80]

I want to be very careful here; Chinese were also lynched in the history of the American West, including the mass lynching of Chinese in Los Angeles in 1871.[81] And the forced removals of Indigenous peoples throughout American history constituted a widespread and genocidal regime with policies spanning from the Trail of Tears to compulsory confinement within reservation borders. At the same time, Shah indexes a complex yet differentiated system of violence that fits Alaska's gold rush era concomitant to the national shift from mercantile to industrial capitalism. Instructive are scholars of lynching in the American South, who contend that the white propensity for racial violence against Black bodies stemmed not from retrograde Southern culture but, rather, reflected white Southerners' capacity for sustained and spectacular white supremacist brutality within the commencement of an incipient industrial modernity.[82] Similarly, lynchings and drivings-out in Alaska were modern phenomena, instantiations of necropower that coincided with modernity's industrial moment.

Lynchings and drivings-out were practices based on dehumanizing violence, yet neither act was random or confused. Both acts were targeted to a specific community, based on each colonized group's threat to settler colonial stability and order. Racially exploitable migrant labor produced the capitalist expansion that colonialism depended on; yet the physical presence of Asian aliens was an impediment to white settlement, denying the promise of opportunity to white settlers. As discussed in chapter 1, this spatial anxiety was also a reproductive one, as the majority-male Asian workforce threatened and thwarted a generative white futurity. Asian bodies were therefore pathologized as spatial excess, and driving out was a necropolitical response that conditioned settler space. Asian migrants were disposable, and, as the bombings that preceded the driving-out emphasize, lethal tactics were used to oppose their presence. Valued as a laboring industrial population, however, they were spared mass annihilation, instead inhabiting Mbembe's "death-world," a "form of social existence in which vast populations are subjected to conditions of life conferring upon them the status of *living dead*."[83]

In contrast, Native life in the colony was the conundrum, the continued presence of Alaska Natives who held distinct knowledge and forms of governance. Settler colonialism narrates its ascendency through an appropriation of Native-ness, celebrating aspects of Alaskan indigeneity as part of its colorful and archaic past, the process Morgensen names, after Patrick Wolfe's theorization of settler colonialism, as "amalgamation and replacement," in which settlers supplant the Indigenous within foundational narratives.[84] Crucial to this is the discourse of the ever-disappearing Alaska Native, which is why, as discussed in chapter 1, the missionary promise of assimilation is central to the project of settler modernity. What we see articulated in both the threat and performance of white vigilante terror is an extension of this logic, the pathologization and punishment of Alaska Natives' failure to be part of modern time. Looking back to the story of the Juneau lynching, murder is the stated crime, but implicitly it is the Native inability to exist properly within frontier forms of economy and socialization, particularly through a discourse that pathologizes Native imbibing and belies alcohol's long colonial history. Russians first introduced alcohol to Alaska, and even though the Russian American Company outlawed the trade of alcohol to Alaska Native peoples in the 1790s, they rationed vodka for their employees (Russian, Creole, and Native) as both an incentive and a tactic to create dependency through financial debt.[85] In contrast, British and Americans in the fur trade utilized alcoholic beverages as a commodity to trade with Alaska Native peoples and to gain an advantage over their Russian counterparts. Alaska Native communities experienced increased exposure to alcohol after U.S. purchase, through contact with army and navy soldiers, in emerging industries such as canning and logging and, especially, in the numerous saloons rapidly established in gold mining boomtowns.[86] The most significant change brought by American possession, however, was the bootlegging of homebrew: the making, distilling, and unsanctioned sale of liquor within the territory. The Tlingit packers killed were caught in this illicit economy, acting as proxy in the dispute between two white bootleggers.

To disentangle the underlying racialization that accompanies discourses of liquor and alcohol, we can look to the specific vocabulary that emerges in

Alaska. The most popular origin of homebrew involved U.S. soldiers teaching Alaska Natives how to produce alcohol from molasses, a liquor that becomes known as "hooch," a term so popular that its usage extended beyond Alaska to enter the national lexicon. "Hooch" derived from the longer Hoochinoo (Xutsnoowú), or "Fortress of the Brown Bear," the Tlingit word for what becomes renamed in colonial vocabulary as Admiralty Island. Xutsnoowú is the same place discussed in chapter 1, whose name elicits laughing incomprehension from Ernestine Hayes's tourist audience, when confronted with Tlingit relations to land and nonhuman persons. "Hooch" similarly supplants Native epistemology and ontology, instead equating Alaska Native people with a colonially imposed substance and its criminalized production, erasing that colonial genealogy and instead correlating racialized drunkenness with Native land. It is not always white soldiers, however, who provide this information in the etymologies of Alaskan homebrew. Chinese working in canneries are also blamed for this problem, said to have taught Alaska Native peoples how to use a mash of flour and sugar to make a liquor known as "sourdough," using the vernacular to describe old-time prospectors, the ingredients that ensure longevity for gold miners corrupted by the putatively devious Chinese. Contrasted with the China Joe story, the flour and sugar that the singular and exceptional Chinese baker used to sustain starving prospectors becomes fermented into another type of sourdough, both a shadow and mockery of the hardscrabble prospector. Signaling an immoral excess that is produced by the Chinese and consumed by Alaska Natives, the Chinese cannery workers as a class, a mass, form a biopolitical threat by thwarting the reproductive life of the white settler using the very substance that once sustained him, as well as obstructing the biopolitical potential for Alaska Native assimilation. As Renisa Mawani elaborates in her study of the figures of the Chinese liquor trafficker and the Native victim in British Columbia, "The prohibition of liquor use among native peoples was long regarded to be an important colonial policy, one that was intended to facilitate the Christianization and moral development of Indians, on the one hand, and to promote and secure white settlement, on the other."[87] The discourse of the Chinese liquor producer threatens white settler futurity in several overlapping ways: as racial contaminant, as an improper class of laborers, and as a menace to the assimilative potential of Native residents.

The deaths of these three Tlingit men were interpellated by these overdetermined discourses of assimilation, criminalization, and moral deficiency. The notion of assimilative failure is compounded by the fact that the Tlingit men killed were all Christian, having been converted by missionaries, their religious belief conveyed when the man known as Boxer recited the Lord's Prayer in English just before being hung.[88] The Tlingit men involved in the altercation may have been inebriated, but so too were the white rum sellers, and as the Tlingit men protested afterward, Rennie came at them first. Self-defense remained an impossibility, however, given the larger carceral dimensions in the territory. Some type of prohibition legislation governed Alaska from the time of purchase to the end of the national prohibition era, from 1867 to 1933 (at which time, prohibition specifically for Alaska Native peoples was extended another twenty years). In the beginning years of American possession, the production, sale, and consumption of all hard spirits was outlawed; while the letter of the law applied universally to all those residing in the territory, prohibition was understood in practice to regulate and control Alaska Native peoples. As the territorial governor reported in 1890, alcohol prohibition was "a dead letter, except in its application to the Indians. Liquors of the vilest quality, it is asserted, are sold openly and in violation of the law."[89] Prohibition, in Alaska, appeared to be universal but was actually enforced only against Alaska Native peoples, demonstrating the temporal logics of settler colonialism, wherein different temporal realities existed for white and Native peoples within the same territorial bounds. Given this juridical asymmetry, only Tlingit inebriation could be marked as criminal, civilizational promise frustrated by putative Native immaturity in contrast to the self-governing capacity of white men. Compare the story of these Tlingit packers with the founding narrative of Joe Juneau and Richard Harris, who could not move past the mouth of Gold Creek because of their drunken state. Taking place along the same route to Silver Bow Basin, one tale of inebriation results in the refinancing and second-chance redemption of colorful and ultimately heroic settler actors, the other becomes an inevitable tragedy blamed on the violent tendencies enacted when Native men could not regulate their alcohol consumption. The biopolitical and necropolitical are marked by a temporal delimitation, effectively erasing colonial violence through colonialist figurations of puerile Native peoples, unprepared for modernity.

Consider the rope, in the stories of the driving-out and the lynching, its appearance in both stories an index of the space-time dimensions of colonial violence. As a tool of maritime and mining industries, the rope functions in these narratives as a methodology of white masculine protection: in the case of China Joe, to protect him from the aggregate violence of industrial capital, and, in the lynching, its collective use protects the miners from individual culpability. The proverbial line in the sand, the rope in China Joe's story is drawn by prospectors to demarcate a separation between dauntless frontier masculinity and the industrial class of wage-earning company miners. Time is spatialized, romantic anticapitalism separated and recuperated for settler founding as well as futurity. China Joe serves as catalyst for masculinized settler subjectivity, but he cannot occupy it, his honorary whiteness always already marked as outside. China Joe's story can move forward in time, pedagogically, yet cannot move forward under spatial terms. He has to remain the exception, the solitary Chinese, even when he isn't. China Joe occupies this space-time contradiction biopolitically, replicating white masculinist origins for Alaska forward to the present, even as he cannot reproduce within Alaska, biologically or socially, always narratively alone. In contrast to the separation of miners, the rope in the lynching acts as an extension of the miners themselves, consolidating their racial control and terror through combined action. Enacting the technology of the rope, in which individual strands are collectively stronger when bound together, white masculinity serves as a weapon. The lynch rope, as symbol of settler apparatus, serves not as a spatial demarcation in this instance, but as a temporal device, violently displaying the power of settler governance to enact differential punishment on Native bodies. Note again, in tourist traveler Edward Pierrepont's description of the scene, where the lynched body "slowly swayed to and fro," as if a giant pendulum whose rhythm, lagging behind white progress, is protracted to induce a fearful civility.[90] In contrast to the spatial excess of Asian immigrants, Alaska Natives were viewed as out of time; as such, colonial terror formations were unpredictable and prolonged.

The published sources, the colonial record, does not afford Tlingit perspectives or understandings of these extrajudicial killings, but Tlingit oral history provides a radically different viewpoint. Tlingit elder Cecilia Kintoow Kunz, a member of the L'uknax̲.ádi or Coho Salmon clan, was born in 1910, and her father, Jake Yaakwaan, was a leader of the Kaagwaantaan clan, the same clan as the men who died. In 1990, she told Tlingit anthropologist and president of the Sealaska Heritage Institute, Dr. Rosita K̲aaháni Worl, a story of the hangings as told to her by Mrs. Keinaanuk from the K̲óok Hít (Box House) of the Kaagwaantaan.[91] As Cecilia Kunz relayed, the three young men were Kaagwaantaan of the K̲óok Hít from Sitka, part of a larger Kaagwaantaan migration to Juneau for work in the gold mines. The young men (two of their names are remembered as Kaakayeik and Kaanax̲tee Éesh) set up a camp along Perseverance Trail across from a makeshift liquor store, and when the owner was robbed by a L'eeneidí man from the Dipper House, he mistakenly came after the Kaagwaantaan men. This amplifies the tragedy of the ensuing altercation, that the men killed were misidentified from the start. The details of the jailing remain much the same in the Tlingit story, but instead of focusing on the hangings, emphasis is placed on Kaakayeik, who escaped jail and was hidden at an Áak'w Ḵwáan house, where he cut off the ball and chain that were attached to him. Rather than risk harm to those who sheltered him, he confronted the settlers on his own. Contradicting the colonial narrative that a rival clan turned him in, Kaakayeik ran out of the house and down the hill, howling like the principal crest of the Kaagwaantaan, the wolf. And white settlers did not shoot and kill him—Kaakayeik killed himself, but not before he killed one of his attackers.

Following the deaths of the three men, several additional and important aspects are communicated in the Tlingit narrative. One is that the Kaagwaantaan uncle of the three young men who were killed, overcome with grief, went to the tidal flats in front of the village, and cried out, "Let the tide come over me, my nephews are gone." Contrary to the pedagogical intent of the lynchings to instill fear and civility among the Tlingit, the deaths elicited an outpouring of emotion, sorrow over the loss of life. And instead of the distortion that colonial punishment was lamentable but justifiable, colonial society was impossible to redeem in the face of the uncle's anguish. What happened next, in response to the Kaagwaantaan uncle's grief, is remarkable. Two men from the Dipper House went down to the bereaving uncle and brought him back to their house. There, the L'eeneidí took responsibility, since it was a member of their clan who robbed the liquor seller, and, as was customary under Tlingit law, they made payment to the Kaagwaantaan for the deaths of the young men. The L'eeneidí gave the Kaagwaantaan land, fittingly, in the area of Gold Creek, and this is how the Kaagwaantaan came to establish the Eagle Nest House and the Box House in Áak'w Ḵwáan territory. The L'eeneidí told the Kaagwaantaan uncle, "You will make your home in Juneau." In contrast to the necropolitical disciplining of "frontier justice," Tlingit jurisprudence stressed reciprocity and balance—the L'eeneidí sought reparative measures meant to increase Tlingit life, land, and relations in response to death and destruction. The Tlingit understanding of the events in 1883 is important not only for refuting the colonial narrative and its normalizing claims to authority, but also for serving as a model for apprehending how we might view China Joe within colonial Alaska but through Tlingit epistemologies and ontologies.

Conclusion: Alternate Affinities

I close with a final reading of China Joe's story, moving him away from frontier intimacy with white miners and into affinity with Alaska Native residents of Juneau. I use affinity deliberately here, to signal an affective measure of intimate alliance, or sociality. In their mode of analysis that accounts for racialized, gendered, and sexualized difference, Grace Kyungwon Hong and Roderick Ferguson pose "strange affinity" to "[imagine] alternative modes of coalition beyond prior models of racial or ethnic solidarity based on a notion of homogeneity or similarity."[92] In the numerous accounts of Joe's life, it is said that he was connected to three groups of people: old-timers, children, and Alaska Natives. His connection to the early generation of prospectors was evident from his Cassiar days and was repeatedly narrated through the myths told about him. His generosity for children surfaces as a common trope about Asian migrant men—without families, they tended to dote on local youth—and Joe was known to make cookies and other treats especially for neighborhood children. The traces of affinity to the Tlingit community are interesting given that no reason is provided, and all of Joe's mythology connects him to white prospectors. It is reported that "during his declining years, Joe only baked for a few old-timers and Natives."[93] A 1910 article explained that he served Alaska Native customers even after he stopped baking for children: "After his shop became the bakery for the Indians exclusively, the toddlers would beg to be taken to their friend Joe for cookies."[94] In these accounts it appears that Alaska Natives were the most numerous and longest lasting of all his customers, and that old-timers and children were considered more auxiliary. As opposed to viewing China Joe as an exceptional member of white prospector fraternity, we might view the old-timers as exceptions to China Joe's regular associates, the Tlingit community. Contrary to the Cassiar mining tale that constructs Joe as the sole baker for a group of white men, these anecdotal remarks suggest an alternative economic role for Joe in gold mining society. These comments also convey segregation, as does the information that once German immigrant Gustav Messerschmidt opened a bakery in Juneau in 1899, Joe became the baker for "the Tlingit and his friends."[95] Could it be that Messerschmidt refused to serve Native customers, leaving Joe to serve a Tlingit clientele? Or perhaps, discrimination worked along another vector, that once Messerschmidt opened his bakery, all white customers fled to him, leaving Joe with only Tlingit patrons? Or, perhaps, an informal combination of both of these arrangements?

Cecilia Kunz, the same Tlingit elder who provided a counternarrative to the lynchings, was born in Juneau and fondly remembered going to China Joe's bakery as a child.[96] Joe would have been in his late seventies or older by then. Though Kunz's childhood recollection is often included within the larger assimilationist narrative of China Joe, more telling, perhaps, is the manner in which Kunz provides an alternate genealogy and epistemology, a

Tlingit understanding of China Joe in connection to the ouster of Chinese miners. In a 1995 talk on Juneau's history, what begins as the expected reminiscence of China Joe's bakery and the sweets he gave to her as a young girl diverges into a recounting of the driving-out. As Kunz recollects, "Before my time, my grandparents that were talking about it. . . . You know, Treadwell let all the Chinamens go. . . . I know my Grandpa told them to come, they came into the house, that's where they spent the night. You see my grandfather is Yeesganaalx̱, the leader of the L'eeneidí Áak'w people. They were some of the things that I'm talking about. I hear it. I didn't see it, I didn't exactly see it."[97] Kunz suggests that the Tlingit may have aided the expulsed Chinese miners and that such action demonstrated her grandfather's clan and house leadership—Yeesganaalx̱ was the powerful head of the Big Dipper House (Yax̱té Hít) of the L'eeneidí or Dog Salmon clan—centering Tlingit polity as the foundation for racial solidarity. Similar to China Joe's tale, Kunz is also repeating oral tradition, but in a drama that located racialized migrants not in settler space but on Indigenous land, and in relation to Native governance. The driving-out took place three years after the lynching, and the Dipper House may have been motivated to harbor other fugitives from settler violence. Or, relatedly, Yeesganaalx̱ may have felt a sense of L'eeneidí responsibility, given the previous conflict with the white miners. Descended from an aristocratic Tlingit family, Cecilia Kunz was a leader in her own right, as the first teacher of the Lingít (Tlingit) language in Juneau's schools and an active member of the Alaska Native Sisterhood from 1929 until her death in 2004. Instead of the colonial personification projected onto the ever-opaque facade of China Joe, Kunz's indeterminacy ("I didn't see it, I didn't exactly see it") allows for an alternative chronicling, a relationality afforded in a glance askew. As Hong and Ferguson emphasize, strange affinities "must emphasize what cannot be known, what escapes articulation."[98] Kunz offers that differentially colonized and racialized peoples might have recognized each other outside of settler colonial optics, even if one cannot "exactly see it," that such traces elucidate imaginable affinities within the violence of Alaska's gold rush economy, potential alliances seemingly impossible within the spatial and temporal logics of settler colonialism.

TODAY, DURING THE SUMMER MONTHS, cruise ship tourists who arrive in Juneau are encouraged to take a historic walking tour, with a Juneau-Douglas City Museum volunteer as their guide.[99] Along the tour, tourists visit notable sites, view local architecture, and hear about the colorful characters that make up Juneau's history, including China Joe.[100] The longevity of China Joe's folktale is demonstrated in this current reiteration, highlighting both the prominence of gold rush narratives and China Joe's place within such tales. Configured as the last frontier, Alaska is the first to be recuperated in American nostalgia, and the telling and retelling of China Joe's story, in particular his racialized and feminized exceptionalism, rationalizes the settler expulsion of Asian labor. Further reading for disavowed violence reveals the lynching of Tlingit men as an additional and connected gold rush story but one that, unlike China Joe's prominent tale, must be elided within the town's foundational lore, highlighting what Lisa Lowe calls, "the economy of affirmation and forgetting."[101] The presence of China Joe's story to tourist audiences signals the shift from colonial narratives that racialized Natives and Asians together in settler orientalist ancestry, as outlined in chapter 1, to frontier tales in which Asian and Native peoples are designated as contradistinctive threats to the settler order. The racialized differentiation that marks this transition is constituted by and, in turn, further shapes, the incipient settler colonialism ushered in with Alaska's gold rush era. In chapter 3, which examines Alaska's industrial development within the cannery economy, Asian and Native connections are further rendered illegible, even as Asian men and Native women work the cannery line together. In chapter 3, I excavate the traces of a 1913 labor union in Ketchikan, Alaska, examining two repeating figures, the Asian male sex worker and the promiscuous Native woman, to ask how failed settlers, unproductive workers, and improper men and women elucidate colonial understandings of land and labor.

CHAPTER THREE

Unbecoming Workers
Asian Men and Native Women in Alaska's Canneries

Live from occupied Duwamish territory
Where Carlos Bulosan once lived to tell the story
— Blue Scholars, "North by Northwest"

Nora told me today that your life's a poem.
There's no time for a rewrite; it doesn't do any
Good to crack open the book out of harm's way.
— Ishmael Hope, "Talking with Nora"

This chapter centers around a trace: in 1913 at a salmon cannery in the Southeast Alaska town of Ketchikan, cannery workers formed a union. Part of the Industrial Workers of the World (IWW), Local 283's membership comprised predominantly Japanese immigrant workers. Little else is known about this union and its activities. Master narratives in Alaskan history fail to note the event took place, let alone any labor activities of Asian workers. Although the story of the Ketchikan local is recuperated by Asian American studies scholars, concomitant with the Asian American movement of the late 1960s and 1970s, no further details are provided. Moreover, the narrative of class struggle in the face of economic and racial injustice resurrected within Asian American studies fails to account for Native women when Asian migrant men and Native women made up the majority of workers at Alaskan canneries by the 1910s. IWW documents also contain traces of this Alaskan union, including retaliation when two of the union's leaders are dragged nearly to death. At the same time that labor studies scholars substantiate this union and its organizing, the ways in which Asian and Native workers are discursively incorporated into larger narratives of multiracial class struggle ultimately elide their participation.

Using the story of the 1913 union in Ketchikan as a departure point, I focus this chapter around the figure of the worker produced by a labor archive that incorporates records and taxonomies within Alaskan history, Asian American studies, Native studies, and labor studies, an archive that alternately illuminates and delimits who a proper worker can be within the construction of the proletariat. Canneries emerged in Alaska during the same period as mining, during the late nineteenth century. Though the cannery industry was initially eclipsed by the monumental gold rush in terms of population, profits, and popular imagination, canneries made a steady increase through the turn of the century, and by World War I, Alaskan canneries packed more than half the world's supply of salmon. The rise in cannery economy also coincided with a new era in Alaska's development, the period following the 1912 Organic Act that organized Alaska into an official, incorporated territory with a territorial legislature.[1] In contrast to chapter 2, the study of the long-standing presence of the China Joe folktale, here we examine multiple types of absences across different intellectual formations. I am not simply tracing elision, however, but questioning the larger role of obfuscation. Rather than simply looking for the proverbial needle in the haystack, I question the haystack itself—how was it formed and how does it function to obscure the needle? In this process, I return to Lisa Lowe's formulation of intimacy, in which she stresses the shadow record between colonized peoples, that even though the "contacts of colonized peoples [are] never explicitly named in the documents, [they are], paradoxically, everywhere implicit in the archive in the presence of such ellipses."[2] I look to this absent presence across different intellectual fields to inform the contours of settler colonial racial capitalism, to ask how different historical formations foreclose who can be seen as a worker, simultaneously rendering illegible connections between Indigenous and alien workers, even as they labor together. I argue that the foreclosure of historical subjectivity shapes and is shaped by powerful disciplining discourses of proper gender and sexuality for colonized and racialized workers. Moreover, settler colonial logics of space and time highlight the different ways in which Asian masculinity and Native femininity are respectively construed as improper labor, or erased from histories of labor altogether.

Later in the chapter, I shift my attention to the concern of presence and how cannery labor is expressed within Alaska Native and Asian American cultural production. Because, as I argue throughout the first half of the chapter, the intellectual fields of Alaskan history and labor studies, as well as Asian American and Native studies, are limited by their determination of a proper laboring subject, I examine an alternative labor archive within literary expression to examine both unbecoming workers and their unbecoming ways. Said again, the labor archive is concerned with productive subjects, whereas Native and Asian cultural productions reject the notion of productive subjectivity in favor of unproductive intimacies. Through close readings of Tlingit author Nora Marks Dauenhauer's poetry and Carlos Bulosan's novel, *America Is in the Heart*, I excavate the figures of the promiscuous Native woman and the Asian male sex worker to ask how unbecoming workers elucidate complex yet contingent meanings of land and labor, central frameworks in Native studies and Asian American studies, respectively. Again looking to Lowe, I utilize her conceptualization of intimacy as a heuristic, as a method for examining the figures that animate colonial discourses, tracing anxiety and elision to comment on intimate constellations and queer affiliations.[3]

Reflecting on multiple (and at times overlapping) elisions and investments, I utilize the concept of "unbecoming" to connect several different registers, the first of which is to signal the foreclosure of subjectivity. Similar to historian Mai Ngai, who charts the genealogy of the "illegal alien" as a legally "impossible" subject, I examine who can and cannot "become" a proper worker based on the racial and gendered logic of the capitalist settler state.[4] I connect this subjective failure to the raced, gendered, and classed disciplinary functions of who is pathologized as a nonnormative subject, exhibiting "unbecoming" or improper behavior or excess. The unraveling of these intertwined functions, unbecoming as historical foreclosure and as social pathologization, signals another way that I am using this framework of unbecoming, as an act of undoing. In deconstructing the powerful cloaking mechanisms of settler colonialism, I attempt to highlight the proximities that settler colonialism engenders without collapsing difference or claiming liberal subjectivity that further enables settler colonial capitalism. Critical to this endeavor is thinking through contingencies of labor exploitation and Indigenous dispossession through theories of racial capital, specifically Iyko Day's reworking of romantic anticapitalism and Glen Sean Coulthard's formulation of colonial accumulation, in order to ultimately comment on land and labor through the incommensurate and nonnormative relationalities between and among Asian migrant men and Alaska Native women.[5]

Ketchikan, the "Salmon Capital of the World"

The town of Ketchikan is situated on the southern coast of Revillagigedo Island, along the southern border of Alaska, within a 300-mile archipelago of more than a thousand islands. The town lies in the shadow of Deer Mountain, where a salmon stream flows into a deepwater channel, the starting point to the protected waterway known as the Inside Passage. American whites settled the area in the 1880s to take advantage of the salmon runs at the mouth of the creek and a strip of level ground that allowed for building and expansion within the sheer verticality of Southeast Alaska. Given the nearness to markets south, this location was prime real estate. The Tongass Packing

Company first established a saltery in 1887, which was soon converted to a cannery.[6]

Of course, white settlers were not the first to discover the natural attributes of this site. Tlingit communities established summer fishing camps at what is now known as Ketchikan Creek, with clans in the Tongass and Cape Fox villages (Taant'a K̲wáan and Sanyaa K̲wáan, respectively) possessing historical ownership claims to the salmon stream as well as other fishing, hunting, and berry picking sites in the area. While the k̲wáan designation describes the geographic area shared by a common wintering village (the word k̲wáan comes from the Tlingit verb "to dwell"), it is Tlingit hereditary clans that collectively own rights to physical property such as salmon streams and hunting grounds as well as symbolic property such as names, songs, stories, and crests. These sacred possessions, tangible and intangible, are collectively known in Tlingit culture as at.óow. The clans in the Sanyaa K̲wáan are the Kiks.ádi, Neix̲.ádi, and Teik̲weidí; and the four clans in the Taant'a K̲wáan are the Dak̲l'aweidí, G̲aanax̲.ádi, Shangukeidí, and Teik̲weidí.[7] Clans from the Tongass and Cape Fox villages maintained ownership and usage from time immemorial on lands encompassing the greater Ketchikan area, including present-day Revillagigedo Island, nearby Annette and Gravina Islands, Prince of Wales Island to the west, the mainland to the east and south, and even parts of present-day Canada.[8] The Haida people moved north from their ancestral homeland of Haida Gwaii (present-day Queen Charlotte Islands in British Columbia) into Tlingit lands, from before colonial contact and into the nineteenth century, occupying the southern portion of Prince of Wales Island to the west of Revillagigedo Island, where the Kaigani Haida retained the villages' original Tlingit names. The Tsimshian people also moved into Southeast Alaska from traditional homelands in British Columbia, but did so as an 800-member congregation following Anglican missionary William Duncan in 1887 to Annette Island, Tlingit land that was expropriated by president Grover Cleveland's administration and was reestablished as a reservation in 1891, the only Native reservation in Alaska.[9]

American settlement at salmon streams during this period resulted in large-scale dispossession of traditional Native fishing grounds. All five species of Pacific salmon can be found in Alaska: chinook or king; coho or silver; sockeye or red; chum or dog; and humpy or pink. Salmon eggs hatch in freshwater streams, spend their adult lives in saltwater seas and oceans, and eventually return during the summer to the streams of their births to spawn and die. Canneries were established in Alaska starting in the 1880s through to the early twentieth century along the coast, dotting the shorelines of the Alaskan

Panhandle in the southeast, the Kenai Peninsula in the south, the Aleutian Islands in the southwest, and Bristol Bay in Western Alaska. Even though gold rushes changed the Alaskan landscape in drastic ways for Native peoples, the rise of canneries in Alaska had an arguably greater impact on Native culture and economy. In Southeast Alaska, Tlingit, Haida, and Tsimshian peoples depended on salmon as a primary food source and as a major cultural and spiritual element in their histories and cosmologies. In 1898, at a territorially convened meeting of leaders from southeast Alaskan villages, Tlingit chief Kah-du-shan delivered a speech denouncing the theft of Native land due to American canneries: "They began to build canneries and take the creeks away from us, . . . and when we told them these creeks belonged to us, they would not pay any attention to us and said all this country belonged to President, the big chief at Washington."[10] As Tlingit scholar and author Nora Marks Dauenhauer has emphasized, this expulsion was not only an eviction from land and resources but simultaneously an American dismissal of the symbolic and totemic value of salmon for many clans. For example, Dauenhauer is a member of the Lukaax̱.ádi clan, their name originating from a salmon river near present-day Petersburg, Alaska, and the clan is known in English by their principal crest, the sockeye salmon.[11] Crests are sacred to the Tlingit, as the spiritual embodiment of a clan's ancestors, haa shagoon, linking them intergenerationally to past and future generations.

Eighty miles south of Wrangell, Ketchikan eclipsed the mining boomtown as Alaska's gateway city, and was part of the Alaska Steamship Company's regular route by 1895.[12] At the time of the town's incorporation in 1900, Ketchikan included a trading post and several salmon canneries. Although halibut fishing, mining, timber, and tourism would develop as important local economies, the town identified most strongly with its salmon industry origins, and in the 1930s an arch was constructed near Mission and Front streets announcing Ketchikan as the "Salmon Capital of the World."[13] Ketchikan was at the forefront of the cannery industry that developed in Alaska in the 1880s and 1890s, as the improvement from salting to canning salmon meat provided a means to deliver a once-perishable product to distant markets; by the 1910s, the growing town was an integral part of the flourishing Alaskan economy, with more than a dozen canneries. Similar to other resource extraction industries that built the Alaskan economy, canneries serviced national and global consumers while cannery towns remained dependent on outside goods and support. As salmon canning operations grew, they became dependent on a large yet seasonal workforce, which was represented by a diversity of laborers. Canneries first relied on an Alaska Native workforce yet quickly recruited Chinese cannery workers, citing increased labor demands. In several instances, this conversion elicited protest from Tlingit clans for being displaced thusly, their grievance firmly rooted in Tlingit jurisdictional understandings of land ownership and use.[14]

In 1886, a tourist author observed Chinese laborers on board her steamship, including those whose destination was a cannery village near Ketchikan.[15] Cannery ledgers for the Alaska Packers Association, the largest canning operator in Alaska, showed "China Contracts" in the Ketchikan area starting in 1891 and, by 1905, detailed tallies of the numbers of Chinese workers aboard each ship sailing to Alaska. In 1909, the language shifted from "Chinese" to "Oriental," a reflection that other Asian workers in addition to Chinese laborers were present. In the 1910s, ledgers contained columns designating Chinese, Japanese, Filipinx, Mexican, and miscellaneous categories.[16] The "miscellaneous" heading may have included Black, Puerto Rican, Korean, or South Asian workers. In one Ketchikan local's recollections of the early twentieth century, the town included whites, Natives, Japanese, and at least one Black resident.[17] Although the canneries depended on seasonal migrant labor, they still relied on a Native workforce, with Native men fishing and Native women canning. As George Yanagimachi, a Japanese American man who worked in Alaska canneries in the 1920s and 1930s, related, of the local Alaskan residents, mostly Native women worked in the canneries, while all the whites were in management.[18] Within this diverse array of workers, a predominant pattern developed, stratified by a combination of race and gender. White managers and engineers oversaw the canneries; Native and white (often Scandinavian) men fished ocean waters with trolling lines or purse seine nets; and Asian men alongside Native women worked the dangerous cannery line cleaning, chopping, and packing salmon into half- and full-pound tins.

The Subjects of Alaska History

Prior to statehood, Asian migrants were the largest racialized group of non-Indigenous peoples to reside or settle in Alaska, and their labor was critical to the development of Alaska canneries; however, histories of Alaska have suppressed their presence. The first extensive history of Alaska published in English, Hubert Howe Bancroft's *History of Alaska, 1730–1885*, covered the Russian colonial period up to Alaska's first Organic Act.[19] In a chapter devoted to fisheries, Bancroft extols the abundance and superiority of salmon from Alaska over the catch in other parts of the United States or world, but, in describing the emergence of canneries in Alaska, he fails to mention Asian laborers, or any details on cannery labor, even though Chinese laborers had been working in Alaska canneries since the 1870s. Bancroft viewed the impediments to cannery production as "the shortness of the season, the difficulty in obtaining labor, the great cost of supplies, the want of communication, and the fact that no title can be obtained to land."[20] Here, at the onset of the Alaskan cannery industry, the issues of land and labor were explicitly linked, or, more implicitly, settler capital success was predicated on both an usurpation of Indigenous land and installation of an exploitable class of workers. Though canneries are a prominent element in histories of Alaska, the dual elision of Asian labor and Alaska Native territorial claims is often repeated by accounts of Alaska that follow Bancroft.[21]

When Asian migrants are marginally noted in larger narratives of the state, they are positioned outside the purview of organized labor, often under a formulation that refuses an Alaskan subjectivity to Asian migrant workers. This idea is exemplified by Ernest Gruening, who served as governor of the Alaska Territory from 1939 to 1953, and as a U.S. senator from Alaska once Alaska gained statehood, from 1959 to 1969. Gruening writes, in his history of Alaska, "Without a single exception the canneries were owned and operated by nonresident corporations whose operators came in the spring, bringing with them all the cheap Chinese and other labor they required, few if any of their employees becoming actual residents."[22] Gruening's account of the canneries was inaccurate on several accounts: the Annette Island Packing Company was (and is) owned and operated by the Tsimshian members of the Metlakatla Indian Community. Similarly, the Klawock Cooperative Association formed in the 1930s as a nonprofit organization in the city of Klawock (on Prince of Wales Island, fifty-six miles from Ketchikan) in order to manage and run a cannery for Native residents. These Native-owned and Native-operated canneries contradict Gruening's emphatic "without a single exception." Alternatively, Chinese and other cannery workers did indeed settle in Alaska, their residence reflected in local newspapers and census reports from 1900 forward. Gruening's rhetorical "few if any" obscures the manifold ways that Chinese and other Asian migrants established ties to Alaska, including, among other activities, permanent settlement. Further, his reasoning implies that migrant laborers were not residents, even though migrant workers lived in Alaska for the duration of the cannery season, lasting several months out of the year. Unlike the mining industry, which succeeded in physically expelling its Asian workers, the cannery economy's dependence on Asian migrant labor only heightened the contradictions of settler colonial capital. The solution was to position Asian transient labor as failure, epistemologically excluding Asian migrant workers from the history and (therefore) the future of the settler state. The fact that Gruening was unable to perceive Native-run canneries or Asian residents reflects a pervasive discourse: that canneries, to be fully realized within settler capital industrialism, had to be imagined within the proper realm of white settler relations, even if materially untrue.

Gruening's equivalency of Chinese workers with cannery corporations through their putative nonresidence highlights Iyko Day's theorization that, under romantic anticapitalism, Asian labor is abstracted as a representation of capital, a misapprehension of capitalist social relations as an antinomical positioning of the concrete (that which is natural, pure, visible) versus the abstract (that which is unnatural, invisible, fungible).[23] As Day demonstrates in the late-nineteenth-century North American West, this misconception resulted in the antagonism between the concrete as anticapitalist and symbolized by white workers positioned against the abstract as capitalism naturalized and embodied as Asian labor. This division is implicit in the discourse of Asian seasonal workers as nonresident, as no dilemma exists in claiming the gold prospectors who temporarily traveled to Alaska as inheritors of the state and its promises of wealth. As discussed in chapter 2, such narratives fostered Alaska's eminence as an enduring frontier produced through heroic white male fortitude and labor, prior and superior to the industrial economy that followed.

An examination of Alaska history demonstrates that it was not only xenophobic and opportunistic trade unions, politicians, and journalists that deployed romantic anticapitalism to displace industrial anxieties onto Asian bodies, but also historians who instantiate the same romantic anticapitalist discourse. Stephen Haycox's monograph, *Alaska: An American Colony*, counters the notion of Alaskan frontier individualism with a national and transnational framework that places Alaska within an American West political economy.[24] Haycox's extensive study, spanning from Indigenous communities prior to Russian colonialism to Alaska in the 1990s, has quickly become regarded as the definitive text on Alaskan history.[25] The salmon industry is a predominant concern to Haycox as the state's principal revenue source in the first half of the twentieth century and because canneries exemplify the colonial power that corporations exert on the Alaskan territory, an attribute and relationship that Haycox repeatedly describes as "absentee." In an otherwise exhaustive history, Haycox provides only cursory attention to Asians in Alaska, mentioning them twice in relation to cannery work, but as intrinsic and representative of the distant and disconnected monopolies that controlled canneries.[26] Haycox characterizes the salmon industry as an "absentee operation, that is, it did not provide local jobs and produced little local revenue," arguing that Asian cannery workers "labored in isolated locations with little economic impact on the territory."[27] Although canneries occupy a central component of Haycox's colonial thesis, Asian workers are configured as absentee or foreign elements, disavowing the labor and residency of Asian migrants. The conflation of the Asian racialized worker with capital essentializes forestalled settlement upon the Asian body, even as the enforced mobility of the cannery economy separates Asian as transient from white as settled. The figure of the alien worker relies on the notion of Asians as an impossible working class under settler colonialism; that is, they can neither become settlers through permanent residence nor contribute to the economy because of their transience. The very discourse of Asian immigrants as impossible settlers elucidates the logics of white settler colonialism as foundational to the construction of the Alaskan state, wherein the use of undesirable Asian labor is what prevented "American" (i.e., white) settlement and, by inference, also delayed statehood.

This is a powerful articulation of what Day describes as the temporal delineation between the concrete and the abstract. Analyzing Chinese railroad workers, Day states, "The connection between the Chinese and the abstract dominion of capitalism evolved through their identification with a mode of efficiency that was aligned with a perverse temporality of domestic and social reproduction."[28] Chinese hyperefficiency was viewed as being both caused by and furthered through a lack of heteronormativity—the gendered racialization of Chinese (and other Asian workers) sign and symptom of their being out of sync with industrial time and, therefore, impossible historical subjects. The romantic anticapitalist notion of Asian workers, unencumbered by heterosexual familial relations, as temporally overproductive is countered through colonialism to simultaneously postpone settler time. Notice, however, that their temporal perversion is enacted as a *spatial failure*; that is, an inability to remain residents or become settlers. Perverse, or queer, occupants of labor time, Asian workers both accelerated and hindered settler capitalist relations, and romantic anticapitalist histories responded by absenting them from both territorial space and economy. Within this ubiquitous discourse, a radical union of Asian workers remained impossible to historical narrative and was likewise obscured within the state archive.[29]

The (Re)visioning of Asian American Studies

Against the backdrop of erasure within Alaskan history, Asian American scholars recuperated the story of a union formed in 1913 in Ketchikan, the narrative emerging out of the Asian American movement of the late 1960s and early 1970s and concomitant to the formation of Asian American studies. Local 283 appeared within the first published anthology of the nascent field of Asian American studies, *Roots: An Asian American Reader*, in the article "One Hundred Years of Japanese Labor in the USA," written by Japanese American journalist and communist Karl Yoneda.[30] The inclusion of Yoneda, born in 1906 and active in union organizing since the 1930s, in the anthology signaled a link to an earlier generation of Asian American activism.[31] In his essay, Yoneda included a section on the IWW, highlighting the union's appeal to foreign-born immigrants, including Asians, and noted, "The IWW established local 283 in an Alaska Ketchikan cannery in 1913. Among its members were 100 Japanese."[32] In this way, Local 283 and the organizing of Asian cannery workers in Alaska is prominent in the genealogy of Asian American labor and rendered legible both for and because of the emergent field of Asian American studies. This story became important to Asian American studies precisely because Asian American studies claimed it as an originating moment. Though Yoneda did not provide specific citation for Local 283 in this article, in his Japanese-language book *Zai-Bei Nihonjin rodosha no rekishi (History of Japanese Laborers in America)*, he attributed one hundred Japanese names on the membership rolls of Local 283 that he received personally from another Japanese American.[33] In this way, Local 283 materialized out of an alternative and informal archive of Asian American activism, substantiated through the field of Asian American studies.

Since its appearance in the anthology *Roots*, the example of Local 283 has been reaffirmed within an Asian American labor and activist lineage. Asian American studies and labor historian Glenn Omatsu explains that the Alaska Cannery Workers Union in Seattle, a union of predominantly Filipinx workers active from the 1930s to 1960s, "draws from a rich legacy. It has its roots in the Industrial Workers of the World Local 283 in 1913."[34] In his essay, "The Hidden World of Asian Immigrant Radicalism," historian Robert G. Lee heralds the materialization of the IWW as a major intervention that allowed an opening for union organization, and contends "hundreds of Japanese, Chinese, and Indian workers flocked to the call of the IWW." As one of several concrete examples, Lee reports, "In 1913, when the IWW established Local 283 in the Alaska Ketchikan cannery, its membership included over a hundred Japanese, Chinese, and Filipino workers."[35] Lee curiously expands Local 283's membership to incorporate Chinese and Filipinx workers, who, though they certainly also labored in Alaskan canneries, are not linked to the union through primary source materials. What Lee's expansion underscores, and what is additionally evident in Omatsu's linking of Local 283 to the Filipinx

Alaska Cannery Workers Union, is the desire within Asian American studies to locate Local 283 in a configuration of, and antecedent to, pan-Asian labor activism.

As generative as the Asian American coalitional interpretation of a 1913 union in Ketchikan is, however, it remains problematic. By envisioning a pan-Asian solidarity in Local 283 and, therefore, in the genealogy of Asian American labor, Asian American studies, in turn, obscures other possible alliances, particularly among other cannery workers who are not considered subjects of Asian American studies. What possible alliances or antagonisms were formed with other cannery workers, who were Mexican, Puerto Rican, or Black? And, given the predominant presence of Native women cannery workers, how might Native women been included or excluded from Local 283? How might Native women have supported or opposed such organizing efforts and why? As much as Asian American labor organizing has been excised from Alaskan history, Asian American studies in turn has occluded the labors of Native women. The framework of antiracist and anticapitalist analysis remains complicit in furthering colonial and settler colonial erasures, a caution to the limits of countering romantic anticapitalism solely through class-based racial justice.

Within Asian American studies, the study of Local 283 has been neither furthered nor scrutinized. To date, no other scholars have examined the origin of its citation, presumably because the case of a union formed in Alaska serves its pedagogical function to assert an early-twentieth-century prototype of Asian American activism. Though the recuperation of Local 283 challenges romantic anticapitalist narratives embedded within labor and state histories, this revisionism also constructs a particular type of heroic subject that not only disregards the Native woman worker but also refuses nonnormative constructions of Asian cannery workers themselves. That is, by attempting to correct the perverse labor time manufactured by romantic anticapitalism, a masculine and heteronormative Asian American subject is subsequently constructed, based on normative categories for intimacy along the lines of race and gender. Take, for example, prominent and founding Asian American historian Ronald Takaki's assessment of Asian American cannery workers in Alaska: "Their leisure hours were times of loneliness, spent drinking or in whorehouses." This statement seemingly contradicts itself—that loneliness may actually have been abated through homosocial, cross-racial, and/or sexual relations deemed unproductive to the nation-state, what Nayan Shah has termed "stranger intimacy."[36] While Asian American men may have formed bonds of union brotherhood across lines of ethnicity, Native women appear only as possible (and unproductive) romantic or sexual partners. Rendered illegible by these differential schemas of intimacies are the possibilities for Asian men and Native women to form working alliances or, as we explore later in this chapter, the prospects of romantic or sexual liaisons among Asian migrant men with each other.

The Gendered Labor of Native Women

Dominant narratives of Alaskan history describe the cannery industry as controlled by outside corporations with correspondingly foreign Asian workers, such perspectives rendering invisible the presence of Native women who also worked in Alaskan canneries. Unlike the greater Pacific Northwest area, where Native labor was supplanted by European and, especially, Asian immigrant workers, canneries in Alaska continued to employ Native workers well into the twentieth century. As historian Chris Friday has demonstrated, cannery work quickly became gendered for Native workers, with Native men employed as fisherman, while Native women were perceived by management to have a cultural disposition to work handling salmon in the canneries.[37] We see here the intersection of several gendered, racialized, and colonial discourses about labor. The overdetermination of the cannery workforce as Asian, an alien laboring class representative of absentee capitalism, is bolstered by colonial discourses that placed Native peoples outside of modernity, particularly industrial labor. Even as these racialized discourses coalesced in spatial and temporal understandings of colonial exclusion, they fractured along gender lines, with Native women imbued with romanticized notions of premodern expertise that, ironically, reinforced their material history within industrial capitalism even as they were written out of histories of the state. This gendered and racial contradiction is evident when the labors of Native men fishing are included in narratives of Alaskan economic and state development, while Native women's labor has been occluded. Although historian Stephen Haycox explains that "many Native fishermen made their summer livelihood selling to the canneries," no mention is made in his lengthy Alaskan history of Native women cannery workers.[38]

Contradicting this pervasive tendency in Alaskan history scholarship, examples of Native women working in canneries are abundant in oral histories and ethnographies of Alaska Native people (most notably, those collected and compiled by early Alaska Native studies scholars Nora Marks Dauenhauer and Richard Dauenhauer).[39] In 1994, Herman Kitka, an eighty-year-old Tlingit elder from Sitka, Alaska, recalled the emergence of canneries and the resulting changes to Tlingit society and economy: "In my lifetime a change in living took place—going to canneries for summer work and seine fishing. . . . All the older men went seine fishing for salmon for two months. The women all worked in the cannery."[40] Native women recounted working in the canneries starting at an early age, such as Amy Kooteen Marvin, who began cannery work at Port Althorp in the 1920s at the age of twelve. She was young enough that she wasn't aware how much she was paid.[41] Alaska Native women working in Southeast Alaska canneries in the early twentieth century received wages ranging from thirty-five cents to a dollar and a half per day, roughly half the wage of Native men.[42] Alaska Native women worked in the canneries as slimers and fillers, and at the patch table: slimers finished gutting the fish coming down the line, washed fish of blood and viscera, and separated fish into different grades; fillers sliced and diced fish and put them into cans; those at the patch table weighed filled cans and added small chunks of salmon if needed.[43] The ubiquitous cannery work among Alaska Native women, widely acknowledged by Native peoples as taking place since the late nineteenth century, cannot be accounted for because of settler capitalist discourses that render cannery labor solely as "absentee" Asian laborers or Alaska Native peoples as outside of industrial modernity. The paucity of scholarship on Native labor is pervasive and extends outside Alaska; as Martha Knack and Alice Littlefield acknowledge, "studies of North American Indian economic life have largely ignored the participation of indigenous people in wage labor, even though for over a century such participation has often been essential for the survival of Native individuals and communities."[44] Knack and Littlefield cite several factors for this omission, including anthropological fascination in viewing Indigenous peoples as part of an unchanging past, indicative of what I discuss as settler temporality, alongside ethnohistorical tendencies to focus on federal Indian policy while overlooking the daily economic practices of Native peoples. This is a particularly powerful combination for erasure in Alaska, where Native peoples have often been affected differently by or excluded from federal Indian policies.

In order to not only assert the presence of Alaska Native women in canneries but to further analyze their labor and experiences, I turn to Yellowknives Dene theorist Glen Sean Coulthard and his reformulation of Marx's theory of primitive accumulation.[45] Coulthard engages this area of Marxist theorization to underscore the violent dispossession of Indigenous lands and polities as foundational to capitalist accumulation but is critical of the way Marx and certain Marxists have applied primitive accumulation as a developmentalist formulation with civilizational and teleological tendencies. A left materialist enunciation of settler time, such western Marxist thought views colonial dispossession and resource extraction as inaugurating capitalist industrialism and marks this process with temporal rupture, a distinction made between backward land-based societies (in Europe, the peasantry) that give way to modern capitalism, a progression, though marked by exploitation, seen as both beneficial and inevitable. Given that settler colonialism is an ongoing process, Coulthard shifts the conceptual focus from a capitalist social relation to a colonialist social relation and, in so doing, centers dispossession rather than proletarianization as the structuring force of domination of greatest effect and concern to Indigenous peoples.

An overarching frame of colonial dispossession foregrounds how the rise of canneries in Alaska had a profound impact on Native land and livelihood. Canneries formed a direct attack on Native economies and political orders. Not only did canneries jeopardize a primary food source for Indigenous coastal peoples and pressure them further into a cash economy, they also flagrantly ignored land owned by Tlingit and Haida clans. Instead of possessing a single, bounded territorial property, clans in Southeast Alaska owned multiple areas of historic and economic importance, salmon rivers and streams being some of the most vital. Ownership of such sites expressed the wealth of clans, but was also reciprocal, meaning clans held responsibilities for the well-being of the land in these places and all the nonhuman relatives who dwelled there. In the face of widespread disorder following the expulsion and theft of Native fishing grounds, Indigenous peoples utilized the seasonal nature of the salmon industry, including the versatile labor practices of Native women within the canneries, to continue customary economies and relationships with and on Indigenous land. Take, for example, the experiences of Jessie Starr Dalton, a Tlingit of the T'a<u>k</u>deintaan clan, born in 1903 in Tenakee Springs, Alaska. She grew up during the era of American industrial development, her mother having witnessed the colonial exchange of flags between Russia and the United States in 1867. As a young adult, the newly married Starr Dalton worked in the Tenakee Springs cannery while her husband George Dalton hand trolled salmon for both the cannery and family consumption. The young couple lived with Jessie's parents, and the family's diverse labors included fish buying, pile driving, and mining, which augmented customary practices of boat building, hunting, trapping, and berry picking.[46] The Daltons' experiences were common, as Tlingit, Haida, and Tsimshian peoples in Southeast Alaska utilized canneries as one practice within a diversified strategy to continue their historic and traditional economies. For Alaska Native peoples, similar to the Navajo, the Ojibwe, and multiple Indigenous nations living on the Round Reservation in Northern California, capitalism failed to be a totalizing force, and many Indigenous peoples in North America in the late nineteenth and early twentieth centuries adapted wage labor, especially seasonal labor such as fishing, canning, and migrant farmwork, to conform to larger Indigenous economies in order to sustain Indigenous identity, culture, and relations.[47] Later in life, the Daltons served as tradition-bearers and educators for younger generations; George Dalton inherited the honorary Tlingit role of peacemaker, and Jessie Starr Dalton received the name Naa Tláa, clan mother within the Raven moiety.

Understanding canneries within colonial social relations also entails shifting what Marx conceptualized as capitalist modes of production to a colonial structure and the attendant relations that both reproduce and refuse ongoing dispossession and oppression. As social reproduction feminists Tithi Bhattacharya and Susan Ferguson have respectively elaborated on Marx's original formulation, capitalism depends on both productive and reproductive labor, the latter the biological reproduction necessary for capitalism's ongoing demand for exploited labor power as well as the individual and societal work and care outside of the point of production that sustains the life of the worker.[48] To understand such relations within a colonial context, Coulthard rephrases "mode of production" as "mode of life," or what might be considered culture, especially in discussing Native cultural resistance to colonial dispossession. More specifically, based on the philosophies of American Indian women, Manu Karuka posits "Indigenous modes of relationship" to focus on processes and affiliations that respond to the expropriation and exploitation enacted by continental imperialism.[49] A similar theorization can also be found within Tlingit epistemology and ontology, in the important concept haa ḵusteeyí, for which an exact English translation does not exist, but which can mean all of the following: "life," "our way of living," "culture," and "real being."[50] With this expanded and Indigenized frame of social relations, Alaska Native women, even as they were incorporated into capitalist modes of production as an industrial proletariat class, worked to further Indigenous ways of living and being through familial and intergenerational relations. Alaska Native women recount meeting and reuniting with women relatives in the canneries, and cannery workers often brought their children with them to the canneries. Young girls transitioned from babysitting younger children to working on the cannery line when old enough. Sally Shx̱aastí Hopkins' daughter Amy Hopkins remembers watching both her younger sister and cousins while her mother and aunts worked in the cannery.[51]

The reproductive registers of ways of life and giving life coalesce through Native women not only raising children in the canneries, but also giving birth within the space of colonial industrialism. Susie Kaasgéiy James, of the Chookaneidí clan, was born in 1890, and her diverse labors included Indigenous economic practices, working in the Todd and Chatham canneries, and selling moccasins, dolls, and beadwork on Sitka's Main Street. She was most well-known, however, for her role and practice as a midwife, which she started at age sixteen; she was said to have delivered more than one thousand babies over the next fifty years, attending births in both dryfish camp and at canneries.[52] Such processes cannot and should not be viewed simply as reproducing the industrial worker, but, given the eliminatory logics of settler colonialism, such practices highlight how Native women in the canneries helped to uphold and further Indigenous life and social relations, even with the disruptions and dislocation caused by the cannery industry. As Kahnawà:ke Mohawk scholar Audra Simpson and Michi Saagig Nishnaabeg scholar Leanne Betasamosake Simpson both argue, Native women's bodies, especially within matrilineal Indigenous nations, must be understood as furthering not only life, but also Indigenous political orders, reminders that Indigenous governance is always prior to settler regimes and, even under threat of colonial dispossession, continues to affirm and practice enduring and alternative forms of sovereignty, economy, and social relations.[53]

In juxtaposing Native women's and Asian men's cannery experiences, it is important not only to recognize that dominant state-based histories limit our understandings of these experiences, but also to consider that the fields of Native and Indigenous studies and Asian American studies use divergent frameworks: respectively, understanding Native peoples' experiences through colonial relations of *dispossession* and Asian immigrants' through capitalist relations of *exploitation*. These contrasting discourses result in the construction of two different, yet mirrored, spaces of cannery life: while canneries served as a homosocial workplace for Asian immigrant men, they existed as a homosocial family space for Native women and their children, even as both communities labored together on the cannery line under colonial capitalism. In an inverse of the temporal perversion of Asian men's economic and social production resulting in spatial failure, Native women's activities in the cannery, reproductive and relational, were regarded by colonial administrators as a type of spatial perversion, collapsing and exceeding capitalist spaces and modes of production.

Producing Solidarity: The Settler Racial Rhetoric of the IWW

Before we turn to imbricated considerations of land expropriation and labor exploitation in Alaska Native and Asian American cultural productions, I address one more set of elisions, produced within labor studies, specifically, histories of American radical unionism. In the February 27, 1913, issue of the *Industrial Worker*, the official newspaper of the Industrial Workers of the World, a small item appeared announcing the formation of Local 283 in Ketchikan, Alaska, with the group renting space in the Socialist Hall. No further description of the group or its activities appeared that season in the newspaper.[54] As Glenn Omatsu reminds us, accounting for Asian American labor "means understanding that union history is as much a history of exclusion and racism as it is of inclusion and solidarity."[55] An examination of IWW discursive practice reveals this doubled history and, moreover, that inclusion and exclusion are co-constitutive elements of producing the white male subject of labor, while simultaneously yet differentially disavowing Asian Americans and Native peoples through spatial and temporal expressions of settler romantic anticapitalism.

The Industrial Workers of the World was founded in Chicago in 1905 by a gathering of anarchists, socialists, and trade unionists around the concept of a revolutionary and internationalist "One Big Union"—worker solidarity across industries, an idea in direct contrast to other U.S. trade unions at the time. Emphasizing that the "working class and the employing class have nothing in common," the IWW advocated for worker solidarity across all boundaries, including nation, race, gender, and citizenship status.[56] It is this central tenet of all-inclusive worker solidarity that merits the highest praise for the IWW, among scholars and activists alike.[57] Even though the IWW led its largest strikes among industrial workers in the Northeast, the union is most often associated with the itinerant workers of the West in the social imagination, focusing on the migrant labor force resulting from the West's extractive economies, such as mining, logging, and canning. The IWW's vision of on-the-job organizing with work slowdowns and wildcat strikes appealed to a workforce that seasonally moved in and out of towns and through multiple industries, and the union's militant stance of direct action over political activity was especially popular to foreign-born immigrants, disenfranchised from the vote.

At its founding convention, the IWW clearly articulated its inclusion of workers of all races, even if there were few workers of color in attendance and, as far as the record shows, no workers of Asian descent.[58] From the start, however, and especially on the West Coast, the IWW actively attempted to recruit Japanese and Chinese workers.[59] In a 1924 IWW meeting in Vancouver, British Columbia, more than 150 members testified on the discrimination that Chinese, Japanese, and South Asian workers experienced, one person present remarking that by 1919 the IWW had as many Chinese members as white workers.[60] Participation is difficult to gauge, however, as many Asian American workers did not join the IWW in its early years because they already had experience organizing their own, culturally based labor associations and viewed the strength of IWW as countering racism within the ranks of white workers.[61] Labor historian Philip Foner argues that the IWW's limited analysis of race could not compel Black membership because the union's stance that there was "no race problem. There is only the class problem," failing to account for Black workers' political rights.[62] Such class reductionism, especially given the presence of active, ethnic-based labor associations, similarly failed to comprehend the brutal exploitation and racially hostile social environment that Asian migrants faced in the late nineteenth and early twentieth centuries on the West Coast, including Alaska.

An example of such racially violent reprisal can be located in the possible trace of Local 283 in an IWW pamphlet printed in 1919, *With Drops of Blood the History of the Industrial Workers of the World Has Been Written*. This pamphlet detailed the persecution of the IWW in the first two decades of the twentieth century, including a litany of martyred members. The concluding example stated, "Two members were nearly dragged to death behind an automobile at Ketchikan, Alaska."[63] While attributing this instance to violence directed against Japanese immigrant workers in Local 283 is speculative, it certainly remains a strong possibility, given the sparse archival fragments that exist on Asian IWW members and IWW activities in Alaska, with Local 283 the only mention of Ketchikan, Alaska, prior to the pamphlet's publication.[64] The fact that these martyrs are not mentioned by name (unlike most of the martyrs in the pamphlet), falls into a larger IWW pattern that obscured the organizing histories of Asian migrant workers. An examination of IWW press reveals more rhetorical support for Asian workers than actual organizing efforts for Asian workers. For the year 1913, several articles and essays in the *Industrial Worker* expounded on the IWW's inclusion of Chinese and Japanese workers, especially as "yellow peril" sentiments took hold among other labor formations, from the historically racist American Federation of Labor to the Socialist Party of California, yet no Asian American workers were actually named.[65] White leaders of national and local struggles, in comparison, were prominently listed.

The IWW's hyperbolic alliance in place of material support for Asian workers carries through to historic and scholarly understandings of the IWW as a radical labor formation. The genealogy of the popular moniker "Wobbly" is perhaps one of best examples of expressed solidarity involving Asian workers. IWW workers became known as "Wobblies" sometime around 1912 or 1913, the same time as the formation of Local 283 in Ketchikan. Many theories have been put forth as to the origin of the term (such as a wobble saw used by timber workers or the wobbling motion of a drunken worker), but by far the most popular is that of the Chinese cook. Variously told as a Chinese cook in a Vancouver restaurant, a Saskatchewan railroad camp, an Oregon lumber camp, and so on, this cook supports the IWW and gives credit, or free food, to striking workers, yet cannot pronounce the letter "double u," so asks if the workers are "I Wobble Wobble" or "I Wobbly Wobbly."[66] With startling similarity to the China Joe folktale analyzed in chapter 2, this etymology, explained in the 1920s by Mortimer Downing, editor of the *Industrial Worker*, "hints of a fine, practical internationalism, a human brotherhood based on a community of interests and of understanding."[67] Or, as more recently described by a radical scholar and a leftist artist, this nickname "was taken up in friendly fashion rather than racist derision."[68] Rather than debate whether the fondness for a Chinese person's accent is solidarity or mockery, however, the significance is to underscore that this genealogy is fundamental to the IWW's expressed multiracial internationalism. This story highlights interracial connection, and the support of Asian immigrant workers for the IWW cause; at the same time, it doesn't answer the question of how, or if, Wobblies in turn supported the Chinese cook and his struggles. Indeed, in this formulation, the Chinese cook's part in the origin of the term "Wobbly" positions him discursively as a conduit for appellation but not as a worker in his own right. He can name the Wobblies, but he cannot be one. Just as with the prospectors who protect China Joe, the IWW's protean antiracism, elevated in later liberal multicultural narratives, bolsters the IWW's superlative radicalism while denying subjectivity to the Chinese cipher who confers their primacy.

In comparison to the IWW's abstraction of Asian workers, attention to Native people as workers was virtually nonexistent. At the same time, the rhetoric of Indian identification was plentiful in IWW literature, with a great number of members and leaders alike hinting at or alluding to Indian ancestry. This lore is reiterated in contemporary histories of the IWW, where it is said that a "considerable number of Wobblies were at least part Indian." Indian identity serves as a particular marker of the IWW worker as a frontier figure: "The early Wobblies were above all famous for their Westerners: the part-Indians and the Yankees, sons and daughters of pony-express drivers, and gold prospectors whose families had kept going West but never escaped poverty."[69] Granted, there were individuals such as Lucy Parsons, of mixed Native, Black, and Mexican descent, who spoke at the IWW founding convention, and the self-identified "half-breed" IWW organizer Frank Little, who liked to joke that he was the only real "red" and authentic "American" in the crowd.[70] The majority of Indian identification, however, was vague and elusive. This "going Native" or "playing Indian," as Shari Huhndorf and Philip Deloria have alternately termed it, occurs throughout U.S. settler history, wherein an appropriation of Indian images or identity by white Americans is equated with notions of rebellion and freedom distinctly American, and representations of indigeneity become co-opted for American national identity.[71] Deloria elaborates that white desires for playing Indian shifted in the twentieth century as a way to wrestle with anxieties of increasing industrialization. Association with Indian identity, then, was a romantic anticapitalist strategy to assert a seemingly natural and authentic American individualism. The part-Indian IWW worker became a particularly powerful figure in this discourse, to contend with seemingly impersonal and oppressive industrial capitalism as heroes and patriots, the rightful heirs to an American West.

The idea that numerous IWW workers were of Indian ancestry relied on the settler logic of Indians as premodern people and is exemplified in the autobiography of William "Big Bill" Haywood. Haywood was arguably the most well-known IWW member, a veteran of the Western Miners Federation strikes of the late 1800s who spent the first decade of his IWW career as a popular orator, traveling to numerous strike lines.[72] In his autobiography, penned from exile in 1929 in the Soviet Union, Haywood typifies the racial rhetoric emblematic of the Industrial Workers of the World. Although many other IWW writers speculate on Haywood's rumored Indian blood, Haywood only hints at the possibility. Haywood demonstrates his abstracted and unnamed respect for Asian workers and similarly goes to great lengths to articulate his admiration for American Indian people and to sympathize with their defense against white settler encroachment.[73] The major difference being, however, that Haywood situates his racial solidarity with Chinese and Japanese as a workers' alliance while positing Indigenous peoples outside of modernity. Most telling is a passage from Haywood's time working in a Nevada mining camp, in which he describes his Indian neighbors.

> Interesting were the Indian dances, where, in a circle cleared on the sagebrush flat, the Indians would gather for their pow-wow and dance sometimes the snake-dance, the ghost-dance, the sun-dance, or some other just as mysterious. Their only music was the drums and the lilt of the squaws. The tunes were plaintive and fantastic, and sounded much alike to me. In the night when the fires were lighted, the hypnotic rhythm of the drums and the springy furtive dance steps of the Indians, accompanied by the low crooning song, were thrillingly weird.[74]

In contrast to the temporal perversion of Asian efficiency, the Native dancers improperly occupy the space of settler capitalism, their circular dance space within the sagebrush illegible infrastructure to the enclosure of both nuclear domicile and industrial edifice. Haywood attempts to name these dances, the "snake-dance" most likely a reference to the common appellation "Snake Indians" that settlers called the Indigenous peoples of the Great Basin, including the Northern Paiute, Bannock, and Shoshone. Native religious ceremonies such as the Sun Dance and the Ghost Dance were outlawed, during both the period Haywood presumably witnessed their practice and the time of his book's publication, the mysteriousness of such ceremonies underscored by the fact that the Paiute prophet Wovoka, whose vision catalyzed the Ghost Dance movement, spent the majority of his life in Mason Valley, Nevada, the site of silver and copper mining. The Ghost Dance movement, which promised the return of deceased relatives (human and buffalo) and the disappearance of white settlers, was birthed in the same space of developing industrial mining. For Haywood, a bewildering spatial overlay is solved through the logic of temporal failure. In Haywood's description, the labors of Native people—dancing, drumming, singing—are described as primitive yet desirable, queerly outside the pale of industrial work. The spatial perversion of Native dancing in the Nevada rangeland is represented through Haywood's visual and aural preoccupation, especially his exoticization of Native women's singing, underlaid with the sexualized and racial violence of epithet. American Indians under Haywood's gaze are marked by a fundamental difference, yet this weirdness is thrilling, that is, desirable to the hoboing Wobbly who lives a proximal life on the frontier, by the lit fires of his "jungle camp." In this formulation, the appeal is to be like an Indian but not an Indian. Hence, white workers who claimed Indian blood made for particularly good members of the international brotherhood of workers, while Indians living Indian lifestyles in Indian communities are viewed to be part of a nostalgic and soon-to-be eclipsed past. The romantic anticapitalist notion of Indian peoples tied to a natural and free yet primitive and stagnant way of life allowed IWW members to disregard Indians as workers while simultaneously using Indian identification to further a mythic concept of the hoboing IWW rooted in American history, on American soil. In the Pacific Northwest and Alaska, in particular, the early-twentieth-century surge in IWW organizing coincided with many Native peoples' growing participation in wage labor. The relationship of Native people to organized labor, including radical labor formations, remained inconceivable when such lasting romantic connotations permeated IWW labor histories.

The IWW discursively positioned itself as including ("liking") Asian American workers while subsuming traits ("likened") with American Indian peoples. Whereas Asian workers functioned as outsiders within, fictive Native ancestors functioned as insiders without. These logics in combination worked to construct the white male as labor's natural and proper subject, rendering invisible the actual organizing struggles of Asian or Native people, a particularly ironic disavowal given the attention to the IWW by labor scholars extolling the union's radical and alternative lifestyle practices. Labor studies, even radical labor studies, joins Alaskan history, Asian American studies, and Native and Indigenous studies in delimiting the proper worker. In this way, labor's archive, constructed through various intellectual projects, circumscribes the laboring subject to normative race, gender, sexuality, and settler status. In the discussions that follow, through engagements with Tlingit poet Nora Marks Dauenhauer and Filipino author Carlos Bulosan, I explore the creative counter archive created by those who cannot become labor's proper subjects. Both authors elucidate quotidian and unbecoming cannery experiences within and beyond the workplace, highlighting the potential for unproductive intimacies.

The Intimate Pleasures of Nora Marks Dauenhauer's Poetry

Nora Marks Dauenhauer (Tlingit name K̲eixwnéi) is arguably the most widely known and regarded Tlingit writer of both scholarly and creative texts, including oral history collections, Tlingit language instruction, poems, plays, and essays, and her creative work in particular lends itself to a lens of intimacy. Dauenhauer focuses on the intimate and everyday relationships between people as in "A Poem for Jim Nagatáak'w (Jak̲wteen)" based on Dauenhauer's relationship with her blind and nearly deaf grandfather:

> I could look at him and get
> really close. We both liked this.
> Getting close was his way
> of seeing.[75]

As Gladys Cardiff notes in her review of Dauenhauer's creative collection *Life Woven with Song*, "getting close" is also Dauenhauer's aesthetic lens.[76] Dauenhauer's poem "Salmon Egg Puller—$2.15 an Hour" intimately and affectively engages her experience working in canneries, the poem's title simultaneously identifying the specific racial and gendered job task on the assembly line and the value assigned through wage labor.[77] Born in 1927, Dauenhauer's first wage-earning job was in a cannery and she continued to work in canneries throughout much of her life.[78] Her poem elaborates on the work entailed as a salmon egg puller as an intimacy with the salmon itself:

> Grab lightly
> top of egg sack
> with fingers,
> pull gently, but quick.
> Reach in immediately with right hand
> for the lower egg sack.
> Pull this gently.[79]

Dauenhauer is engaging with the discourses extolling the gendered aspects of Native women's work in the cannery, and their innate ability to "pull gently." As the cannery industry developed, employment became increasingly gendered, with Native men regarded as having "little desire to give themselves over to company control," especially when they would often leave cannery work to hunt or fish for their families and communities.[80] Native women were racialized very differently by cannery and government officials as having an "immemorial instinct" for working with salmon, and were often assigned as slimers, those who cut and gut the salmon first coming down the line, or as egg pullers tasked with the specialized skill of removing eggs to be marketed as roe caviar or for sushi.[81] Such officials deployed settler logics to naturalize the cannery labor of Native women derived from a timeless past and, in doing so, effaced their presence as industrial workers. Such romanticization was anything but natural, however, as Dauenhauer intersperses the image of gentle pulling with the monotonous repetition of the assembly line: "Do this four hours in the morning," then "work four hours in the afternoon" and, after the dinner break,

> Go back for two more hours,
> four more hours.
> Reach,
> pull gently.[82]

This juxtaposition expands the scope of this "gentle" work to the rapacious demands of industrial capital and the embodied result—sore, swollen fingers.

In their racial and gendered assumptions, cannery operators failed to comprehend the complex survival strategies that cannery work enabled. As noted in earlier discussions, seasonal work allowed Native families and communities to continue Indigenous economies and cultural practices even while confronting rapid changes due to extractive economies. In a time when canneries facilitated dispossession from traditional fishing grounds, the temporary work they demanded ironically provided a means for Alaska Native communities to continue cultural practices without governmental interference, following the seasonal round of Indigenous food gathering and production. Dauenhauer's family caught and dried their own salmon in addition to the women and children working in the cannery and the men fishing for cannery tenders. Native studies focuses on the land dispossession caused by canneries, and canneries are formulated through the lens of migratory labor in Asian American studies, but it is the intersection of the cannery's contradictory demands of land expropriation and labor exploitation that reveals Native economic strategies in response to colonial capitalism. Glimpses of this connection are revealed in the poem when Dauenhauer describes one of the first steps of the salmon egg puller:

> reach inside the salmon cavity
> with your left hand,
> where the head was.[83]

This generalized description could describe either a procedural instruction in Dauenhauer's cannery job or the Indigenous practice of drying salmon for winter, as heads are typically cut off as a first step. The difference lies in Tlingit relations to salmon during food production, as embodied in the salmon head. In a childhood recollection, Dauenhauer describes chum and coho salmon caught at her clan's salmon stream thusly: "All of the salmon heads were gray and black; they were beautiful."[84] Her admiration is immediately followed by the announcement that her father is already preparing his "favorite treat," the finest coho heads and tails to be eaten raw. Dauenhauer's childhood story highlights the material, cultural, and spiritual importance of salmon: that the heads are beautiful leads to her father's desire to eat them, and, conversely, her father's enthusiasm for salmon heads reinforces their beauty, all taking place during the family's yearly seasonal fishing at their owned and known salmon stream. While Native lifeways prize the head of the salmon as the choicest eating, in industrial canning practice the head is disposed of, separated physically and economically from the rest of the salmon that is cut, canned, and shipped for eating in far-flung locales across the globe.[85] Dauenhauer's poem acknowledges the shift of working with salmon and its preservation in an industrial setting, recognizing both settler and Tlingit production dependent on salmon though also suggesting the disembodied salmon as a metonym for dispossession, the missing head that the narrator reaches for.

We might also read "Salmon Egg Puller" as a comment on and response to the Asian male cannery worker constructed by Asian American studies. Many of the intimate details and repetition of the cannery assembly line in Dauenhauer's poem are echoed in social histories of Asian laborers in Alaskan canneries. At the same time, the tone of Dauenhauer's poem differs from the accounts in Asian American studies. She opens the poem with the line, "You learn to dance with machines," underscoring the specific cultural strategies of the Tlingit in the face of settler colonial capitalism. We might understand this dance as a rejoinder to the "thrillingly weird" surveillance of the IWW's romantic anticapitalism, wherein Dauenhauer poetically carries the Tlingit cultural practice of dancing into both the space and time of industrial capital. In contrast, the narrative of cannery labor constructed by Asian American studies is one of worker opposition to exploitation, in which dancing with the machinery of industrial capitalism is not a viable, or even preferable, option. This difference, read alongside the erasure of Native women in accounts of the 1913 union, suggests a narrative impasse between Asian American studies and Native and Indigenous studies, as well as a productive inquiry into the articulations and disarticulations of colonial constructs of race and gender, labor disputes, and Indigenous strategies for survival. In speculating whether Native women participated in, opposed, or were excluded from union organizing, we might also ask whether issues of wages, safety, and worker control were of priority to Native people ensconced in battles for land and cultural survival. We see here that Asian American studies' overdetermination of labor cannot account for more expansive subjectivities and modes of resistance. A critical engagement with settler colonialism therefore requires Asian American studies to address a more capacious framework for migrant labor attentive to issues of Indigenous land dispossession and Indigenous self-determination.

Dauenhauer gives voice to Indigenous considerations in an autobiographical essay in which she reminisces that the cannery experience was fraught with racial discrimination, stressing the substandard housing of Native families compared to the bunkhouses of white workers. But even with this admission, she remembers the era fondly: "I guess we had fun."[86] Not to minimize or romanticize the harsh working conditions of either Native or Asian cannery workers, it is this idea of pleasure or joy in the intimacy of the cannery experience itself I wish to explore further. As noted above, Dauenhauer opens her poem with the line, "You learn to dance with machines," with the imagery of dancing continued throughout the poem. In the territorial period, when Alaska Native dancing and ceremonies were banned by missionaries and government officials, dancing during the workday was a way to sustain culture, and, similar to the continued connection to salmon and salmon economy within seasonal wage labor, dancing formed a contestational maneuver, small and intimate, that remained outside the purview of cannery operators and government agents. Learning this new form of dance, with machines, can be seen as a metaphorical strategy that facilitated the later emergence of the Tlingit renaissance of the 1960s and 1970s, a heritage revival that Dauenhauer herself was instrumental in leading. Returning back to Dauenhauer's image of beautiful salmon heads, we might also consider the "salmon-trout head," the elaborated ovoid shape foundational to Pacific Northwest/Alaska Southeast visual arts known as formline, that the salmon head jettisoned by settler colonial racial capitalism can be found in cultural revival.[87]

Dauenhauer also addresses social reproduction and Indigenous modes of relation as a mother in this poem (and as she describes, a "housewife," even though she labors all day in the cannery).[88] Twice in the poem she repeats the line, "Attend to kids, and feed them," describing her activity during lunch and dinner breaks. At the end of the day, "Attend to kids who missed you."[89] Here, multiple meanings are revealed: her alienation from the Tlingit food source of salmon as she feeds her children away and apart from the cannery line and its work of food preparation; her wage labor (at $2.15 an hour), however, provides a means by which to feed her children; and an additional subtext, that the seasonal and temporary nature of the profit-driven, corporate cannery allows her to continue traditional salmon gathering practices with the next generation. As a space of and for laboring Native women, the homosocial aspect of "Salmon Egg Puller" is further stressed in Dauenhauer's direct form of address. In using the second person, Dauenhauer directs her poem to other salmon egg pullers—given the racialized and gendered stratification of the cannery system, Dauenhauer is addressing other Native women. Although literary critics often highlight Dauenhauer's pedagogic project to educate non-Natives, in this poem she is not only detailing strategies for coping but also suggesting cultural sustenance and revival for Native women. This oppositional narrative is similar to her popular "How to Make Good Baked Salmon from the River," another poem in which Dauenhauer uses the second-person form of address.[90] As Tlingit scholar Caskey Russell notes, Dauenhauer's prescriptive form of address echoes traditional Tlingit oratory and is "part pragmatic recipe for preparing salmon, and part exhortation to sensual enjoyment and spiritual wholeness."[91] Similarly, in "Salmon Egg Puller—$2.15 an

Hour," Dauenhauer provides instruction to other Native women cannery workers on how to survive the grueling physical demands of the job as well as keep culture and family intact. A pragmatic sensuality is conveyed not only in the dance with machines, but also in the aftereffects of the workday:

> When fingers start swelling,
> soak them in Epsom salts.
> If you don't have time,
> stand under the shower
> with your hands up under the spray.[92]

The unapologetic sensual imagery of Native women dancing on the cannery assembly line and soaking/spraying their swollen fingers intervenes in the pathologization of Native women as promiscuous. The writings of prominent Alaskan officials, most notably missionaries, abounded with preoccupation of Native women's perceived negative sexual behavior.[93] Such authors constructed Native women on the one hand as oppressed under Tlingit polygamous marriage yet also as debased by their participation in modernity. We see the intersection of these two discourses when Alaska Native women or Native culture is blamed for Native women's prostitution, even though sex work emerged as a growing industry within and among all racial groups during colonial and territorial expansion. As one government report described, Native women participated in "indiscriminate prostitution . . . with the consent, and often under the escort of their husbands, fathers, or other male relatives."[94] Such accounts reveal the depths of the colonial discourse that Native women were available for non-Native men's sexual desires, even to the extent that Native men were viewed as facilitating this process. Rather than apprehend the possible prostitution of Native women as a response to colonial changes, including the sexual demands of non-Native men and the emergence of a market economy, this colonialist fantasy shifts culpability onto Native men and the representation of a debased Native family/community.[95] If, as Indigenous feminists theorize, the image of the sexually available Native woman constitutes the corresponding idea of Indigenous land to possess and settle, the above quotation illustrates the colonial fantasy of Native community approval for dispossession. Further, it deflects from the foundational use of coercive sexual violence in the formation of the Alaskan colony, first implemented by the Russian promyshlenniki, fur trappers and traders, but expanded under British and American colonialism.[96]

The figure of the licentious Native woman was also implicitly linked to Native peoples' mobile and manifold labor practices. The territory's leadership was vexed, similar as in discourses of sex work, by Native women's participation in forms of wage labor such as cannery work. Indigenous involvement in the emergent Pacific Northwest/Alaska Southeast industrialization of the early twentieth century functioned as a mode of resistance to the Christian missionary facet of colonialism that compelled Native peoples to settle into permanent American homes as nuclear families. Historian Coll Thrush explains colonial administrators' opposition to migrant labor: "It often seemed to agents that such travel undermined efforts to 'civilize' Native people. From the Makah Reservation, for instance, whole families headed to the hop fields, leaving agency schools empty, Bibles unread, and lessons unlearned.... Efforts to define who belonged where rarely worked out as planned."[97] Indeed, Dauenhauer herself did not learn English until she was eight years old and forced to attend school; before then she was hidden with other children on the family boat, away from truant officers who "detained families such as ours, forcing them to settle in towns."[98] Leanne Betasamosake Simpson stresses that such enforcement by missionaries and colonial administrators attempted to control women's bodies and political orders, with settlement a particularly egregious retaliation to deeply relational, matrilineal, clan-based governance. She highlights the fundamental and willful ignorance when "rhythmic, seasonal, [travel] through the territory gets positioned as 'nomadic,' rather than as a political and governing structure and process that facilitated a gentle and sustainable use of our lands and waters, a decentralized national leadership, and an intensification of personal and political relationships with a diversity of human and nonhuman nations."[99]

Refuting the colonial normative view that positioned the behavior and choices of Native women as deviant, Dauenhauer provides a representation of joyous and unruly survival. What exceeds heteropatriarchal colonial dictates is precisely what Dauenhauer's cannery worker uses to survive the workday—her own body and sensations. I take my cue from Mark Rifkin who formulates an "erotics of sovereignty" to examine Indigenous sensory experience as articulating a politics of decolonization. Rifkin formulates "an Indigenous structure of feeling [that refers] to a sensation of belonging to place and peoplehood excluded from settler governance but that remains present, most viscerally in the affective lives of Native people."[100] It is within Dauenhauer's poetry that Native women's laboring bodies are sustained in a loving self-care and recuperated from both the material violence of dispossession and the epistemic violence of erasure. As Dauenhauer advises, "Next morning, if your fingers are sore, / start dancing immediately."[101] As Native women work with each other on the cannery line, Dauenhauer configures dancing as a complex and sensual remedy for surviving and enduring the embodied effects of colonial expropriation and exploitation.

Carlos Bulosan: Queering Labor and Land

Carlos Bulosan's *America Is in the Heart*, a novel based on Bulosan's own life as a Filipino migrant worker in the United States during the 1930s and 1940s, is arguably the most canonical Asian American literary text centered on labor and labor organizing. Born in 1913 in the Philippines to an impoverished farming family, Bulosan arrived in the United States in 1930 as part of a larger wave of Filipinx immigration facilitated by U.S. imperialism in the Philippines that paradoxically included Filipinx as colonial subjects during a period of Asian exclusion policies.[102] The contradictory incorporative logics within unincorporated territories (and here we could consider both the Philippines and Alaska) also underscore a resultant paradox of arrivant colonialism: to position anticolonial class politics in the service of settler nationalist belonging, a trajectory typified in Bulosan's arc from poor peasant to American communist. Read for gender and sexuality, however, Bulosan's novel provides a site for critically engaging with figurations of nonnormative Asian American men and Native woman. Similar to Dauenhauer's poetry, Carlos Bulosan's literature provides a view of the salmon industry from the vantage of those who labored in canneries; in Bulosan's case including descriptions of social life between Filipinx men and Alaska Native women. To consider the queer in Bulosan's text reveals affiliations that exceed and reconfigure Bulosan's preoccupation with the (destructive) powers of Native and Asian sex and sexualization.

The simultaneous fear and fascination with Asian male sexuality within colonial discourses is illustrated in the repeated yet fleeting documentation of Asian sex workers in the canneries.[103] This presence in the archive is presumably due to the profitability for foremen and labor contractors, but can also be read implicitly as a form of anxiety and surveillance toward Asian male sexuality. This anxiety is present in Asian American representations of the migrant worker as well. Karl Yoneda, the Japanese American communist and labor organizer who introduces Ketchikan's Local 283 to Asian American studies, was himself involved in organizing cannery workers in the 1930s. He became active in cannery organizing after attending a government hearing on canneries for a Japanese American newspaper. In his autobiography, Yoneda specifically mentions Asian sex workers in detailing the oppressive conditions presented at this hearing: "Boys, some as young as fourteen, were recruited or smuggled aboard ships 'to serve' the foremen or contractors. A few homosexuals were hired, who changed into women's attire as soon as ships left port."[104] Several aspects of this description merit mention. "Boys" are distinct from "homosexuals," that is, young men who are engaged in sex work are being exploited, whereas cross-dressing men (or transgender women), presumably also sex workers, are themselves exploiting the masculine norms of the cannery. In both cases, however, sex workers are located outside the parameters of identity roles prescribed for male cannery workers. Notions of improper or perverse behavior subsumed more complex narratives that registered labor through sex, sex workers' exploitation, and even, possibly, pleasure. Yoneda's account typifies what historian Peter Boag names as the "re-dressing" of the American West, in which gender transgression, particularly male to female cross-dressing, is rendered effeminate and degenerate, and outside of a recuperated heroic and virile history.[105]

Yoneda's text also highlights that discourses of deviant working-class sexuality are also always discourses of nonnormative racialization. Nayan Shah elucidates this point in his study of queer sociality as expressed in the cross-racial encounters (including male-on-male sex) of migrant South Asian workers in the North American West.[106] As Shah explains, "Drawing racial and civilizational distinctions of dress, behavior, recreation, and livelihood shored up white supremacy and nationalism. At the same time, it naturalized subordination of racialized migrants' presumed incapacity for maintaining the 'natural' gender binary and inequality."[107] In this way, the surveillance and criminalization of Asian migrant men's sexual and relationship practices reveals the disciplining desires of the heteronormative, nationalist, and settler colonial state. Resuscitating the figure of the Asian sex worker and positioning him/her/them as laborer critically intervenes in the normative tendencies of Asian American historical revision, while also providing a means through which to critique the overdetermination of the Asian migrant as failed settler. The failed masculinity of Asian sex workers stands as a powerful symbol of all Asian migrant workers in demonstrating their multiple failures in terms of properly gendered subjects, workers, and citizens as contestational to a heteronormative settler colonialism that depends on the disciplining of gender, race, labor, and national belonging.

The figure of the Asian male sex worker is available through a queer reading of Bulosan. Here I take my cue from Melinda De Jesús, who focuses on the homosocial and homoerotic passages in *America Is in the Heart* to demonstrate the subversive subtext in this canonical novel.[108] The narrator Carlos's transition from growing up in the Philippines to a life as a migrant worker is marked by his labor in an Alaskan cannery, as it is his first job in the United States. In this way, Alaska can be considered a liminal space, or land, that Carlos passes through in his "progress" from Filipino colonial subject to American national subject, illustrating the overlay between arrivant colonialism and liberal multiculturalism. At Rose Inlet, one of the canneries in the Ketchikan area, Carlos is befriended by Filipino "oldtimers" Conrado and Paulo. Carlos pays special attention to Conrado's "wise, sensuous mouth" and later emphasizes Paulo's desirable "curly hair" and "his even, white teeth."[109] It is homoerotic passages such as these that De Jesús points to in arguing that Asian American studies has focused on Filipinx migrant workers' sense of thwarted heterosexuality (due to legal and social blocks to white women) while ignoring the intense relationships between and among the men themselves. While Carlos remains asexual and innocent in his encounters, we see in Bulosan's homoerotic descriptions the trace of the Asian male sex worker. Such homoerotic admiration, instead of being configured outside of labor, as Karl Yoneda does in his detailing of Asian sex workers in the cannery, strengthens the brotherhood of workers as Carlos describes his relationship with Conrado and Paulo as "the beginning of a friendship that grew simultaneously with the growth of the trade union movement and progressive ideas among the Filipinos in the United States."[110]

As a literary text that includes some of the most detailed descriptions of cannery labor, Bulosan's novel unfortunately replicates the figure of the promiscuous Native woman. At Rose Inlet, Paulo begins a relationship with an Alaska Native woman named La Belle. As the cannery season progresses, however, Carlos makes it clear that La Belle has taken up with a number of different men. When La Belle gets pregnant and has a baby, the Filipino men believe the father to be an Italian fisherman. La Belle, however, claims Conrado as the father. Carlos describes this scene as one of conniving entrapment, and expresses dismay when Paulo steps up to claim the child and remain with La Belle in Alaska, saying that he will "stay with this dirty Indian girl."[111] Bulosan as narrator cannot comprehend Paulo's decision and never sees Paulo again. In her feminist reading of Bulosan's novel, Rachel Lee argues that heroic and brotherly affections of Asian migrant men rely on "the successful regulation of sexuality," wherein eroticized women embody the failure of comradeship.[112] What are we to make of the disarticulation between Lee's and De Jesús's respective feminist and queer readings of *America Is in the Heart*? Bulosan's novel can be both highlighted for its homosociality and critiqued as a celebration of heroic worker solidary through abject racialization of Native women. Lisa Lowe's formulation of intimacy as a heuristic provides a third reading. Because Bulosan locates Asian and Native cannery workers together in the space of the cannery, we are able to establish a nearness, an intimacy, between figurings of queer Asian American men and promiscuous Native women, and even comment on their co-constitution.

I turn now to a telling passage in *America Is in the Heart* as it recounts intimacy between Asian men and Native women at the cannery that is not constituted through colonialist misogyny:

> It was only at night that we felt free, although the sun seemed never to disappear from the sky. It stayed on in the western horizon and its magnificence inflamed the snows on the island, giving us a world of soft, continuous light, until the moon rose at about ten o'clock to take its place. Then trembling shadows began to form on the rise of the brilliant snow in our yard, and we would come out with baseball bats, gloves, and balls, and the Indian girls who worked in the cannery would join us, shouting huskily like men.[113]

In this passage Bulosan offers an alternate configuration of freedom, outside of the workday activities of cannery labor. This freedom occurs only at night, and this night is described as perverse: an Alaskan dusk of "trembling shadows." This queering of the land is premised by the place of Alaska and its long daylight summer hours. Bulosan is also invoking a metaphor used by Alaska Native peoples to describe the first half of the twentieth century as a "time of twilight," the in-between space in which Native peoples struggled to creatively maintain cultural traditions in the face of American colonial industrialism.[114] Similar to the sensual strategies in Nora Dauenhauer's poetry, Bulosan highlights the need for pleasurable space within the environment of the cannery. In fact, it is within the contradictions of unproductive pleasure that a more complex relationship between racialized and colonized workers emerges.

This passage complicates both Lee's and De Jesús's readings of *America Is in the Heart*. For Lee, Bulosan constructs women as the other to worker, but in the scene above, Bulosan underscores comradery with Native women. A subtle double move is at play here—Bulosan cannot construct Alaska Native women as oppositional and malicious to labor (as he does with white women, be they prostitutes, romantic interests, or labor organizers) because of the gendered and racialized intimacy that the cannery constructs—the line is worked by Asian migrant men and Indigenous women in the same space-time. Yet Bulosan recognizes Native women as workers in the precise moment they are engaged in an activity unproductive to the cannery owners, playing baseball together. This is not the social reproduction theorized by Tithi Bhattacharya and by Susan Ferguson, Asian men and Native women neither the target nor beneficiaries of Fordist management, their unions not the reproduction that capitalist expansion desires. By exploring this simultaneously pleasurable and unproductive intimacy between Native and Asian cannery workers, Bulosan not only acknowledges Native women in the canneries but also suggests an alternate engagement for Asian American studies that is not dependent on heroic, or productive, figures. Further, it gestures to alliances formed outside worker claims to production, to a more capacious antiracism that might account for Indigenous presence, a reckoning necessary to topple both capitalism and colonization.

Similar to Dauenhauer's poetry, this passage from *America Is in the Heart* exudes sensuality: snow inflamed with sun, shadows that tremble, an eroticism that concludes with Native women "shouting huskily like men." Following De Jesús's treatise that Bulosan creates a queer subtext with his homosocial and homoerotic language, Native women are imbued here with a hale masculinity, and in their butchness they become part of Bulosan's internationalist fraternity of worker solidarity. When Bulosan goes on to describe Filipinx and Native workers who leave the game to "run off into the moonlight" to sexual liaisons, their physical intimacy is queered by the preceding narrative of jocular and eroticized ball play. Echoing Dauenhauer's recollection that "we had fun," Bulosan links the description of baseball games to nighttime trysts with the double entendre, "We played far into the night."[115]

Even though Bulosan forecloses this complex scene with the limited portrayal of entrapment by a promiscuous Native woman, it is not before he provides an intimate relationship, a queer kinship, between Native women and Asian men that echoes Dauenhauer's focus on pleasurable freedoms. In doing so, he allows for an alternate reading of La Belle, Paulo, and Conrado's intimacies, because Asian sex workers are ostensibly brought into the canneries to prevent sexual relations with Native women. The antireproductive quality of sex work can then be seen as acting in the capitalist service of white settler colonialism—by preventing Asian migrants from forming familial relationships with Native women and establishing permanent residence, immigrant-to-immigrant homosex becomes productive in the maintenance of the mobile migrant workforce. Asian and Native relationships would bring Asian immigrant workers into the sociality created by Native women cannery workers and their Indigenous modes of relation, in opposition to colonialist extractive relations. It would be mistaken to read this as the triumph of heteronormativity, however. As Indigenous feminist studies scholars such as Chris Finley and

Scott Morgensen remind us, Native reproduction is always queerly nonnormative to the disciplining of both heteropatriarchy and the settler state.[116] In matrilineal, clan-based Alaska Native societies, children born from Native and Asian relationships would be considered Native, politically and culturally, threatening the futurity of the white settler state while furthering Indigenous life and relations.

Conclusion: Unproductive Pleasures

The labor archive constructed by Alaskan history and labor studies naturalizes the productive worker as white, male, and settler. Though Asian American studies challenges romantic anticapitalist subjectivity through the verification of Local 283, claims to a heroic proletariat reinforce settler subjectivity by effacing both Native women workers and nonnormative Asian laborers. The queer temporality of racialized alien labor results in a spatial failure: they are positioned foreign and nonresident to the settler state. For Native women, their queer spatiality, their intergenerational occupancy of the assembly line, signals a temporal contradiction: they are positioned outside of modern time even as they labor in it. More than just an explanatory model of settler colonial racial capitalism, when Alaska Native women's and Asian immigrant men's experiences are taken together, land expropriation and labor exploitation no longer present discrete or competing frameworks, but, rather, settler colonial racial capitalism can be considered within the processes and logics of overlapping and contradictory racialized, gendered, and economic oppressions and opportunities, backgrounded by the Indigenous land dispossession wrought by colonial accumulation. Read in this way, the intimacies between and among Native women and Asian men in Southeast Alaska are central to understanding settler colonialism in Alaska and beyond, specifically the coconstitution of an emergent industrialism and a heteronormative nation-state. The literary works of Nora Marks Dauenhauer and Carlos Bulosan recuperate the debased figures of the promiscuous Native woman and the Asian sex worker to embrace unproductive pleasures and contestations, highlighting that nonnormative resistance and potential collaboration are central to two interrelated projects: Native nationhood that is predicated on neither heteropatriarchy nor the nation-state, and a politics of decolonizing antiracism.

In the chapters thus far, I've explored how settler colonial logics condition Alaska Native and Asian peoples differentially. Alaska Natives are viewed as outside of settler colonial time, their participation deemed impossible as modern laboring subjects. Conversely, Asian residents are afforded modernity, particularly as industrial workers, but cannot be part of settler colonial space and are either physically expelled or discursively framed as failed settlers. In chapter 4, I look at the life and photography of Japanese immigrant Shoki Kayamori to explore the ways in which Kayamori's oeuvre captures Asian immigrants within Alaska Native understandings of place as well as the complex sovereignty strategies of mid-twentieth-century Alaska Natives, approaches that exceeded settler temporality. Kayamori's suicide remains a haunting presence, and reading his death alongside the internment of the Unangax̂ people articulates an elided militarization and surveillance that reinforces the argument that colonialism and modernity are always intertwined processes.

CHAPTER FOUR

Picture Man
Photographer Shoki Kayamori and Settler Militarism

This story begins in the early 1970s in Yakutat, Alaska, inside the attic of a derelict church, decades after missionaries departed their post in this rural Native village. A local couple has been living temporarily in the church after their trailer burned down, but now plans are made for demolition. In cleaning out the mission house, the couple and their friends discover a number of glass plate negatives tucked among other discarded and forgotten objects. The photographs are stacked in small crates or scattered across the floor, the outlines of the images beginning to peel and bubble. In the intervening years, children have been in the attic and some photos lie cracked and broken. Townspeople attempt to enlist various government entities to print the photographs but are unsuccessful. In the late 1970s, the people of Yakutat raise half the funds to develop the photographs with the Alaska State Library. Though it is unclear how this collection of photos came to be abandoned in a church attic, it is immediately and collectively known among Yakutat residents that these images are the work of the deceased photographer Shoki Kayamori.[1]

In the 1910s, Japanese immigrant Shoki Kayamori traveled to Yakutat, Alaska, to work the cannery season, and stayed for the remainder of his life.[2] (Figure 4.1 shows a landscape view of Yakutat taken by Kayamori.) Events in this chapter overlap with the moment examined in chapter 3—Asian migrant labor in Alaska's canneries in the 1910s—and takes us through the interwar years to World War II. For close to three decades, Kayamori documented the quotidian activities of the village's denizens, capturing a simultaneously Native and multiracial Yakutat in portraits and during community events. As World War II escalated, Kayamori committed suicide amid rumors that he was a spy, with his avocation of photography specifically cited by government officials to warrant suspicion and possible detention.[3]

Based on nearly 950 existing Kayamori photographs archived at the Alaska State Library, the Sealaska Heritage Institute, and Yakutat City Hall, and interviews conducted with Yakutat residents on the meanings and usage of his photographs, I examine Kayamori's visual archive: his photographic history and representation of the people, place, and events of Yakutat from the 1910s

FIGURE 4.1 Photograph of Yakutat, Alaska, showing the Libby, McNeil, and Libby cannery, fishing boats along the wharf, and houses on the hillside behind. Alaska State Library, Seiki (Shoki, Fhoki) Photograph Collection, ca. 1912–1941, photo by Shoki Kayamori, ASL-P55-206.

to the early 1940s.[4] I argue that Kayamori's corpus demonstrates a liminal intimacy across racial and gendered boundaries with Yakutat's Native community, simultaneously representing the indigeneity and racial heterogeneity within Alaska under American colonialism. Kayamori's photographs and his own lived history in Yakutat represent the complex and dynamic relationships between Indigenous peoples and racialized immigrants, demonstrating not only asymmetrical and uneven relations of power within extractive economies and colonial dispossession, but also the very encounters that settler colonial logics render illegible. As Kayamori's images reveal, Asian and Native experiences of settler colonialism are never discrete but, rather, are contingent and overlapping processes that produce multiply authored counternarratives.

I am interested in the ways that Kayamori as a racialized and gendered subject, an immigrant who settled but was denied the citizenship of settlers, identified and represented his subjects in ways different than those of the canonical cohort of European American photographers. Lorenzo Veracini makes a distinction between settler and immigrant, noting that, "Settlers are *founders* of political orders and carry their sovereignty with them.... Migrants can be individually co-opted within settler colonial political regimes, and indeed they often are. They do not, however, enjoy inherent rights and are characterised by a defining lack of sovereign entitlement."[5] How did the foreclosure of citizenship, the inability to attain what Veracini names as "sovereign entitlement," influence Kayamori's life and work? Kayamori's identity as a resident photographer, especially within a Native community, is shared by other Asian North American immigrants who lived and worked in the North American West during the early twentieth century. Japanese immigrant Frank Matsura documented the Native, Asian, and white inhabitants of Washington's Okanogan County from 1903 to 1913, and Chinese Canadian C. D. Hoy similarly photographed First Nation residents, and Chinese and white migrants and settlers, in the Cariboo region of interior British Columbia from 1911 to 1923. Scholarly attention to these two photographers underscores their importance in challenging national narratives of manifest destiny as well as the concomitant myth of the "vanishing Indian," particularly because of their proximal intimacy with their subjects, whether Native, Asian, or white.[6] This cohort of Asian North American photographers, including Kayamori, could not conform to heteronormative and racially normative citizenship, and subsequently their disenfranchisement within the settler state facilitated their documentation of the overlapping lives of racialized migrants and Indigenous inhabitants.

Kayamori's photographic representations and status as resident documenter signal a liminal positionality within both the Native community he inhabited and the nascent settler nation-state. The framework of liminality within anthropology demonstrates the radical possibilities of social marginality, but I'm most interested in how liminality has been taken up within Asian American studies.[7] As Asian American studies scholars have asserted, the liminality of the Asian immigrant can be located within the legal preclusion of citizenship, wherein racialized policies work in tandem with discourses of foreignness.[8] Historian Mae Ngai elaborates that "illegal aliens, alien citizens, colonial subjects, and foreign contract-workers [were] all liminal status categories that existed outside the normative teleology of immigration, that is, legal admission, permanent-resident status, and citizenship."[9] In Kayamori's case, however, it is not just distance from white normative citizenship that establishes his marginality, but also his affiliation with Alaska Native residents of Yakutat. Instructive, here, are Asian American studies scholars who have framed Asian Americans as liminal figures within racial construction, particularly within a Black-white paradigm.[10] Leslie Bow, for example, configures Asian Americans in the U.S. South as racial anomalies, stressing that "what anomaly reveals is not merely a more nuanced account of racialization, but the counter-narratives that interrupt the work of the dominant, the partial stories that characterize the *unevenly* oppressed."[11] Kayamori similarly inhabits an anomalous position within Alaska, and his photography depicts people in ways that exceed the racialization of dominant settler ideology.

I want to caution, however, against viewing Asian American liminality only within racialized terms, or as conditioned by the settler state. To do so overlooks Kayamori's relationality to Alaska Native peoples, who may have been conditioned by racialized and colonized liminalities but remained in some aspects independent and certainly prior. In relation to Tlingit community, Kayamori was also liminal, and occupied a simultaneous insider/outsider position as a long-term documenter who was trusted to represent community members to themselves, yet did not appear himself within the social fabric that he photographed. Because he did not establish traditional kinship bonds through marriage into the Tlingit community, the ongoing intimate connections his photography established serve as a powerful articulation of intimacy from the failed settler subject position of alien resident. His liminal position as a racialized and anomalous settler allowed him to build community across racial and gender boundaries, but through a photographic practice that also continued to reestablish his marginal position.

Given this nexus of multiply liminal positions, I am specifically interested in how Kayamori's work speaks back to settler colonialism. I argue that because of his liminal position in Alaska's settler colonial project, Kayamori's photography represents multivalent expressions of space and time that extend beyond the limitations of settler colonial logics. In capturing the everyday images, ordinary and intimate, of Yakutat and its residents in the early twentieth century, his photographs refuse the exclusion of racialized migrants within settler colonial space, instead documenting, borrowing from Renisa Mawani, the "colonial proximities" of racialized migrants and Native inhabitants.[12] In this way, through his own liminal aesthetic, Kayamori reveals settler colonial Alaska as a simultaneously racially heterogeneous and Indigenous space.

Kayamori's in-between status reflects a level of ambiguity and multivalence in his photographs, providing representations that intervene in the static and timeless notion of the vanishing Indian as well as the progressive teleology of the assimilation project. I am interested particularly in the ways that Kayamori, as a liminal subject and photographer, records Kevin Bruyneel's political concept, "third space of sovereignty," after postcolonial scholar Homi Bhabha's formulation of third space to denote an Indigenous form of expression and resistance "that resides neither simply inside nor outside the American political system but rather exists on these very boundaries, exposing both the practices and the contingencies of American colonial rule."[13] If, as Bruyneel argues, the spatial and temporal logics of settler colonialism supposed that Native sovereignty exists outside the nation, and that claims to sovereignty are reduced to archaic rather than modern times, Kayamori's representations explode the inside-outside and traditional-modern binaries by showing Native people generally, and Tlingit people specifically, engaged in everyday and multifaceted responses to colonial change, irreducible to essentialized notions of timeless cultural practice or assimilationist inevitability. In this way, Kayamori's photographs both expose and reject the logics of settler colonial time and its disavowal of Native subjects. At the same time that Kayamori is able to document Alaska Native third-space strategies under colonial modernity, he himself remains liminal to the creation of such spaces, and I suggest that his possible yet unrecorded participation in Alaska Native political organization also challenges the logics on which space-time colonialism depends.

Kayamori's liminality as a racialized immigrant and failed settler subject, though generative to and because of Yakutat's Tlingit community, becomes a liability within the militarized buildup of World War II, when his local association is violently disciplined by soldiers stationed in Yakutat. Particularly revealing is how his avocation of photography is oppositionally assessed by military administrators and Yakutat's Indigenous community, respectively viewed as either a marker of culpability or a sign of belonging. Kayamori's suicide in particular provides a haunting trace that intervenes in historical accounts of World War II as a progressive event that propelled Alaska, with a newly acquired modern and militarized infrastructure, into statehood.[14] A combined Asian American and Indigenous studies examination of Kayamori's suicide, read alongside the internment of Unangax̂ and mixed Native-Japanese peoples, elucidates disavowed violence and surveillance that reinforces the argument that in Alaska, settler colonialism and militarism are always intertwined processes, a conjunction that Jodi Kim has termed "settler modernity."[15] Doing so allows us to view Alaska as a site that not only joins settler colonialism and overseas empire in the late nineteenth century but also connects that imbrication to a reanimation in the mid-twentieth century period that witnesses the post–World War II rise of an American military empire, specifically in the imperially imagined region of the "Asia-Pacific."

As a writing strategy throughout this chapter, I propose various entry points into Shoki Kayamori's life and photography as a way to stress the multivalency of his work and influence, as well as to make legible different intersections that may not be evident within the structure and logics of dominant narratives within settler colonial Alaskan history. I provide multiple origins for telling Kayamori's story, restarting the narrative from different beginning points, to signal the ways in which Kayamori's photos, as a (lost and) found archive, necessarily resist order and linear progression. More importantly—and in some small measure my attempt to reflect the influence that Indigenous epistemologies and lifeways had on Kayamori—I suggest a narrative form not dependent on settler time or space.

The Racial and Gendered Proximities of Kayamori's Photography

> *This story begins in 1912, when a young Japanese migrant worker leaves the port of Seattle aboard a northbound clipper ship. He travels through an archipelago, the panhandle of Alaska, passing tall mountains that reach down to the water's edge, their limestone cliffs carpeted with sphagnum moss and lichen, while dense forests stretch for the sky. Ravens chatter at the shoreline and eagles circle in the sky above. Moving past misty islands and alongside glaciers, he arrives in Yakutat to work at the maroon and black cannery seated at the head of a bay. There, he works as a cooker, boiling tins of humpy and chum salmon. At the end of the summer, his fellow sojourners—Japanese, Chinese, Filipinx, Puerto Rican, Mexican, and Black—return south on their seasonal migration. A few, like this worker, choose to stay, making their home on Native land, within Native communities.*[16]

Shoki Kayamori was born in 1877 in the Japanese village of Denbo, part of what is present-day Fuji City in Shizuoka Prefecture.[17] He arrived in the United States in 1903 and, by 1910, was living in Seattle with other Japanese lodgers, records listing his occupation as a "cleaner & passer" at a dye works.[18] He was a member of a cohort of Asian American laborers in the Pacific Northwest, the Alaskan Southeast, and on the West Coast whose livelihoods were limited because of racially hostile working and living environments expressed in both institutional and extralegal maneuvers. The Yakutat that

Kayamori arrived at in the early 1910s was a Native village—the original inhabitants of the area were Eyak, but by the twentieth century, Yakutat was predominantly Tlingit, with a number of Eyak and Athabascan intermarriages. During the eighteenth century, the area was visited by Russian, British, Spanish, French, and American traders and colonizers; as part of Russia's imperial expansion, the Russian American Company built a fort in Yakutat in 1796, which was destroyed by Tlingit in 1806. At the northern edge of Tlingit territory, Yakutat is located at the terminus of the archipelago that makes up Southeast Alaska, as the multitude of islands opens to the expanse of the Gulf Coast. As such, it was situated outside of gold rush access points and most tourist routes; therefore, most non-Native inhabitants came in relation to the cannery, to pursue homesteading, or as part of missionary efforts. At the time of Kayamori's arrival, residents in the Yakutat area numbered 271, a third of whom made up the cannery workforce.[19]

That Kayamori made the decision to permanently reside in Yakutat underscores his status as a liminal subject, particularly his ambivalence to settler logics through choosing spatial intimacy within an Alaska Native community. Kayamori was in his mid-thirties when he came to Yakutat and had already lived and worked in the United States for almost a decade. What motivated a Japanese migrant worker to settle in Alaska, ending his previous history of temporary and mobile employment? Given the environment of anti-Asian hostility described during this period, perhaps the remote village of Yakutat appealed to a racialized immigrant. In Yakutat, Kayamori would still be a minority, but not in a majority-white environment. Here, he lived in a majority-Native community, his permanent settlement contradicting the predominant framework in both Alaskan history and Asian American studies that configures Asians in Alaska as migrant and seasonal workers, an overdetermination that elides Native and Asian intersections and relationships. It is important to assert that all non-Indigenous peoples such as Kayamori participate in settler colonialism, but we might also ask after the importance of looking to the desires of racialized migrants who chose to live in Native communities. In the early 1900s in Alaska, multiracial communities that were overwhelmingly male formed as a result of the racial and gendered demands of colonial economic development. At the same time, Alaskan villages and towns remained predominantly Native. Kayamori's choice to live in Yakutat reflects the simultaneous multiracial and Native dimensions of early-twentieth-century Alaska, and, in turn, he represented this imbrication in his photography.

As a liminal subject, Kayamori was able to move beyond the discursive bounds of settler colonial space, visually expressing both indigeneity and racialization in his work. Kayamori began taking photos soon after relocating to Yakutat, as one photograph in his collection has been identified as being taken in the winter of 1913.[20] Kayamori documented Yakutat's denizens for the next three decades, recording townspeople, events, and the surrounding environs in portraiture, action shots, and landscapes. The wide variety of his photographs reveals how integral he was to the local community, and the events he photographed include weddings, funerals, school plays, Fourth of July footraces, Alaska Native Brotherhood and Sisterhood gatherings, clan house meetings, dances, basketball games, fish arriving at the cannery, and at least one clan-based ceremony, or ḵu.éex'. "He was just part of the whole big family in town," recalled MaryAnn Paquette, a Yakutat Tlingit of the people of Copper River clan (K'inéix̱ Ḵwáan), Owl House (Tsísk'w Hít), born in 1924. "Whenever something was happening, he was there."[21] Paquette's statement underscores the belonging that Kayamori likely sought and, to some extent, achieved.

Kayamori's photographs document the racial diversity of Alaskan villages and towns during this time period, brought on by the colonial expansion of resource extraction industries such as canning, logging, and mining. In the photo of Lon Wun Gee Café (figure 4.2), the Chinese proprietor stands behind the counter while four Native men sit on stools at the bar, the young George Bremner's swinging legs appearing as a blur. The subjects in Kayamori's photos have been identified by Yakutat residents as Tlingit, white, Japanese, Chinese, and Filipinx, while those unidentified might also be South Asian, Latinx, or Black.[22] Kayamori provides representations of the racially diverse and predominantly male communities that emerged within Alaska's colonial development, overlying and alongside Native communities in transition. It is the juxtaposition of Kayamori's work in total, however, in the immense volume of his daily photography that reveals the mutual constitution of racialized immigrant and Native communities, exposing the myriad contingencies among the colonial projects of land dispossession, enforced assimilation, economic exploitation, and exclusion legislation, and the affinities and affiliations among those racialized and gendered by such structures.

Kayamori's ability to capture the myriad lives of those in Yakutat stems from the fact that he resided there as a local and permanent member of the community—he lived alongside his photographic subjects. I position Kayamori as a local mindful of the scholarly and activist critique of the "local" resident within the context of Asian settler colonialism in Hawai'i, as a liberal multicultural construction that elides Indigenous sovereignty as well as Asian immigrant complicity in settler governance and power.[23] In the case

FIGURE 4.2 Photograph of Lon Wun Gee's café. Proprietor Lon Wun Gee stands behind the counter and Tlingit customers sit on barstools; left to right, Dick Albert, George Bremner, Sam Henniger, and Richard Reese. Alaska State Library, Seiki (Shoki, Fhoki) Photograph Collection, ca. 1912–1941, photo by Shoki Kayamori, ASL-P55-007.

of Kayamori, however, his residence is deployed not as an instrument of settler multiculturalism but as marker of his place-based connection to his Native neighbors, suggestive of the grounded relationality proposed by Byrd and colleagues.[24] Kayamori's connection with the Native community of Yakutat included hunting and gathering practices as well as participation in the colonial cash economy. Don Bremner, a Yakutat Tlingit (of the Beaver House in the Galyáx̱ Kaagwaantaan clan) is the son of John Bremner Sr., who was one of Kayamori's closest friends. Don Bremner asserts that Kayamori's employment mirrored that of the Tlingit community, consisting of the occasional odd job (cannery cooker, store clerk, dog trainer) but ultimately sustained from living off the land, an arrangement often termed in anthropology as "mixed subsistence." Bremner recounts his father, John Bremner Sr., telling him that Kayamori had a camp on the Ankau River near a coho salmon stream and trapping sites.[25] Here, I want to carefully avoid romanticizing

FIGURE 4.3 Portrait of Mary Thomas. Alaska State Library, Seiki (Shoki, Fhoki) Photograph Collection, ca. 1912–1941, photo by Shoki Kayamori, ASL-P55-270.

Kayamori's possible participation in traditional Tlingit economies, cognizant that Native understandings of sustenance—material, political, and spiritual— extend beyond colonially and governmentally imposed notions of subsistence as simply survival but, rather, are more accurately expressed in a Tlingit epistemology as haa atx̲aayí haa k̲usteeyíx̲ sitee, or our food is our Tlingit way of life.[26] Kayamori may or may not have been part of larger cosmological and spiritual practices encompassed in Alaska Native ways of living, but his practices of hunting, fishing, and trapping as acknowledged by Bremner point to Kayamori's intimacy with Tlingit or Eyak economies and ecologies. If, as Thomas Thornton argues, haa ḵusteeyí, the Tlingit way of life, was known and practiced through relational and place-based pathways and projects, Kayamori was, to some extent, living according to Tlingit space and (seasonal) time.[27]

Unlike European Americans who went "Native," Kayamori's affiliation was not initiated as part of a larger system of colonial economic relations, such as fur trapping, dependent on marriage or sexual partnership with Native women. Instead, his intimacy with other Yakutat residents was formed in ways illegible to the heteropatriarchal settler state. Kayamori is repeatedly described as a bachelor, and those who remember him say he never dated. As Asian American studies scholars have critiqued the oversimplification of configuring Asian migrant communities as (heterosexual) "bachelor societies," Kayamori's example offers a generative reading of bachelorhood that facilitates an alternative framework of intimacies in a colonial context that, borrowing from Lisa Lowe, are not limited to sexual or marital encounters.[28] Take, for example, Kayamori's photo of Mary Thomas (figure 4.3). She stands in front of a Sitka spruce tree (*Picea sitchensis*) near Kayamori's house, which emphasizes the photographer's localized status, as he took the majority of his portraits on the porch of his small cabin or, like this photo of Thomas, to the side of his house in the trees. The young Tlingit woman wears a polka dot dress and sweater, her hands tucked comfortably in her pockets. Whether on her initiative or Kayamori's, she playfully perches on a large rock, her enthusiasm displayed in her smile directed to the camera. This portrait of Mary Thomas suggests an intimacy with Kayamori across race and gender boundaries, and one that was not predicated on romantic relations.

Kayamori's portraits stand in contrast to Alaska-based commercial photographers who relied on the profitability of racial and gendered stereotypes to sell their images. For example, the studio owned and operated by William Howard Case and Horace Draper photographed seminude images of Tlingit women, most likely for consumption by miners in Alaska. Three models appear topless in their photographs: "Stene-Tu," "Kaw-Claa," and "Sha-e-dah-kla." As anthropologist Sharon Bohn Gmelch has analyzed, these photographs, along with captions depicting the women alternately as "maiden," "clutch," "Amazon," and "princess," relied on and perpetuated stereotypes of Tlingit women as racially exotic and sexually willing.[29] The term "clutch" was particularly overladen with sexually violent connotations, originating in the Chinook trade jargon word for woman, "klootchman," which developed specifically for Native women that colonial traders sought for sexual purposes.[30] Notably, these women also posed in Case and Draper photographs wearing Chilkat blankets and in dancing regalia, highlighting the "economies of Otherness" which undergird both ethnography and pornography and highlight the intersection of colonial, white supremacist, and misogynist desires.[31] In contrast, Kayamori's photo of Mary Thomas lacks the spectacle of otherness, instead focusing on the everyday appearance of a young Tlingit woman. Even Lloyd Winter and E. Percy Pond, Juneau photographers whose photos ranged far beyond the stereotypical images of Case and Draper, rarely showed Tlingit women smiling in their photos.[32] Of course, there may have been many reasons for their stern countenances, including the wishes of those photographed. The juxtaposition is informative, however, to point to the importance of Kayamori's photo of Mary Thomas and others like it, for they demonstrate familiarity, the sheer rapport, Kayamori had with his photographic subjects.

The visual economy of Kayamori's photographs underscore Native viewership of Native images. Although historically recognized commercial photographers may have been based in Alaska, they also profited (in finances and reputation) from selling their photographs to presses outside the territory. For Kayamori, on the other hand, his photographs of the community were viewed almost exclusively by the community themselves. The Native consumption and reception of photography is evident in the portrait of Jack and Emma Ellis (figure 4.4), in which photographic prints of Native people are displayed on the wall behind them. Gmelch asserts that Tlingit consumption of photographic images of themselves and family members reveals an important and agential response Tlingit people formed to this emergent technology. To emphasize her argument, Gmelch points specifically to two of Kayamori's portraits in people's private homes that show previous photographs taken in the background, including the photo of Emma and Jack Ellis.[33] That Native viewers were the intended audience of Kayamori's photos is also revealed in the appearance of Kayamori's photographs in museum exhibits and oral history collections, where prints of his work are donated from the personal collections of Native families.[34] When I interviewed Tlingit elder Lorraine Adams, she arrived with several framed photographs of family members taken by Kayamori.[35] Similarly, Don Bremner described a wedding photo of his parents taken by Kayamori and, when showed a print taken from the glass plate negative, remarked that the photo he remembered growing up had been cropped by Kayamori to highlight his parents.[36] Given the rich history of Tlingit visual culture, considering Native consumption, and even connoisseurship, of Kayamori's

FIGURE 4.4 Portrait of Jack and Emma Ellis in what appears to be their home. Alaska State Library, Seiki (Shoki, Fhoki) Photograph Collection, ca. 1912–1941, photo by Shoki Kayamori, ASL-P55-599.

photographs suggests an understanding of his images as artistic representations to convey identity, history, and status even as missionaries and anthropologists alike were predicting the end to such artistic achievements by the Tlingit.[37]

Accounting for Native viewership imbues Kayamori's work with a doubled meaning of the gaze, both the gaze of the photographer and that of the Native viewer. Returning to Mary Thomas's portrait (figure 4.3), we may read her friendly smile as a sign of familiarity with Kayamori as photographer, and also as one of self-awareness and self-representation. She is posing not just for Kayamori but also for the intended viewer—herself, her family, and her peers. The doubled gaze also signals Kayamori's liminality, as this configuration renders him simultaneously as insider and outsider: his proximity and intimacy to his Native subjects facilitates their viewership, yet in this formulation Native consumption articulates a sense of collective ownership that excludes Kayamori from the defined community, or at least renders him to the margin. As we see in the discussion that follows, this insider/outsider status repeats itself in Kayamori's images of Tlingit responses to colonialism and also haunts the circumstances involving Kayamori's death and the accounting of that event.

Documenting the Third Space of Sovereignty

> In the beginning a glacier covered Yakutat Bay. The Kwáashk'i Kwáan were Copper River people living at Chitina when their Raven chief killed a giant moose and used the moose horn to make a large ornate dish, which he displayed when he hosted ku.éex', clan-hosted ceremonies. After the Raven chief died, fighting ensues over the dish. As one group at Chitina takes the dish, the other group leaves, heading out onto the glacier.
>
> The people walk for a long time, and they meet starvation on the glacier. When they see a wolverine in the distance, they walk toward it. Once they get closer, the wolverine transforms into an island, bristling with trees. They walk still. Soon after, the people see a rabbit sitting in the snow and follow it. For two days and nights they walk to the rabbit and then see the rabbit is the top of a mountain, fluffy fur all white snow. This mountain is known in Tlingit as Yaas'eita Shaa, the mountain behind Icy Bay. Later, after the Russians come, the peak is also known as Mount Saint Elias.
>
> The people dance down the mountain, first to Icy Bay and then to Yakutat. In the beginning, a glacier covers Yakutat Bay. In the beginning, there were already people there. Yakutat is not a Tlingit name, but Eyak for "lagoon" or "a lagoon is forming here." As the glacier melts, the people make their home in Yakutat.[38]

Yakutat figures prominently in histories of Alaska, particularly anthropologic studies of its Native people. Yaas'eita Shaa or Mount Saint Elias, the second highest peak in North America, rises in the distance from the village, and it is this snow-covered mountain that Vitus Bering of the Imperial Russian Navy first spotted in 1741, leading to his being credited with "discovering" an already peopled land, now known as Alaska. The mountain is an important named-place in the ontology of Yakutat Tlingit, particularly the Kwáashk'i Kwáan or K'inéix Kwáan clan, and their origin story. Yakutat Bay was also a stopping point for the 1899 Harriman expedition to Alaska. The two-month-long survey of the Alaskan coast was the largest and most publicized expedition of its time. Financed by railroad magnate Edward Henry Harriman, the expedition passengers and crew included scientists and artists, who collected a hundred trunks of specimens and produced more than 5,000 drawings and photographs that were later catalogued and compiled in a thirteen-volume edition. The expedition included naturalist John Muir and photographer Edward Sheriff Curtis.

The most prolific photographer of North American Indigenous peoples, Curtis remains one of the most controversial. Curtis opened his studio in 1890, and over the next several decades, he photographed more than eighty tribes in the United States, including Alaska and Canada, published in the monumental twenty-volume series, *The North American Indian*.[39] He formed an impressive archive of more than 40,000 negatives with a lasting importance to museum curators, (art) historians, and Indigenous people seeking images of family ancestors. At the same time, Curtis's work and popularity depended on the construction of a "vanishing race" of Indian peoples, his importance elevated by the faulted notion that his photographic subjects were doomed to extinction. Influenced by the pictorialist art movement, Curtis's photos were characterized by soft focus, shadowed lighting, and sentimental staging to evince highly evocative and romanticized images. Curtis aspired to represent what he perceived as precontact and premodern activities, even if it meant supplying wigs and costumes to his subjects.[40] As Curtis participated in the Harriman expedition in his early years of photographing Native North Americans, Alaska marks a formative point in Curtis's genealogy that led to his enduring fabrication of Indigenous peoples as forever disappearing.

As much as he promulgated the trope of the vanishing Indian, Curtis was not the sole architect of the stereotype; the mythic image enjoyed popularity with Alaskan officials prior to the Harriman expedition, particularly among missionaries. Missionary activity in Alaska was led by the superintendent of Presbyterian missions in Alaska and U.S. general agent for education in Alaska, Sheldon Jackson, and relied on the teleologic progression from "savage" to "civilized." In her study of colonial photography of the Pacific Northwest, Carol Williams asserts that portraits of Christian converts "[exemplified] the pedagogical use of the camera and photography by missionaries who tried to prove the efficacy of their contributions toward Indian conversion and acculturation. The category of the 'good,' or in the missionary case, 'reformed,' Indian was consistently invoked as the ideal model (in contrast to the bad or resistant Indian)."[41] As examined in chapter 1, Alaska Natives were subsumed within this civilizational discourse, but through an orientalist lens, an abstracted Asianness that exceptionalized (and foretold) their assimilation while paradoxically ignoring the material history of Asian laborers migrating into the American territory.

FIGURE 4.5 Nurse leading a tooth-brushing lesson outside the Mission School, which later became the Covenant Church. Alaska State Library, Seiki (Shoki, Fhoki) Photograph Collection, ca. 1912–1941, photo by Shoki Kayamori, ASL-P55-395.

Kayamori, as a failed subject to settler spatiality, outside and illegible to assimilationist discourse, documented the colonial encounter without the same overriding civilizationist teleology. Take, for instance, his photo of a tooth-brushing lesson outside the Mission School, one of the Alaska missions run by the Swedish Mission Covenant of America (figure 4.5). The scene shows the mission nurse demonstrating proper tooth-brushing techniques while her class of Native students (and one white teacher's aide) emulate her example. The scene takes place outside, presumably because the students must spit on the ground. We view the scene from the nurse's back, while the gaze is directed at the students and their responses. While some of the students engage in the collective brushing, others appear wary about the activity. One young man in front eyes the nurse with a frown and holds the brush up to his closed mouth. A small girl to the side holds no brush, her hands clasped in front of her dress as she fixes the nurse with a serious stare.

The pedagogical project of introducing hygiene to the "uncivilized" Native is no longer the theme of this event; instead, Kayamori captures the chaos and indeterminacy of the moment. In contrast to Curtis's soft-focus sentimentality, Kayamori records this moment in a frank and open style, and through the students' responses, he illustrates multiple reactions to colonial dictates, a range of accommodation and resistance.

It is not only Kayamori's social intimacy with the community but also his specific social location as a racialized subject that allows for counternarratives to settler colonialism's civilizing project to emerge. Kayamori's photograph stands in stark contrast to the many images of the Sitka Industrial Training School (discussed in chapter 1), a part of the Presbyterian mission schools in Alaska. Taken by missionaries, staff, and commercial photographers, photos of the Sitka Industrial Training School normalized the civilizing discourse of the school itself: boys were dressed as soldiers, girls wore virginal white dresses, genders were segregated, students stood in orderly rows, and photographs were typically static and posed. These photos functioned to witness the "miraculous change Tlingit children were undergoing," and were published in school newspapers and sent throughout the United States to raise funds among national donors for the school's continued work.[42] Photographers of the Sitka Industrial Training School promoted the colonial assimilation policies of the missionaries and furthered naturalized discourses of colonial and industrial progress dependent on a visually demarcated representation of settler colonial temporal logics.

That Kayamori's photograph does not reiterate these concepts suggests that his racialized subjectivity as an Asian immigrant meant that he held little investment in the colonialist premise of white superiority and supremacy. Or, perhaps, his racialized subjectivity provided an affinity with his Native neighbors, an affective alliance with their ambivalence to colonial desires. Above all, Kayamori's marginalization from settler colonial arrangements undergirds this image, as his photo stands as antipode to the representations of the Sitka Industrial Training School. Instead of being static and posed, this photo and others like it show missionary instruction for what it was: an encounter. Kayamori's photos of Yakutat highlight the process of settler colonialism, as a structure *and* an event. While missionary photographers relied on the settler colonial temporality of a before-and-after transformation, Kayamori documents the transition, with all its possible ambiguities and tensions. He represents Native students as dynamic participants rather than miraculous converts and, in doing so, reveals that missionary narratives of assimilation were never absolute or inevitable. In the tooth-brushing lesson, instead of order and progression, the natural landscape dominates: patches of snow and scraggly trees surround the scene and everywhere an unruly contestation threatens to erupt. Kayamori's photographs that illustrate instruction at the Yakutat school or clinic similarly show students in action, rather than as the end product of assimilation. In these photos, Native children demonstrate a range of actions, from curiosity with the instruction to disinterestedly looking away and, in one case, mugging for the camera.[43] Not without a sense a humor, Kayamori's photographs inform the viewer that whether or not these students succeeded in good tooth brushing or other hygienic habits bore little upon their perceived colonial success, undermining the necessity or desirability of assimilation.

Like missionaries, anthropologists were also influenced by the ideology of the vanishing Indian, but instead of trying to assimilate Native peoples, they sought to study and preserve what they perceived as premodern. Anthropology stakes a specific claim to Alaska and its Indigenous inhabitants, and anthropologist Frederica de Laguna is most important to Yakutat. After World War II, de Laguna set out to conduct an archaeological, historical, and ethnographic study of Tlingit culture. Working north to south, her first stop in scouting possible sites was Yakutat. She ended up staying six weeks, returning for the summer of 1952 and the spring of 1954, forming lasting relationships with her informants. Two decades later she published *Under Mount Saint Elias: The History and Culture of the Yakutat Tlingit* as part of the Smithsonian Contributions of Anthropology series.[44] A three-volume text of more than one thousand pages, it remains a foundational work that provides an invaluable resource for and about Yakutat Tlingit specifically and Tlingit culture generally. De Laguna's study also contains Shoki Kayamori's first published photographs, courtesy of Mr. and Mrs. Harry K. Bremner's personal collection, providing the first printed attribution given to Shoki Kayamori's work: "Photograph by Fhoki [sic] Kayamori, a Japanese photographer who lived in Yakutat from 1912–1941."[45] De Laguna was a student of Franz Boas, as discussed in chapter 1, a founding scholar of the American field of cultural anthropology who extensively studied Indigenous people in Alaska and the Pacific Northwest. As a proponent of salvage anthropology, Boas attached findings to the problematic notion that Native culture was static and separate from colonial influences. Salvage anthropologists erased Native participation in wage labor such as canneries and Native usage of introduced technology such as sewing machines.[46] Although anthropology differed from missionary education, the two practices depended on a particularly flawed presumption, an extension of the demarcated before-and-after photograph, that Native

FIGURE 4.6 A dance at Billy Jackson's house, ca. 1921. Alaska State Library, Seiki (Shoki, Fhoki) Photograph Collection, ca. 1912–1941, photo by Shoki Kayamori, ASL-P55-348.

peoples cannot be traditional and modern simultaneously. As such, anthropological discourses suppressed capacious representations of Tlingit people and their activities that exceeded the limited and colonial binary of traditional versus modern.

Kayamori, in contrast, represented the Native community of Yakutat in more complex ways, demonstrating a counternarrative to salvage anthropology and the field's attachment to settler colonial time. His photo of a 1921 dance at Billy Jackson's house (figure 4.6) shows dancers in motion, wearing a mix of regalia and Western dress. Undesirable to a salvage ethnography that erased perceived aspects of modernity, this event takes place inside a European American-style dwelling, a ceiling lamp hangs over the dancers, and wallpaper lines the walls.[47] These juxtapositions also counter Edward Curtis's representations of Indians in a "pure" and frozen past—the prolific photographer was known to manipulate images, erasing objects such as clocks, parasols, suspenders, and wagons.[48] In contrast to Curtis's anachronistic project, Kayamori depicts Native subjects in historical and material time and space. This photo also challenges the presumed gaze of the ethnographic viewer, that is, of the non-Native modern subject viewing the soon-to-be vanishing Indian, as the lower third of the frame depicts the Native audience in attendance. Although Boas was known to be critical of what he perceived to be Curtis's unscientific portrayals of Native peoples, they shared a practice of erasing Native participation in what they regarded to be modern time. As this photo illustrates, Tlingit people engaged in a number of activities and strategies that incorporated different levels of what could be conceived as traditional and modern but all were undeniably Native.

Instead of an abstract and ahistorical representation for an outside colonialist audience, this activity marks a specific and contextual event. The dance at Billy Jackson's house was part of a fundraiser to build an Alaska Native Brotherhood (ANB) hall, according to husband and wife Bert Adams Sr. and Lorraine Adams, Yakutat elders and longtime members of the Alaska Native Brotherhood and Alaska Native Sisterhood (ANS).[49] One prominent example of how Tlingit people responded to colonial pressure was the formation of the Alaska Native Brotherhood in 1912, followed by the companion organization Alaska Native Sisterhood in 1913. Founded by the first generation of Alaska Natives in Southeast Alaska (majority Tlingit but also Haida and Tsimshian) that was educated in the mission schools, the initial agenda of the ANB/ANS stressed citizenship rights and education, but after 1918, the ANB organized mainly through legal battles, most notably land claims. There is a general consensus that the ANB, particularly in its early years, sought Native rights through a Christian assimilationist approach.[50] Such a stance was not simply the influence of missionaries, however; it also reflected the ambiguous legal position of Alaska Natives and the centrality of a civilizing discourse in that status. As discussed previously, the 1867 Treaty of Cession between Russia and the United States distinguished "uncivilized tribes" from other "inhabitants of the ceded territory," and only the second group received rights to be admitted as citizens of the United States.[51] Legal rights of citizenship, therefore, hinged on demonstration of civility and, until the Citizenship Act of 1924, U.S. government administrators scrutinized citizenship claims through what they perceived as adoption of white social norms alongside a disavowal of Indigenous culture. This created an inherent contradiction that, as Paige Raibmon describes, "a civilized Aboriginal existence was an oxymoron. Only once a Tlingit *community* was no longer discernible could a Tlingit *individual* qualify as civilized. But the absence of Tlingit community would erase the traits that marked individuals as Tlingit."[52] We can locate the political predicament Alaska Natives experienced by placing their ambiguous status as anticipatory to U.S. federal Indian policy that legislated the end to formal treaty making in 1871. As Kevin Bruyneel elaborates, this period "came to represent the beginning of a postcolonial challenge for indigenous politics. The challenge would be to reclaim this 'neither-nor' [neither assimilated nor other] location as a third space of sovereignty to express indigenous political identity, agency, and autonomy in resistance to the impositions of American colonial rule."[53] Rather than seeing the progressive and assimilationist stance as universally informing the vision of the ANB, Kayamori's photographs imply such rhetoric was strategically deployed to gain rights within Alaska's contradictory and racialized legal codes. Renouncement of Native customs, therefore, operated as tactical articulation (especially to settler administrators), while internal organizing remained tied to forms of Native culture and polity. Former ANB grand camp president and noted Tlingit leader Rev. Dr. Walter Soboleff (Tlingit name Kaajaakwtí, of the L'eeneidí, or Dog Salmon clan) elucidated this complexity when he stated that the ANB and ANS relied internally on Native governance along clan lines, what might be considered an example of what Audra Simpson terms "nested sovereignty," in which Native political orders exist within, even if unrecognized by, settler political orders.[54]

Kayamori's photo points to a larger conception of community-based self-determination that contradicted a universal or absolute disavowal of Native culture. In contrast to the limitations imposed by settler colonial time, Kayamori documented the flexible and contingent nature of Tlingit political resistance in his photo at Billy Jackson's residence. Even with the Alaska Native Brotherhood's progressive and assimilationist stance against Native customs, dancers in regalia fundraised to build a hall for the organization. Here, Tlingit cultural practice materially supported the ANB and ANS, and, conversely, the ANB/ANS is shown to support continued Tlingit cultural practice, regardless of what was tactically communicated to missionary supporters. The example of the dance at Billy Jackson's house is echoed in a Presbyterian missionary's complaint that Peter Simpson, Tsimshian co-founder and leader of the ANB, hunted and fished on the Sabbath, and also "played at the Native dances."[55] Though this religious official viewed the ANB leader's participation in Native dances as an apparent transgression from ANB aims, ANB members expressed a third space of sovereignty that challenged such facile temporal demarcations; moreover, in maintaining cultural practice, they were not "playing" at dances but, perhaps more accurately, "playing" with the missionary dictates for Christian assimilation, a code-switching that allowed for an uninterrupted Tlingit polity that eventually enabled the ANB's leadership to assert sovereign land claims from the 1920s forward.[56]

Shoki Kayamori documented this third space of sovereignty, serving as the unofficial photographer of the ANB/ANS in Yakutat. He covered the numerous events taking place at the ANB Hall, including the 1931 ANB convention hosted in Yakutat, with attendees from throughout Southeast Alaska. Jack and Emma Ellis (figure 4.4) are most likely dressed for this convention, with Jack Ellis wearing his ANB sash draped across his suit. Don Bremner asserts that Kayamori did not just photograph the ANB, he was also a member: "How could anybody think that he was just here to visit? No, he lived his life here.... He was . . . part of the town and the Alaska Native Brotherhood."[57] Histories of the ANB do not acknowledge Kayamori as a possible (and non-Native) member, but Bremner is adamant that he was told this by his father and his uncle, both active leaders in the ANB. What would it mean to view Kayamori not only as a photographer with an intimate alliance to his Native neighbors, but also as a member of the Alaska Native Brotherhood, one of the earliest Indigenous political rights organizations in North America? Is it such a fantastic claim not simply because Kayamori is non-Native, but because the logics of settler colonialism render such incorporation illegible? Considering Kayamori as a possible member of the Alaska Native Brotherhood allows for a reassessment with the concept of third space, as Kayamori is able to photographically represent the ANB's strategic deployment of the third space of sovereignty, yet he, himself, cannot be represented by it. As documenter of the ANB, he still remains marginal, outside. Jodi Byrd critiques the formulation of third space for an inability to disrupt the very binary formation that it is responding to. As she elaborates, "Focused as it is on the dialectics initiated by formal administrative colonialisms, Bhabha's ruptured discourse is more difficult to mobilize along the axes of other/others, where racialized and colonized peoples, existing in the same geographical space, interact with one another as well as the colonizer."[58] It is not simply that Kayamori is situated outside the colonizer-colonized axis of white-Native but also that he occupies a dissimilar space-time within settler logics. In this way, Kayamori both depicts and disrupts third space, exposing the opportunities and limits within structures that cannot account for differentially racialized and colonized conditions and, as we see in the discussion that follows, Kayamori's photographic representations not only fail to articulate his belonging, but are also viewed by the settler state as the sign of criminality.

World War II and the Haunting Violence of Militarism

This story begins in 1941 as U.S. entry into World War II looms, and hostility toward Americans of Japanese descent spikes. In the sleepy fishing village of

Yakutat, rumors and behind-the-back whispers circulate, speculations surface concerning the unofficial town photographer, known to residents as Kayamori, popularly called "Picture Man." Having lived in Yakutat for almost three decades, Kayamori's hair is now graying, and he makes his living as the cannery's night watchman. Once sought after to document the cannery's latest technological invention as well as the newest family member, Kayamori is now pariah, alongside accusations: outsider, traitor, spy. His prominence as a noncommercial photographer is exactly what arouses suspicion.

> *This story begins with an FBI file.*
> *It begins with the bombing of Pearl Harbor.*
> *It begins with a beating by army soldiers.*
> *It begins with a suicide.*
> > *Begins with a death certificate.*
> > > *one word.*
> > > *one sentence.*
> > > *one question.*
> > > *"drug?"*
>
> *It begins with an unmarked grave that no one living can remember.*[59]

The death of Shoki Kayamori, and the circumstances leading up to it, highlights a rupture in the third-space visuality of Kayamori's documentation of Yakutat Tlingit activities, and should be viewed not as a casualty or aberration of wartime exigencies but, instead, as an instantiation of the disavowed and constitutive violence on which militarized inclusion depends. Alaska, as an understudied site of World War II militarism, at least as it connects to the postwar rise of U.S. hegemony as a military empire, emerges as an unexpected node of American imperial expansion in Asia and the Pacific. Once Alaska's long colonial history is considered, the reprisal of its connections to American imperial desires makes evident the recursive and enfolded nature of settler colonialism and imperialism, emphasizing militarization as the key colonial mechanism in the mid-nineteenth century, yet also originating from American Alaska's foundation in army and navy rule. World War II and the concomitant militarization in Alaska proved a key moment in the economic and political development of the territory within the larger structure of the U.S. nation-state. Because of fears of Japanese occupation of the Aleutian Islands, coupled with Alaska's strategic location between the United States and Asia, Congress made the decision to remilitarize Alaska in 1940; during the course of the war, the U.S. War Department sent approximately 300,000 military personnel to the territory.[60] As part of this militarization, the U.S. Army Corps of Engineers arrived in Yakutat to build an airfield that would serve as a refueling and service base to the Aleutian Islands and points north (Anchorage and Fairbanks). An entire base was built to accommodate the airfield, including a fueling dock, rifle range, numerous roads, and living quarters, while the beachfront was fortified with cannons and tanks, perched just inside the tree line.[61]

The influx of thousands of soldiers, greatly outnumbering the local population, which in the early 1940s still hovered around two hundred, changed the village in critical ways. Yakutat became not only the locale for the largest airfield in Alaska at the time but also an R&R spot for off-duty soldiers. In this way, the militarization of Alaska not only installed a system of infrastructure but also pulled Alaskan residents into American popular culture and its attendant discourses. The ANB hall began to show U.S. government newsreels on the war, and also sponsored food sales and dances that soldiers were invited to. Once the base was built, socializing between soldiers and Yakutat residents increased in scope. The USO sponsored movies and other forms of entertainment, and soldiers traded with children, giving them candy; youngsters, in turn, translated for their parents, who provided items such as moccasins for purchase.[62] The socializing between soldiers and residents was highly gendered, as one elder remembers that it was the single women in Yakutat who were invited to weekend dances on the base, accompanied by their mothers as chaperones, transported by troop carriers.[63] Outside of the social aspects, the war was viewed as bringing economic opportunities to the community, mostly in the form of construction jobs.

Not everyone, however, remembered this era fondly. Native elder Lena Achkwéi Farkas, who was a young child during World War II, attributed increased alcohol access and consumption to the soldiers and their social activities.[64] The U.S. military was also criticized for environmental contamination caused by chemicals and wastes disposed on the land, and for the void in employment left in the wake of its postwar departure. Building from a long colonial history of land dispossession wrought by military enforcement, Tlingit resident and World War II soldier Sig Edwards's land was taken by the army to build a dock, with promises of return, but the army subsequently sold the fueling dock to Standard Oil.[65] The most common complaint, however, was that of surveillance. Residents were not allowed to leave Yakutat without permission, and taking photographs was forbidden. Alaska Native cultural and economic practices in the area surrounding the village, such as berry picking and seaweed harvesting, were met with distrust.[66]

This atmosphere of suspicion must have been deeply felt by Yakutat resident Shoki Kayamori, during a period that witnessed an increase in anti-Japanese sentiment throughout Alaska and the nation. Similar to treatment of other Japanese Americans on the West Coast, first-generation Japanese (Issei) were accused of sabotage, while the second generation (Nisei) were generally suspect.[67] In a village as heavily militarized as Yakutat, inundated with soldiers and the material and social infrastructure of the armed forces, apprehension was particularly directed against Kayamori. In late 1940, Kayamori's name was included on an FBI list of those who should be investigated; a year later, FBI records officially classified him as a suspect to be detained in a national emergency.[68] The day that Pearl Harbor was bombed, soldiers stationed at Yakutat attacked the stooped and graying sixty-four-year-old Kayamori. MaryAnn Paquette, a teenager then, said the army "hushed it up [but] everybody in town knew what happened."[69] Two days later, a community meeting was held to discuss the United States' declaration of war. MaryAnn's younger sister, Elaine Chuu Shah Abraham, remembered that Kayamori was noticeably absent. As she recalled, "Somebody said, 'Where's Mr. Kayamori?' He was the only one that wasn't there. It was already evening; it was about seven o'clock in the evening; and you know it's dark, very dark. Several of the men took lanterns up to his house, and they found that he had committed suicide. He did not leave a note."[70] Kayamori had apparently donned a suit, written a will, and expired in his armchair, the military doctor who wrote his death certificate suspecting that he had ingested a drug.[71]

Following his suicide, some speculated whether Kayamori could have been a spy during the time he was living in Yakutat.[72] Many more residents vehemently bristled at the accusation. Federal agents questioned Yakutat's minister and postmaster about Kayamori's correspondence after his death; years later his son asserted that espionage claims were the result of "stupid hysteria. He was a tremendous individual. . . . I bet my bottom dollar that Kayamori was no spy."[73] Don Bremner emphatically rejects any notion that Kayamori was disloyal and, further, positions Kayamori as an insider based on his photographic production:

> How many photos would it take to convince the world that he was part of our community, part of our lives? Would it be, say, ten nice ones? Or ten general ones? What about six hundred to prove that he was part of our life because if you think of the time that it takes for the kind of photographs he took of this land, of the wildlife, and the people, that almost the bulk of the photos are of people. So, how could anybody think that, well, he was just there to visit. No, he lived his life here. This was his place. This was his life. Hundreds of photographs prove it.[74]

Bremner's assertion contrasts sharply with FBI suspicions that targeted Kayamori because of his photographic activities. In describing the reasons he was to be investigated, the Juneau field office noted that Kayamori was a "Japanese citizen [and] . . . has worked in Yakutat fish canneries for a long period of time. Is reported to be an enthusiastic photographer and to have panoramic views of the Alaskan coast line."[75] Juxtaposing Don Bremner's and the FBI's comments reveals radically different configurations of land and labor. For the FBI, Kayamori's identification to the Japanese nation-state predominates, and his labor as a cannery worker further signals his immigrant worker status. Moreover, the only labor that is recognized is cannery work; his photography is regarded only as proof of suspicious activity. And land, in this formulation, is limited to the geopolitical. In contrast, Bremner elucidates Kayamori's photography as labor and, importantly, the labor that should be utilized in understanding Kayamori's connection to place. Here, land is populated with people and animals, and has a purpose unto itself. Liminality affords creative possibilities, but it is also an unstable process. Larger structures of power cannot be disregarded. This moment is instructive, however, to show two social systems and economies, that of the larger settler state and that of the Tlingit people. Kayamori's photographic oeuvre marks him simultaneously outside and suspect to the American nation-state at the same time it constructs him as an insider to Yakutat.

The forced relocation and imprisonment of Japanese and Japanese Americans during World War II and their attendant disenfranchisement constituted what Caroline Chung Simpson calls an "absent presence" in U.S. social life that deeply shaped subsequent Cold War culture.[76] I suggest that Shoki Kayamori and his photographs exist as spectral presences to signal traces disavowed in progressive narratives that celebrate the World War II militarism that propelled Alaska into its modern and realized statehood. As sociologist Avery Gordon reminds us, haunting is "something akin to what it feels like to be the object of a social totality vexed by the phantoms of modernity's violence," and Kayamori haunts even his own archive. His photographs demonstrate Native responses to colonialism and participation in American modernity long before World War II militarization, positioning the war not simply as a liberatory project but also as part of a larger continuation of Alaskan colonization, which has always relied on and been exceptionalized through militarism.[77] A spectral reading of his death disrupts discourses that military modernity and U.S. cultural absorption in Alaska was total or complete, and accounting for Kayamori's suicide makes legible as well Native fears and anxieties around World War II relocation and incarceration. While recalling Kayamori specifically and the interaction of Natives and Asians in Yakutat generally, Tlingit elder Lorraine Adams revealed that her grandfather was Japanese, and the community hid the Japanese ancestry of her mother, herself, and her siblings during World War II, fearing for their safety.[78] Internment policy in Alaska called for the evacuation of all males over the age of sixteen with mixed Alaska Native and Japanese parentage. Native wives of Japanese men endured social ostracism and financial hardship after their husbands (and sons) were imprisoned outside Alaska, and some wives and children made the difficult decision to "self-intern." Such actions, as well as the protection that Yakutat's community afforded Lorraine Adams's family, underscore the importance and power of Indigenous kinship even within and in evasion of military carceral policies.[79]

Centering the history of World War II relocation and incarceration in Alaska also highlights Unangax̂ internment in Southeast Alaska. Also known as Aleut (a name given to them by Russian colonizers), the Unangax̂ people, whose name in their own language translates to "the Seasiders," live on traditional homelands along the lower Alaska Peninsula and the Aleutian Island chain in Southwest Alaska, 900 islands that stretch across 1,100 miles to Attu Island, which lies 300 miles from Kamchatka Peninsula in Russia. As the first Indigenous people Russians encountered in Alaska, and as skilled seafaring hunters, Unangax̂ were heavily affected by the Russian empire's frenzied quest for fur pelts. An estimated population of 8,000 to 20,000 Unangax̂ prior to Russian contact was reduced to 2,000 by the time of American purchase through conflict, disease, and the toll of the coercive labor system employed by the Russian empire. Colonial practices extended to control of movement and forced relocation, including the consolidation of small villages into larger centers, the settlement of Unangax̂ to the previously uninhabited Pribilof Islands to harvest fur seals, and the transport of Unangax̂ men to other points throughout the Russian empire, such as Southeast Alaska, and as far away as Fort Ross in California.[80] By the 1940s, Unangax̂ survived and sometimes thrived on the land they had lived on for at least 10,000 years, participating in a mix of commercial economies such as fur seal harvesting, fox trapping, and fishing, overlapping with Unangax̂ cultural and economic practices. The colonial antecedent of forced relocation, however, found a powerful reiteration during World War II, interrupting their legacy of continuous occupation on the Aleutian Islands.

While conditions for interned Unangax̂ paralleled some of those of Japanese Americans imprisoned on the West Coast, the official rationale for internment differed. The Aleutian Islands are strategically located between the United States and Japan, and while American military intelligence warned of an impending Japanese attack, disagreement and indecision was rife among the various government administrators involved: Office of Indian Affairs, Fish and Wildlife Service, the Alaska Defense Command, and the Alaska territorial government. The Office of Indian Affairs could not agree internally whether or not to evacuate the Unangax̂, and the navy stated they would not protect Unangax̂ villages west of Dutch Harbor. No governmental body would take responsibility; the Office of Indian Affairs deferred to the navy, while the navy expected the OIA to make the final decision.[81] Even under the guise of Native advocacy, governmental administrators relied on colonial tropes to oppose evacuation. Acting territorial governor E. L. Bartlett called a meeting of civilian agencies in March 1942 to discuss evacuation; the minutes from the meeting summarized that "No general attempt should be made, even in the case of actual enemy attack, to evacuate Eskimos or other primitive natives from Alaska. It is felt that these people could never adjust themselves to life outside of their present environment, whereas they could 'take to the hills' in case of danger and be practically self-sufficient for a considerable period."[82] Bartlett's sentiments highlight the space-time colonial connection, that Alaska Native people living in rural villages away from white settlers were somehow successful only because they were people out of time and could not safely endure traveling to more modern environs.

Not only did public officials deploy notions of Unangax̂ people as backward, uncivilized, and therefore in need of protection, but often this colonial racialization was overlaid with orientalist figurations, signaling a heightened return to settler orientalist discourse. In 1935, Jesuit missionary and geologist Bernard Hubbard, known as the "Glacier Priest" for his more than thirty expeditions to Alaska, derided the Unangax̂ as "hardly advanced beyond" the "Stone Age." Hubbard, like Boas before him, made the erroneous assumption that Alaska Natives, in Hubbard's case Iñupiat, Sugpiat, and Unangax̂ peoples, shared linguistic and therefore racial ancestry with Asians. After spending several years in the 1930s with the Iñupiat of King Island in the Bering Sea, Hubbard concluded, "Convinced from my few years of association that the Eskimo was Tartar-Mongol in origin and probably the refugee of the Kubla Khan debacle of the thirteenth century, I wished to establish the race as one tribe, not several, as unilingual, not multilingual." Compared to his paternalistic and romanticized assessment of the Iñupiat, Hubbard viewed Unangax̂ racialization less favorably, complaining that the "old Aleuts were a bloodthirsty lot" and were "probably Asiatic degenerates."[83] Hubbard would go on to serve as an adviser to the U.S. military during and after World War II. Characterizing Unangax̂ through combined orientalist and primitivist terms continued leading up to and during World War II. A *New York Herald Tribune* reporter assigned to Alaska during World War II depicted for readers, "The Aleuts might be described as sawed-off Indians with slant eyes. They have an admixture of Oriental blood, which may be an additional reason why they hate the Japs."[84] Government officials also contributed to this discourse, including the Indian Service teacher and principal in Unalaska calling for Unangax̂ evacuation with a particularly gendered form of this racialization. He argued that the "natural unmoral propensities of the native Aleuts," coupled with his observation that U.S. soldiers found young Unangax̂ women "exotic," justified Unangax̂ relocation. In doing so, he exhumed settler orientalist notions that targeted and blamed Alaska Native women for colonialist misogyny and violence.[85] Given settler orientalist government and public rhetoric, and the fact that white residents of Unalaska were not forced to evacuate, many Unangax̂ understood themselves to be racially targeted for evacuation and, even more, as Unangax̂ scholar Eve Tuck and co-author K. Wayne Yang suggest, "the stated rationale was the protection of the people but another likely reason was that the U.S. Government feared the Aleuts would become allies with the Japanese and/or be difficult to differentiate from potential Japanese spies."[86] Tuck and Yang's suspicions are not without precedent: the U.S. military detained Unangax̂ men on suspicion of being Japanese prior to their forced relocation, as when men from the village of Biorka hiking to Unalaska were intercepted and confined for nearly two weeks.[87]

Government indecision and inaction shifted only when the Japanese military bombed American naval facilities at Dutch Harbor and nearby Fort Mears on June 3 and 4, 1942, followed by the Japanese invasion of the islands of Kiska on June 7 and Attu on June 8. The U.S. military coordinated a chaotic and disorganized evacuation in June and July, before confirming a final destination for the Unangax̂. Many communities were given only a few hours to vacate, and when the military evacuated the island of Atka, they burned the Unangax̂ village to prevent possible use by Japanese troops.[88] Nearly 900 Unangax̂ from nine villages were relocated to abandoned sites throughout Southeast Alaska, including a deserted gold mine and several defunct canneries. At a Funter Bay cannery closed for more than a decade, Unangax̂ arrived to find ramshackle bunkhouses named the "China House" and the "Filipino House." That the derelict sites racialized by Asian labor were refashioned for Unangax̂ confinement highlights the assemblage of Indigenous dispossession, racial capitalism, and carceral militarism.

Take, for instance, the site of Killisnoo Island, to which the Unangax̂ of Atka were forcibly relocated. Connected to the larger Tlingit village of Angoon three miles north, Killisnoo beach due east of the island was originally inhabited until a great sickness was said to have driven the remaining residents to Angoon, thought to be the smallpox epidemic of 1836–39. In the 1870s, the Northwest Trading Company established a herring processing plant and whaling station on Killisnoo Island, recruiting Tlingit to work in the factory or fish for the company. One of the earliest American colonial ventures in Alaska, the company town saw the establishment of a Presbyterian mission school as well as a Russian Orthodox church by the end of the century. After the Tlingit ixt', or medicine person, Teel' Tlein, died in a workplace explosion and Tlingit demanded compensation of two hundred blankets from the company, in accordance with Tlingit law and in order to restore balance, the U.S. Navy, under Naval Commander E. C. Merriman (the same military officer en route to Juneau when the Tlingit there were hanged by miners) bombarded the village of Angoon, burning canoes and food cached for the winter.[89] In the years following, the plant changed ownership several times, and by the early twentieth century, after expanding to include salmon canning, Tlingit, Haida, Creoles (Russian-Sugpiat families from the Russian colonial era), Chinese, Japanese, Filipinx, and European immigrants worked and lived on Killisnoo. After a fire destroyed thirty buildings and houses in 1928, most Tlingit workers moved back to Angoon and, when the plant finally closed in 1931, Killisnoo was abandoned except for a small community of Japanese men and Tlingit wives, families that faced disruption and evacuation due to Japanese American internment.[90] Unangax̂ arriving from Atka added another layer to this historic palimpsest punctuated by colonial and military violence, having survived the burning of their village and disembarking with only the clothes on their backs.

Accommodations in the relocation camps were abysmal. Housing was overcrowded and lacked privacy—in one relocation center, internees had to initially sleep in relays. The government and military expected the Unangax̂ to rehabilitate their deserted quarters, yet did not provide the necessary supplies or materials. The sanitary conditions at the Southeast Alaska camps were particularly egregious; at the Funter Bay cannery, one outdoor toilet on the beach serviced nearly thirty Unangax̂, and without proper plumbing, people laundered clothes in rainwater that collected on the ground and sidewalks. Unangax̂ were without their guns or gear necessary to hunt and fish, and initially subsisted on clams dug from the beach. The lack of plumbing and heating throughout the camps was particularly worrisome, and illnesses such as influenza, measles, pneumonia, and tuberculosis were widespread. Medical attention was nonexistent, few camps had doctors or nurses, medical supplies were scarce, and Unangax̂ had no access to their traditional plant medicines.[91] As historian Dean Kohlhoff has documented, the mortality rate of Unangax̂ averaged 10 percent in the relocation camps, significantly higher than prior to World War II, and the villages of Makushin and Kashega lost a quarter of their community members during the war.[92] Young children and the elderly were the most affected by illness and death, a blow to Unangax̂ survival both for the cultural knowledge and wisdom lost through the traumatic passing of elders and for the devastation to a younger generation that could carry on Unangax̂ ways of living and being. Unangax̂ protested and petitioned government officials for adequate accommodations and supplies, but changes were slow to come, improvements often taking more than a year. In stark contrast to the widespread governmental neglect, the Tlingit of Angoon are credited by the Atkans at Killisnoo for providing clothes, supplies, and, most importantly, ongoing deliveries of salmon, keeping the Unangax̂ alive their first winter of confinement.[93] Having survived their own episode of colonial military violence, the Tlingit of Angoon extended what we might consider Indigenous internationalist support for the Unangax̂ of Atka.

For Unangax̂ from the Pribilof Islands, their World War II experiences extended a long history of colonial treatment by both the Russians and Americans. In 1788, Russians captured Unangax̂ hunters from Unalaska and Atka and forcibly relocated them to the Pribilof Islands, roughly 200 miles north of Unalaska and the principal breeding grounds of the North Pacific fur seal. Unangax̂ over several generations labored in the fur seal harvest for the Russian American Company. Soon after Alaska's colonial transfer in 1867, the United States formed consecutive twenty-year leases with American firms that oversaw Unangax̂ residents in exchange for their labor in the fur seal harvest. Given that the Alaska Commercial Company and the North American Commercial Company were modeled on the Russian American Company, which itself was based on the East India Company, the economic and social structures of dominance for the Pribilof Unangax̂ more closely aligned with what is known in settler colonial studies as franchise colonialism rather than with settler colonialism. By the late nineteenth century, overhunting and exploitation of the northern fur seal resulted in poverty, poor working conditions, and racial segregation for the Unangax̂ on the Pribilof Islands of St. George and St. Paul, a situation that was not ameliorated with the conversion to federal government control of the islands starting in 1911. By the 1940s, the Pribilof Islands were under the management of Fish and Wildlife Service (FWS) within the Department of the Interior. That the United States had continued and fostered a colonial relationship was highlighted by the absolute authority of government agents, who could summarily fine and imprison Unangax̂. The FWS agent and caretaker of St. Paul considered the Unangax̂ wards of the government and, as such, had never provided voting rights on the island.[94] The Unangax̂ from the Pribilof Islands were interned at Funter Bay on the west coast of Admiralty Island (Xutsnoowú in Tlingit territory, the same land discussed in chapters 1 and 2), the residents of St. Paul placed in an old cannery, and, across the bay, the Unangax̂ of St. George made the best of an abandoned gold mine. The U.S. government revealed their colonial capitalist priorities when, under threat of never being allowed to return home in the future or as a community, they compelled interned Unangax̂ men to travel back to the Pribilof Islands for the 1943 fur seal harvest, leaving more than 300 women, children, and elderly men in unbearable living conditions in Funter Bay. The callous and extractive ambitions of the American government echoed Russian colonial practices, what Gwenn Miller has termed an "economy of confiscation," whereby Russian fur traders took women and children hostage to compel men to hunt sea mammals to obtain furs.[95] Indeed, because the Pribilof seal hunting party also took the doctor, medical supplies, and the two-way radio, the Department of Interior endangered the lives of those left behind in Funter Bay, who endured influenza and measles outbreaks that summer.

Mirroring the indifference that marked their initial evacuation, officials delayed the permanent return of Unangax̂ to their home villages for more than a year after danger from Japanese military action had passed. Again, governmental agencies balked at taking responsibility for the logistics and costs of arranging return and, in some villages, return was deemed impossible because Unangax̂ homes were being used to billet U.S. troops. When Unangax̂ finally made the journey back to their homelands (Pribilovians in 1944 and Unangax̂ on the Aleutian Islands in 1945), they returned to find extensive damage perpetrated by U.S. military forces—homes looted and churches desecrated. Theft took on an extreme character, and very little personal property remained. Troops stole boats, fishing gear, radios, woven baskets, and even family photos. The avarice of military personnel extended to pilfering religious icons from the churches and ripping keys from pianos. Servicemen appeared to not only be motivated by greed but also demonstrated wanton and hostile destruction by smashing dishes, breaking furniture, and mutilating religious objects before departing. The navy at Akutan reported that not one home was spared from looting. For the Unangax̂, such widespread and extensive damage confirmed the racist treatment of their relocation and further fueled suspicions that they were being conflated with the Japanese. As Unangax̂ survivor of internment Dora Dushkin surmised, "You would think we were the enemy. We were not."[96] Similar to the community at Yakutat, additional hardships for returning Unangax̂ included environmental degradation caused by hazardous waste such as spilled oil, chemical drums, and live munitions. The Office of Indian Affairs cited toxic homesites and decreased population to deny permission for Unangax̂ from Makushin, Biorka, Kashega, and Attu to return to their home villages. This created tensions when these communities were relocated to other villages already strained with rebuilding efforts.[97] The U.S. government offered a pittance for restitution, providing to each Unangax̂ on average thirty-two dollars for personal property damages. This would remain the extent of U.S. compensation until the Unangax̂ fought for redress in the 1970s, initially seeking to sue both the American and Japanese governments, and eventually allying with Japanese American efforts.

The American Civil Liberties Act of 1988, also known as Public Law 100–383, addresses and attempts to colonially reconcile both Unangax̂ and Nikkei (persons of Japanese descent) experiences of forced removal and confinement during World War II; however, the legislation is generally recognized only for Japanese American redress. Although a much smaller number of Unangax̂ were confined compared to Nikkei (900 versus 120,000), accounting for Unangax̂ internment, and reading it against Japanese American internment illuminates the intertwined processes of racism and colonialism in Alaska, specifically, and in the United States more generally. Congress opens the act with a statement of purpose, including acknowledgment of the injustices of evacuation, relocation, and internment; an apology for such acts; and the government's intent to provide restitution for losses suffered.[98] Then, in section 2 of the act, Congress articulates divergent statements to those of Japanese and Unangax̂ descent. In addressing those of Japanese ancestry, Congress states that a "grave injustice" of internment occurred because of "racial prejudice, wartime hysteria, and a failure of political leadership." Such actions resulted in "fundamental violations of . . . basic liberties and constitutional rights," and Congress reiterated its apologies.[99] The congressional statement to the Unangax̂ people noticeably lacks any articulation of racial prejudice or acknowledgment of infringed rights. Instead, the act summarizes Unangax̂ evacuation and relocation as being "under United States control and in the care of the United States, until long after any potential danger to their home villages had passed." The injustice for the Unangax̂ is articulated as the failure "to provide reasonable care for the Aleuts, and this resulted in widespread illness, disease, and death." And, in lieu of an apology, Congress states that, "there is no remedy for injustices suffered... except... compensation."[100] In the case of the Nikkei, forced removal and incarceration is framed as an issue of racial discrimination and civil rights. In contrast, the grievances of the Unangax̂ are viewed under the implicit yet overarching rubric of an imperfected colonialism; that is, Native peoples are considered as wards of a government that failed to care for them properly. Separating their claims ignores the racial discrimination undergirding government indifference to Unangax̂ endangerment and suffering, as well as the military confinement and colonial guardianship of Japanese Americans during World War II. This separation illustrates the level of differential logics under which American colonialism operates. Even as Japanese Americans and Unangax̂ made common cause in seeking redress, racial and colonial injustices were rendered discrete and disparate.

Indigenous studies scholars such as Glen Sean Coulthard and Asian American studies scholars such as Quynh Nhu Le offer salient critiques of redress and other forms of state-sanctioned reconciliation as conceding to settler authority to mediate injustice and, ultimately, fortifying coloniality.[101] Tlingit scholar Nancy Furlow argues, however, that apologies also function outside settler parameters and within Native juridical understandings, making them necessary prerequisites for restoring balance and healing internal to Indigenous forms of epistemology and religion.[102] To that end, certain colonial violences remain one-sided knowledge. In contrast to the U.S. government's apology for Japanese American and Unangax̂ internment, the U.S. military has thus far made no amends for their late nineteenth-century bombardment of Tlingit villages. For the people of Angoon, who aided the Unangax̂ forcibly relocated to Killisnoo, the lack of acknowledgment is particularly poignant. Even after the Tlingit of Angoon sustained refugees of a similar colonial assault (both Aangóon K̲wáan and the village of Atka burned by U.S. military forces), their entreaties to the military and invitations to the U.S. Navy to participate in commemorations have been met with silence, an apology yet to be uttered.

In Alaska colonial brutality has always been dependent on and found expression through military rule and occupation, elucidating the historical antecedents of army and navy rule in Alaska, including the bombardment of Native villages Kake and Wrangell in 1869, and Angoon in 1882. As Setsu Shigematsu and Keith Camacho argue in their analysis of the regionalization of Asia-Pacific as constructed through U.S. and Japanese imperialisms, a figuration that elides Pacific Islander indigeneity and sovereignty, militarism is always constitutive of and an extension of colonialism.[103] Situating Alaska as a connected node within this system expands both the periodic and geographical scope of the settler and imperial nexus of the Pacific, and allows for another site of intersectional analysis for Pacific Islander, Indigenous, and Asian American studies. Consider that the U.S. military included Alaska in its Pacific theater of war, and the Aleutian Islands were a key point for naval intelligence gathering, within a larger constellation of islands within Asia and Oceania.[104] And, certainly, the Unangax̂ were caught between Japanese and American colonialisms. The World War II military buildup in Alaska, frequently termed the "fortification" or "garrisoning" of Alaska, enabled settlement to a greater degree than had any of the preceding extractive economies. Alaska's non-Native population grew dramatically through the military and construction of military infrastructure as soldiers and construction workers flooded into the territory, both during and following the war. As Army Colonel Simon B. Buckner Jr., commander of the Alaska Defense Force, declared, "Our soldiers will make the Alaska of the future," signaling the anticipatory designs of space-time colonialism through settler militarism.[105] In 1939, only 524 military personnel were stationed in Alaska; by 1943, that number had risen astronomically, to 152,000.[106] Alaska's postwar emergence as a critical node in the American empire of bases throughout Asia and the Pacific, alongside an achieved white majority population, bolstered a narrative of modern progress whose momentum would succeed in gaining statehood in 1959, an instantiation of the conjunction of settler colonialism and militarism that Jodi Kim terms "settler modernity."[107] A project that joined settler colonialism and overseas empire in the late nineteenth century, Alaska also reanimates that imbrication in the mid-twentieth-century period that witnesses the post–World War II rise of an American military empire, specifically in the imperially imagined "Asia-Pacific" region. The interconnected traces of Kayamori's death, mixed Native-Japanese internment, and Unangax̂ internment in Southeast Alaska highlight the need for an intersectional epistemology that can account for the colonial violence inherent in settler modernity and prioritize decolonial strategies within transpacific critique.[108]

Conclusion: Kayamori's Legacy

There exist only a few photographs thought to be of Shoki Kayamori, and only one that has been positively identified by those who knew him (figure 4.7). The photograph was unnamed in the first labeling of his found archive, but Yakutat elders were adamant in verifying Kayamori as the man posed outside a hunting tent, holding two hunting dogs on a short leash, a rifle grasped in his other

FIGURE 4.7 Photograph of Shoki Kayamori at hunting camp. Blur at bottom of image possibly indicates self-portraiture. Alaska State Library, Seiki (Shoki, Fhoki) Photograph Collection, ca. 1912–1941, photo by unknown, possibly Shoki Kayamori, ASL-P55-140.

hand. After his death, Kayamori was buried across the bay from Yakutat on Kahntaak Island, with only U.S. soldiers in attendance. The military subsequently paved over the burial site to build a naval ramp and neglected to move his grave.[109] In the years since, local residents have attempted to locate the site, but the abundant growth of Southeast Alaska's temperate rainforest has rendered their efforts unsuccessful.[110] Kayamori's photographic archive, including elusive representation of the photographer, remains his monument.

As a racialized immigrant who resided in Yakutat, Kayamori documented Yakutat as both a historic Tlingit and Eyak place that remains majority Native, as well as a multiracial node in U.S. settler colonial economy. Because Kayamori could not attain settler citizenship, his liminal position made possible intimacies across race and gender with his photographic subjects. In this way, Kayamori's photographs provide generative and multiply authored representations of the colonial encounter in Alaska, one of the most important being the articulation of a third space of sovereignty, Native forms of resistance that are neither inside nor outside the system that also refuse the colonial temporal binary of traditional versus modern. As those in Yakutat reclaim the haunted history of Kayamori and the visual culture he helped facilitate and sustain, so too must the fields of Native and Indigenous studies and Asian American studies account for the epistemic erasure located within the colonial history of Alaska. Doing so exposes colonialism and modernity as co-constitutive structures of domination that both enact and are reinforced through settler military violence. Alternate understandings of colonized and racialized affinities, illegible to settler militarism, affirm a different horizon of possible relations.

Epilogue

In response to the U.S. executive order for the World War II removal and detention of all persons of Japanese descent on the West Coast, Juneau High School (JHS) in Juneau, Alaska, held a special early graduation ceremony for John Tanaka, valedictorian for the class of 1942. The school gymnasium was packed with students and local townspeople. When the regularly scheduled graduation took place in June, Tanaka's classmates placed an empty chair during commencement to honor Tanaka and acknowledge his absence and, by extension, that of the rest of Juneau's Japanese American community. In 2010, nearly seventy years after Japanese American World War II incarceration, a group of Juneau High School graduates from the class of 1958 (including John Tanaka's younger sister Mary Tanaka Abo), initiated a project to build a memorial, the first of its kind in Alaska, to honor Juneau's Nikkei residents who were interned. With participation from other JHS alumni, former internees and their families, and the broader Juneau community, the Empty Chair Committee organized and fundraised for several years. They commissioned Seattle artist Peter Reiquam who designed and constructed a bronze sculpture depicting a wooden folding chair. Approximately one and a half times life size, the chair rests atop floorboards that are etched with the names of the fifty-three internees from Juneau, the Japanese kanji for peace, and a narrative about John Tanaka and Japanese American internment. Reiquam purposely left the edges of the boards uneven, giving the appearance of being ripped from the floor, to represent the Japanese Americans' sudden deportation from their homes and community. The sculpture was placed in Capital School Park in July 2014, next to the original site of the Juneau High School. Yadaa.at Kalé, or Mount Juneau, rising behind it, the chair looks out over Gastineau Channel in the distance. A number of educational and ceremonial events coincided with the installation of the memorial sculpture, including an exhibit organized by the Juneau-Douglas City Museum, "The Forced Incarceration of Juneau's Japanese Community, 1941–1951."[1]

This book opened with my childhood version of John Tanaka's graduation story, although I wasn't told, or didn't remember, his name. Similarly, my dad chose to highlight the community's support for Tanaka's early graduation rather than the more metaphorically poignant empty chair. These differences highlight, on an intimate scale, my interest in stories and the power they hold—to shape history and memory, to sanction or occlude certain narratives. As I conclude this book, I am excited to know that the Empty Chair Project examines and expounds on Juneau's Japanese American community before, during, and after World War II, as well as challenging the previous elision of Japanese American internment within Alaskan history. I was privileged to attend the dedication ceremony for the sculpture in July 2014. Standing with 300 people in the Juneau drizzle, I was moved in witnessing the reflection and reckoning of my hometown toward a former injustice. Just as an empty chair serves as a powerful symbol of the missing Japanese Americans from Juneau and other parts of Alaska, however, additional evacuations are yet located in this particular story, disappearances that link Japanese American internment in Alaska with Alaska Native experiences, within a larger matrix of racial discrimination and colonial dispossession.

As I've endeavored to demonstrate, Alaska Native peoples and Asian migrants and settlers in Alaska share a long history of connection through a differential and colonial racialization and gendering. Starting with the American purchase of Alaska from Russia, Native peoples were racialized through a settler orientalist discourse that linked them to Asian origins, a fictive descendance to discount Indigenous sovereignty and naturalize dispossession. Though Alaska Natives peoples' imperial racialization as Asian would be superseded by settler colonial differentiation, the idea of indigeneity constructed through imagined Asian connection would find a lasting articulation in the colonial epistemology of the Bering Land Bridge hypothesis. As the gold rush era brought both boomtown economies and a crush of non-Native settlers into the Alaskan territory, gold rush narratives centered on romanticized ideals of white male triumph over land and labor. Even as gold rush narratives furthered the gulf between legible Asian and Native connections, differential and contingent violences exposed Native and Asian affinities. Within the shift from mercantile to industrial capitalism in the early 1900s, Alaska officially became an incorporated territory in 1912. Although the emerging cannery industry relied on the labor of Asian migrant men and resident Native women, Alaskan history, labor studies, Asian American studies, and Native studies all obscure this connection through an investment in manufacturing a proper laboring subject. It is only within Alaska Native and Asian American literary authors' exploration of unbecoming subjectivities that other forms of affective belonging become recognizable. Likewise, the liminal intimacies of a Japanese immigrant photographer within an Alaska Native community facilitate a visual record of the multiple associations between racialized and colonized peoples that exceed the logics of settler space and time.

Alaska was (and is) both an Indigenous and racially heterogeneous place, attributes Alaska shares with other colonized spaces. But what should be a basic and obvious premise is obscured by settler colonial logics. Throughout this book, I have shown that Asian immigrants were either materially expulsed or discursively disregarded as belonging to Alaska. This formulation of Asians as failed settlers constructed white settlers as the proper heirs to a future state, and is the defining feature of what I consider settler colonial space. Conversely, the overarching settler discourse of Native peoples is temporal, what I term settler colonial time. Settler society recognized Alaska Native peoples within the space of Alaska, yet failed to acknowledge them as modern subjects if they were perceived to choose Native traditions and practices. This idea of failed modern subjectivity blamed Native culture for the wide-ranging violence required to settle on and extract resources from Indigenous lands. Read together, this space-time colonialism obfuscated the very land and labor that settler colonialism depended on, let alone the intersection of these double disavowals. It is impossible to fully comprehend Alaska's history when Asians cannot be located in the space of Alaska, and Native peoples cannot be understood as participants in historical time.

I have attempted to take seriously the imperative to deepen the connected analyses of imperialism, settler colonialism, and racial and gendered formations, yet my investments in this project are not only scholarly. As my interest in the Empty Chair Project indicates, the questions of differential and relational colonization and racialization in Alaska are very much discussed outside of academia with lasting importance to the present day. In Alaska history, World War II is viewed as marking a turning point, in which the military provides the modern infrastructure needed for statehood, achieved in 1959. This narrative of modern progress undergirds the movement to statehood in the Cold War era, a discourse of modernity that succeeds only with a concomitant disavowal of racial and colonial violences. From the point of American purchase forward, American colonization of Alaska is made possible by the dispossession of Indigenous land, alongside exploited Asian and Native labor. At the same time, the American colonial project narrates itself as a modern ascendancy through the disavowal of this colonized land and racialized labor. Rather than see the internment of Alaska's Japanese and Japanese American residents as a wartime anomaly to the premise and promise of liberal democracy, I suggest viewing internment along a larger continuum of racialized and colonial violences. How might an empty chair also symbolize the specter of

Shoki Kayamori? Instead of a chair missing its high school valedictorian, an absence recognized through the action of Tanaka's peers, it is Kayamori who is missing from Yakutat's town gathering, only to be found at home in his armchair, having committed suicide. If, in John Tanaka's case, the empty chair functions as a representation of the absent Japanese and Japanese American residents of Juneau, a metonym for internment, Shoki Kayamori's deathly presence serves as counterpoint, the chair and its occupant a gruesome refusal of removal and incarceration. The chair left unfilled, both in 1942 and its reconstitution as a public memorial, serves as a tangible maker to invoke belonging for racialized immigrants and to remediate racial injustice while Kayamori's chair, filled with his suicided form, cannot be similarly resolved; instead, his death remains a disquieting sign of and rejoinder to colonial military violence.

That Alaska Native peoples and Asian migrants and settlers in Alaska have been brought into an intimate constellation through the overlapping imperial, colonial, and settler colonial dimensions of Alaska exists in traces of the Empty Chair Project and the story of John Tanaka. These entanglements, formed even prior to World War II, are reflected in Ernestine Hayes's memoir *Blonde Indian*. Hayes describes the Juneau café "that allowed Native men and women to work as staff and even welcomed Natives and Filipino people as customers."[2] This is the City Café, owned and operated by John Tanaka's parents, Shonosuke and Nobu Tanaka, where Hayes's own mother worked for a period of time.[3] The intersecting lives of Japanese, Filipinx, and Alaska Native workers and customers connect policies of wartime racism to longer trajectories of Native dispossession and racial capitalism, and the shared economy and sociality that resulted. The effects of internment on mixed Native and Japanese families is elaborated by Randy (Akagi) Wanamaker, a prominent Tlingit and local Juneau leader.[4] As part of the Empty Chair memorial project, Wanamaker details the life of his Japanese grandfather, Kiichi "Henry" Akagi who arrived in Alaska at the start of the twentieth century to work at Killisnoo, a location whose deep colonial history is discussed in chapter 4. Like Kayamori, Akagi was an Asian migrant worker who stayed and made his home in Alaska and in relation to Alaska Native peoples. Akagi married twice, both times to Tlingit women, but his wives had passed away by the 1930s. During World War II Henry Akagi was imprisoned at a Santa Fe detention facility along with other Issei men. One of his sons, William, was interned at Minidoka, Idaho, while his other son, Joseph (Wanamaker's father), eschewed his Japanese heritage to identify as Tlingit and fight in the army's Seventh Infantry Regiment.[5] In a different example connected to the Empty

Chair Project, Alice Tanaka Hikido, another of John Tanaka's sisters, provides a video interview on her family's evacuation from Juneau and their internment experience. She connects the various Japanese American families and single male laborers that were spread throughout Alaska and their collective experience of removal and detention when she summarizes their departure out of Alaska on an Army transport ship, saying, "We were all in the same boat."[6] How might this symbol of a shared experience connect with the internment of the Unangax̂ people, taken from their Aleutian and Pribilof homes, their forced removal and relocation to southeastern Alaska also facilitated by military ship transportation, perhaps even on the literal "same boat"? Regarding overlapping removal experiences illuminates a filled ship as a powerful metaphor alongside an (empty) chair—together they speak to the absences and presences that highlight militarization, modernity, and settler colonialism as intertwined processes. The image of a filled ship also invokes the driving-out of Chinese miners in 1886 and, in contrast to involuntary transport, a ship filled soldiers and ordnance conveys the sheer brutality of colonial violence expressed in the bombardment of Tlingit villages. Reflecting on the polyvalent registers of a ship's representation—as tourist, as mobile labor, as cargo, as expeller, as weapon of destruction—we might consider both the nearness and the incommensurability between colonial enterprises of eviction and eradication.

The racial and gendered entanglements between Alaska Native and Asian peoples in colonial Alaska underscore the importance of understanding the complex, enfolded, and, at times, contradictory construction and function of imperialism and settler colonialism. Just as this book seeks to demonstrate that racialization and colonization are distinct yet interdependent processes, neither can we collapse racial justice and decolonization nor view them as disparate projects. Colonial imaginaries may be tenacious, but they are never absolute. Recognizing the historical past of shared antagonisms and affinities between Asian immigrants and Alaska Native peoples within imperial and settler constellations means we must endeavor as partners to condition the possibilities for a mutually liberatory future, beyond dispossession, exploitation, and extraction.

Notes

Abbreviations

ASL   Alaska State Library Historical Collections, Juneau, Alaska
DAD   *Daily Alaska Dispatch*
IW   *Industrial Worker*
JE   *Juneau Empire*
NARA National Archives and Records Administration, Washington, D.C.
NYT   *New York Times*
SHI   William L. Paul Sr. Archives, Sealaska Heritage Institute, Juneau, Alaska

A Note on Terminology

1. I follow this same system when describing individual Asian ethnicities (e.g., "Chinese," "Chinese American," "Japanese," "Japanese American," etc.).
2. See Hudson and Mason, *Lost Villages*, vii.
3. In the Revised Popular orthography, Tlingit is spelled (and pronounced) Lingít. The popular orthography was first developed by Constance Naish and Gillian Story in the 1960s, aided by Tlingit speakers George Betts and Robert Zuboff. See Dauenhauer and Dauenhauer, *Haa Shuká*, 38–48.
4. Twitchell, Lingít Yoo X̱'atángi website.
5. Silva, *Aloha Betrayed*, 13.
6. Kale Bantigue Fajardo makes a similar move inspired by Silva in his ethnography of Filipino seafaring masculinities. See Fajardo, *Filipino Crosscurrents*, 191.

Introduction

1. For more on John Tanaka and his family, see Hikido, "Tanaka"; Grummett, *Quiet Defiance*.
2. Maria Shaa Tláa Williams, "Preface," in *Alaska Native Reader*, xiii.
3. Huhndorf, *Mapping the Americas*, 30.
4. Maria Shaa Tláa Williams, "Alaska and Its People"; Langdon, *Native People of Alaska*.
5. The arrival of Alaska Native studies as a distinct field is affirmed by the collection *The Alaska Native Reader*. See Maria Shaa Tláa Williams, *Alaska Native Reader*. See also Leonard et al., *Transforming the University*; Thornton, *Being and Place*; Miller, *Kodiak Kreol*; Reedy-Maschner, *Aleut Identities*; Breinig, "Alaskan Haida Stories"; Breinig, "In Honor of Nastáo"; Tuck, "ANCSA as X-Mark." Additionally, several works within Native and Indigenous studies and American studies more broadly incorporate aspects of Alaska Native studies. See Huhndorf, *Mapping the Americas*; Raibmon, *Authentic Indians*; Cruikshank, *Do Glaciers Listen?*

6. As of June 2020, there are 229 federally recognized tribes in Alaska. The United States officially ceased treaty making with American Indian tribes in 1871.

7. Case and Voluck, *Alaska Natives*, 24; Treaty of Cession.

8. Case and Voluck, *Alaska Natives*, 63–65.

9. U.S. Congress, "Inhabitants of Alaska," 4.

10. Buchholdt, *Filipinos in Alaska*; Inouye, Hoshiko, and Hashiki, *Alaska's Japanese Pioneers*; Guimary, *Marumina Trabaho*.

11. Swineford, *Alaska, Its History*; Wickersham, *Old Yukon*; Gruening, *State of Alaska*; Hinckley, *Americanization of Alaska*; Naske and Slotnick, *Alaska*; Haycox, *Alaska*. Hinckley provides the best examination of Asian immigrants in Alaska, including both Chinese cannery workers and Chinese miners, in his monograph.

12. Good examples of this type of scholarship are two foundational texts in Asian American studies: Chan, *Asian Americans*, and Takaki, *Strangers*.

13. Azuma, *Between Two Empires*; Bascara, *Model-Minority Imperialism*; Choy, *Empire of Care*; Isaac, *American Tropics*; Jung, *Coolies and Cane*; Kim, *Ends of Empire*.

14. Lowe, *Immigrant Acts*.

15. In making this argument, I join a number of scholars in Asian North American studies centering a settler colonial framework and, more broadly, engaging Indigenous studies. See Carpenter and Yoon, "Asian/Native Encounters"; Lai and Smith, "Alternative Contact"; Medak-Saltzman and Tiongson, "Racial Comparativism Reconsidered"; Leong and Carpio, "Carceral States"; Day, *Alien Capital*; Le, *Unsettled Solidarities*; Tiongson, "Asian American Studies"; Jafri, "Desire, Settler Colonialism"; Fugikawa, "Domestic Containment."

16. Mawani, *Colonial Proximities*, 5. Mawani is one of several scholars working at the intersection of Native studies and Asian Canadian studies. See also Day, *Alien Capital* and "Alien Intimacies"; Le, *Unsettled Solidarities*; Lai, "Epistemologies of Respect"; Yu, "Global Migrants"; Lo, "Model Minorities"; Wong, "Decolonizasian"; Patel, "Two Indians"; Upadhyay, "South Asians on the Tar Sands."

17. Lawrence and Dua, "Decolonizing Antiracism."

18. Though beyond the scope of my project, the comparative and relational aspects between Hawaiʻi and Alaska certainly merit further study.

19. Trask, *From a Native Daughter*; Fujikane and Okamura, *Asian Settler Colonialism*; Saranillio, "Asian Settler Colonialism Matters"; hoʻomanawanui, "This Land." In her project that examines race and indigeneity in Hawaiʻi, J. Kēhaulani Kauanui demonstrates that a white-Hawaiian-Asian triangulation developed in Hawaiʻi, a formulation that linked white supremacy and colonialism with anti-immigrant sentiments but that, ultimately, worked to dispossess Kānaka Maoli (Native Hawaiians) through a discourse and policies based on blood quantum. See Kauanui, *Hawaiian Blood*, 16–21, 91–96.

20. Fujikane, "Introduction," in *Asian Settler Colonialism*, 20.

21. Japanese residents were the largest single ethnic group in Hawaiʻi by 1900, and accounted for nearly 40 percent of the population by 1940 (37.3 percent compared to 23 percent white and 23 percent Kānaka Maoli). See Whitehead, *Completing the Union*, 18–31.

22. Jean Potter, *Alaska under Arms*, 88.

23. Saranillio, *Unsustainable Empire*.

24. Byrd, *Transit of Empire*, xix. As a Chickasaw scholar, Byrd's conceptualization of arrivant and arrivant colonialism as separate from yet intersecting with settler colonialism is grounded within the history of her nation and other tribes of the southeastern United States and their adoption of and participation in the enslavement of Black peoples within plantation economies. This strategy resulted in the Chickasaw, Cherokee, Choctaw, Creek, and Seminole being known in American colonial vernacular as the "Five Civilized Tribes," but ultimately failed to prevent the forced removal of the five tribes from their homelands to Indian Territory west of the Mississippi River.

25. Byrd, *Transit of Empire*, 53.
26. Lowe, "Intimacies," 203.
27. Lowe, "Intimacies," 203.
28. Robinson, *Black Marxism*.
29. Day, *Alien Capital*. Though Day's book centers on Asian racialization within settler colonial capitalism, her triangulated model of settler-Native-alien addresses Black as well as Asian racialization. Within an analysis of labor within settler colonialism, Day notes that Black Americans became an undisposable alien labor force while Asian Americans represented an alien labor force whose exploitation was marked by disposability. See Day, *Alien Capital*, 25–34.
30. Tuck and Yang, "Decolonization"; Day, *Alien Capital*, 21.
31. Day, *Alien Capital*, 23–24.
32. Vine Deloria, *God Is Red*, 63.
33. Bruyneel, *Third Space*, 2. See also Rifkin, *Beyond Settler Time*.
34. Philip Deloria, *Indians in Unexpected Places*; Raibmon, *Authentic Indians*.
35. O'Brien, *Firsting and Lasting*, xxii.
36. Chong, "Orientalism," 183. See also Chong, *Oriental Obscene*; Robert Lee, *Orientals*; Wu, *Yellow*.
37. Thank you to Manu Karuka and Alyosha Goldstein for our ongoing conversations troubling these categories and structures of domination. See Vimalassery, Hu Pegues, and Goldstein, "Colonial Unknowing."
38. Byrd, *Transit of Empire*, xv, xix; Arnett, "Between Empires and Frontiers," 3–4.
39. Karuka, *Empire's Tracks*, xii.
40. The phrase "anticipatory geography" comes from the respective scholarship of Juliana Barr and J. Brian Harley. See Barr, "Geographies of Power," 7; Harley, "Rereading the Maps," 532.

Chapter One

1. Collis, *A Woman's Trip*, 118.
2. Collis, 124.
3. Collis, 121. It should be noted that the colonial trade jargon colloquially known as "Chinook" does not refer to an Indigenous nation, but instead the more accurately termed Wawa emerged out of European and Indigenous contact because of the fur trade on the Pacific Northwest coast. See Lang, *Making Wawa*.
4. See Dillehay et al., "New Archaeological Evidence"; Steeves, "Decolonizing the Past"; Fitzhugh, "Yamal to Greenland."

5. For example, Yupiit and Iñupiat peoples exist in larger circumpolar configurations of the Arctic. (Iñupiat are part of a network of Inuit communities in Russia, Canada, Greenland, and Scandinavia. Yupiit live in Siberia and Alaska on both sides of the Bering Strait.) Yup'ik and Iñupiaq histories of movement and migration, therefore, do not necessarily contradict Bering Land Bridge theories, though, importantly, they are multidirectional. Other Alaska Native groups' histories, however, are not as aligned, and, as Maria Shaa Tláa Williams argues, the "hyperfocus" on outside origins elides Indigenous histories that are "more complex and much more interesting because they are related to both physical and metaphysical cosmologies." See Maria Shaa Tláa Williams, "Alaska and Its People," 5, 7.

6. Vine Deloria, *Red Earth, White Lies*; David Hurst Thomas, *Skull Wars*.

7. Said, *Orientalism*.

8. Byrd, *Transit of Empire*, 39.

9. Hinckley, "Inside Passage," 71; U.S. Department of the Interior, *Eleventh Census*, 250.

10. Robert Campbell examines travelers' depictions of nature and Native peoples and the ways these images helped shape American imperial, white supremacist, and capitalist ambitions. Throughout Campbell's excellent study are myriad examples of tourists interpellating Alaska Native peoples in relation to perceived Asian bodies or traits. See Campbell, *In Darkest Alaska*. Similarly, Sergei Kan demonstrates the importance of the figure of the Alaska Native as elaborated by tourist narratives, and, like Campbell, he reveals Asian connections, particularly what Kan calls an "anti-Asian bias." See Kan, "Half a Mile." I build from Campbell's and Kan's scholarship, because the associations they draw, while obviously of interest, are neither author's primary focus.

11. Piatote, *Domestic Subjects*.

12. Wolfe, "Elimination of the Native."

13. The total acreage fell from 155 million acres to 52 million. See Wolfe, "Elimination of the Native," 400.

14. Hayes, *Blonde Indian*.

15. Survivance is a term and concept theorized by Anishinaabe author and scholar Gerald Vizenor as "an active sense of presence, the continuance of native stories, not a mere reaction, or a survivable name. Native survivance stories are renunciations of dominance, tragedy and victimry." Vizenor, *Manifest Manners*, vii.

16. De Acosta et al., *Natural and Moral History*.

17. Foucault, *Order of Things*.

18. Fabian, *Time and the Other*, 15–16.

19. Sumner, *Cession of Russian America*.

20. Sumner, 24. Sumner and Agassiz were on personal terms, and corresponded regularly. See Irmscher, *Louis Agassiz*, 110–111.

21. Agassiz biographer Christoph Irmscher cautions that singling out memorable scientific racists such as Agassiz obscures the entrenched racial thinking of the era. See Irmscher, *Louis Agassiz*, 268–69.

22. Sumner, *Cession of Russian America*, 25. In presenting this nomenclature, Sumner also presents the hypothesis of the Bering Land Bridge but calls it "doubtful." He provides no other explanation for Asian origins.

23. Sumner, *Cession of Russian America*, 25. Interestingly, Sumner doesn't make note of what type of "intermixture" is causing this racial ambiguity—it is unclear whether he is con-

cerned with Sugpiaq intermarriage with other Native groups or whether he is referring to the long and complex history of Sugpiaq intermarriage with Russian fur traders, promyshlenniki. If the latter, he creates an interesting phylogeny in which supposed Asiatic indigenes in their encounter with Russian colonizers become less Asian and more Indian.

24. Sumner, *Cession of Russian America*, 25.

25. Sumner, 27.

26. Sumner, 28. Sumner's description of those he calls Aleut (who may be either Unangax̂ or Sugpiaq, or both) is taken from George Simpson, the Canadian governor of Hudson's Bay Company in the mid-1800s. Sumner's characterization of Aleutians is a direct quotation from Simpson.

27. Miller argues this coercive labor system is what distinguishes Russian fur economy from other colonial fur trades in North America. See Miller, *Kodiak Kreol*; and Miller, "Perfect Mistress."

28. Bradford, *Scenes in the Life*, 81; Bradford, *Harriet Tubman*; Larson, *Promised Land*, 163–66; Clinton, *Harriet Tubman*.

29. Baker, *William H. Seward*, 4:170. See also Paolino, *Foundation of American Empire*, 4–5.

30. Seward, *Immigrant White Free Labor*, 2. See also Paolino, *Foundation of American Empire*, 82.

31. Seward, *North American States*.

32. Seward, 12.

33. U.S. Congress, "Indian Commissioner's Annual Report."

34. U.S. Congress, 1029. In this instance Colyer is quoting a government official speaking about "Aleutians," who may be Unangax̂ or Sugpiaq, or both.

35. U.S. Congress, "Indian Commissioner's Annual Report," 1032, 1042.

36. U.S. Congress, 1029.

37. U.S. Congress, 995.

38. Bhabha, *Location of Culture*, 122.

39. Colyer's recommendations passed the Senate Committee on Indian Affairs but stalled at the congressional level. Congress was hesitant because of the administrative structures required for Colyer's plan, and also disinclined because of publicity surrounding Native and army conflict in Alaska, as well as corruption charges related to the Alaska purchase. A general appropriation was made to the Department of the Interior, which ultimately was not spent on Alaska Natives. See Haycox, "Questionable Ethnical Type," 159.

40. U.S. Congress, "Inhabitants of Alaska," 3–4.

41. U.S. Congress, 4.

42. U.S. Congress, 3.

43. Byrd, *Transit of Empire*, xvii.

44. Pratt, *Imperial Eyes*.

45. On the tourist desire for sublime landscapes, see Campbell, *In Darkest Alaska*; on the tourist gaze directed at Southwest Indian peoples, see Dilworth, *Imagining Indians*; on tourist engagement with Indians of the Pacific Northwest and Southeast Alaska, see Raibmon, *Authentic Indians*. I purposely use the term "authentic" from Raibmon to describe non-Native desires for a mythic representation of a Native subject divorced from modernity, ironically articulated as "authenticity."

46. Woodman, *Picturesque Alaska*, 132.

47. Finck, *Pacific Coast*, 243.

48. Muir, *Travels in Alaska*, 197.

49. William Dall was a naturalist, specializing in mollusks. He was a member of the Scientific Corps of the Alaskan Western Union Telegraph Expedition in 1865 and also surveyed the Alaskan coast in 1871. See Dall, *Alaska and Its Resources*, 373–432.

50. Livingston Jones, *Thlingets of Alaska*, 28. Ft. Wrangel was renamed Wrangell in 1902.

51. Fabian, *Time and the Other*, 7–8.

52. Ismail, *Abiding by Sri Lanka*, xxii (emphasis in original).

53. Raymond Williams, *Marxism and Literature*, 110. See also Gramsci, *Prison Notebooks*.

54. Raymond Williams, *Marxism and Literature*, 132.

55. Rifkin, *Settler Common Sense*. Quynh Nhu Le continues Rifkin's expansion of Gramsci with an expansion of her own, formulating "settler racial structures of feeling," to engage the simultaneous yet differential settler normalization of Asian and Native containment. See Le, *Unsettled Solidarities*, 62.

56. See Cruikshank, *Do Glaciers Listen?*, 179–210; Campbell, *In Darkest Alaska*, 18–45.

57. Pierrepont, *Fifth Avenue to Alaska*, 163. See also Wardman, *Trip to Alaska*, 128; Scidmore, *Alaska*, 181.

58. Woodman, *Picturesque Alaska*, 189. See also Collis, *A Woman's Trip*, 180; Taylor, *Touring Alaska*, 153.

59. Tchen, *New York before Chinatown*, 130.

60. Yaw, *Sixty Years in Alaska*.

61. For more on the Sitka tour, see Raibmon, *Authentic Indians*, 157–69. As Raibmon details, three cottages were built in 1887; by 1905 there were fifteen.

62. Collis, *A Woman's Trip*, 121.

63. Collis, 124.

64. Piatote, *Domestic Subjects*, 109–10.

65. Kaplan, *Anarchy of Empire*, 26.

66. Raibmon, *Authentic Indians*, 167–68.

67. Taylor, *Touring Alaska*, 153.

68. Hallock, *Our New Alaska*, 91–92.

69. Pierrepont, *Fifth Avenue to Alaska*, 177.

70. Swineford, *Alaska, Its History*, 94, 99.

71. Finck, *Pacific Coast*, 112–99; Pierrepont, *Fifth Avenue to Alaska*, 44–51, 99–109.

72. Woodman, *Picturesque Alaska*, 132; Finck, *Pacific Coast*, 243.

73. Muir, *John of the Mountains*, 394.

74. Bhabha, *Location of Culture*, 122–23.

75. Bhabha, 123.

76. Boas, *Ethnography of Franz Boas*, 5–6.

77. Boas, 98. Boas's theory about Tlingit and Haida language origins has since been discounted.

78. Haven, *Archaeology of the United States*. Part of Boas's insistence on the Bering Land Bridge was due to his public disagreement with University of Pennsylvania professor of linguistics and archaeology Daniel Garrison Brinton, who hypothesized that a North Atlantic Land Bridge existed during the last great ice age and that the ancestors of America's

Indigenous peoples were from Europe not Asia. Ascribing to similar scientific racism as Agassiz, Brinton's thesis allowed him to postulate both that Indigenous peoples in the Western Hemisphere had been isolated for tens of thousands of years (and were therefore uniformly inferior) and that the progenitors of the human species were Europeans. See Brinton, *Races and Peoples*; Brinton, *Essays*.

79. Woodman, *Picturesque Alaska*, 110–11.
80. Young, *Mushing Parson*, 437.
81. Hayes, *Blonde Indian*.
82. Buttenwieser, "*Blonde Indian* (Review)"; Gercken, "*Blonde Indian*."
83. Hayes, *Blonde Indian*, 11.
84. Hayes, 34.
85. Hayes, 28.
86. Hayes, 29.
87. Hayes, 75.
88. Hayes, 134.
89. Hayes, 136.
90. Hayes, 138.
91. Goeman, *Mark My Words*.
92. Hayes, *Blonde Indian*, 145.
93. Hayes, 145.
94. Hayes, 145.
95. Hayes, 145.

Chapter Two

1. This opening scene is an original composite of the many iterations of the China Joe tale, excepting the opening lines, "Day had broken cold and gray, exceedingly cold and gray," which are taken verbatim from Jack London's short story, "To Build a Fire."

2. Rickard, *Through the Yukon*; Murphy, "Frontier Incidents at Juneau"; Buteau, "My Experiences"; Levi, *Boom and Bust*, 124. For an example of a tourist description of China Joe's story, see Higginson, *Alaska*, 87, 120.

3. Hinckley, "Prospectors, Profits"; R. N. DeArmond, *Founding of Juneau*, 146; Stone and Stone, *Hard Rock Gold*, 10–11; Sherry Simpson, *Juneau*, 31.

4. "China Joe Sees Things," *DAD*, February 28, 1905; "China Joe Entertains," *DAD*, January 23, 1909; Yule, "China Joe"; "When the Chinese Were Driven Out," *Alaska Sourdough*, December 5, 1911; "China Joe Dies of Heart Failure," *DAD*, May 19, 1917; "China Joe Is Found Dead in His Old Home," *Alaska Daily Empire*, May 18, 1917; Ann Chandonnet, "Evergreen Cemetery Is Final Home to Pioneers," *JE*, October 3, 1999; Ann Chandonnet, "China Joe: Baker, Prospector, and Benefactor Was 'One of Us,'" *JE*, August 15, 2003; I-Chun Che, "China Joe: Man of the Golden Rule," *JE*, October 10, 2004; Kim Marquis, "Presentation to Pay Tribute to Juneau Pioneer," *JE*, January 28, 2008; Jack Marshall, "Accumulated Fragments: Douglas Island's Deep and Sometimes Dark History," *JE*, March 11, 2012; "C.W. Carter Presents a Memorial Plaque of China Joe to Juneau," *DAD*, October 9, 1960; Brett Dillingham and Mark Whitman, play script, "The Story of China Joe" (1992), "China Joe" Papers, MS 217, Folder 4, ASL.

5. Kingston, *China Men*, 160–62. I consider *China Men* a "biomythography," as a work that defies genre categorization, and borrowing from Black lesbian author Audre Lorde, who conceptualizes biomythography as a combination of history, biography, and myth. See Audre Lorde, *Zami*. For another example of China Joe's appearance within an Asian American context, see Che, "Lonesome Land."

6. Haycox, *Alaska*, 166–67. Anthropologist Julie Cruikshank details how Skookum Jim, his sister Kate, Dawson Charlie (all First Nation Tagish), and Kate's non-Native husband George Carmack discovered gold near the Klondike River in 1896, starting the rush. Cruikshank provides an exemplary study comparing official gold rush literature with Tagish oral accounts. See Cruikshank, "Klondike Gold Rush Narratives."

7. It should be noted that the Klondike Gold Fields and the Cassiar were located in the Yukon territory and the Province of British Columbia, respectively. The routes to get to these locations, however, passed through Alaska.

8. *Seattle Post Intelligencer*, Klondike Edition, July 17, 1897.

9. Seattle was also transformed by the Klondike Gold Rush, advertising itself as the "Gateway to Alaska and the Yukon." It is estimated that nearly three-quarters of the 100,000 miners to depart for the Klondike were initially outfitted in Seattle.

10. Ingersoll, *Gold Fields*, 80.

11. Service, "Cremation of Sam McGee," in *Spell of the Yukon*, 50; London, "To Build a Fire," 525.

12. For a more comprehensive study of Jack London's short stories and their themes of white racial mastery, see James McClintock, *White Logic*. Though focused on California and not Alaska, Colleen Lye importantly links the literary nationalism of West Coast authors, including Jack London, to the American construction of Asian stereotypes that move between the two poles of "model minority" and "yellow peril," a formation she terms the "Asiatic racial form." See Lye, *America's Asia*.

13. "Lee Hing, or 'China Joe,'" Lit Site Alaska website; "China Joe Dies of Heart Failure," *DAD*, May 19, 1917. The last quote comes from the memorial plaque on his gravesite, "China Joe" Papers, MS 217, Folder 3, ASL.

14. Beattie, "China Joe."

15. R. N. DeArmond, *Founding of Juneau*, 49.

16. Tlingit elder Cecilia Kunz (discussed later in this chapter) told Tlingit anthropologist and president of the Sealaska Heritage Institute, Dr. Rosita Ḵaaháni Worl, that it was actually a Tlingit named Geinax Éesh who showed Juneau and Harris where to find gold, while noting that descendants of Kaawa.ée maintained his role in the origin story with pride. Both may be true, as Juneau and Harris had to be guided twice, and also reflect capaciousness and grace on Kunz's part. This information comes from Cecilia Kunz, as told to Rosita Worl, "The First Murder in Juneau," courtesy of Rosita Worl. The information about Sheep Creek Mary comes from Rosa Miller, Tlingit elder and leader of the L'eeneidí or Dog Salmon clan. Sheep Creek Mary was also L'eeneidí. Miller quoted in Ann Chandonnet, "Chief Kowee: Shaman, Chief, and Guide," *JE*, June 13, 2003.

17. China Joe's 1881 deed for sale. "China Joe" Papers, MS 217, Folder 1, ASL. The driving-out, however, was recorded in national press.

18. Anderson, *Imagined Communities*.

19. Wolfe, *Settler Colonialism*, 33.

20. *Alaska Journal*, May 6, 1893.

21. As historian Erika Lee points out, no other immigrant group was required to maintain identification cards to demonstrate lawful residence until 1928, when such stipulations were applied more universally. In this way, Lee demonstrates the certificates required by the Geary Act serve as a precursor for alien receipt cards (i.e., "green cards"). See Erika Lee, *At America's Gates*, 42.

22. "Juneau's One Chinaman Celebrates," *Alaska Searchlight*, February 2, 1897; "China Joe Sees Things," *DAD*, February 28, 1905; "'Chinese Joe' Entertains," *DAD*, January 23, 1909; "China Joe Is an Authority," *DAD*, February 20, 1912; "All New Years Are Alike to Juneau's 'China Joe,'" *JE*, February 5, 1913.

23. "China Joe Sees Things," *DAD*, February 28, 1905.

24. London, *Call of the Wild*, 19.

25. "When the Chinese Were Driven Out," *Alaska Sourdough*, December 5, 1911.

26. Yule, "China Joe."

27. Rickard, *Through the Yukon*; Murphy, "Frontier Incidents"; Buteau, "My Experiences"; Levi, *Boom and Bust*, 124; Sherry Simpson, *Juneau*, 31.

28. R. N. DeArmond, *Founding of Juneau*, 146; Stone and Stone, *Hard Rock Gold*, 10–11.

29. Brett Dillingham and Mark Whitman, play script, "The Story of China Joe" (1992), "China Joe" Papers, MS 217, Folder 4, ASL; Fern Chandonnet, "Alter Remembered as Cold-Weather Pioneer," *JE*, October 30, 2002; Dale DeArmond, *Juneau*, n.p.

30. Levi, *Boom and Bust*, 124; Atwood and Williams, *Bent Pins to Chains*, 48.

31. R. N. DeArmond, *Founding of Juneau*, 146; As Hie deed for property, "China Joe" Papers, MS 217, Folder 1, ASL; *Thirteenth Census of the United States*, Microfilm T624, Records of the Bureau of the Census, Record Group 29.

32. R. N. DeArmond, *Founding of Juneau*, 146; Ann Chandonnet, "China Joe: Baker, Prospector, and Benefactor Was 'One of Us,'" *JE*, August 15, 2003; I-Chun Che, "China Joe: Man of the Golden Rule," *JE*, October 10, 2004.

33. Chong Thui probate records, "China Joe" Papers, MS 217, Folder 1, ASL.

34. Thank you to Josephine Min-Hwa Pegues for translation assistance.

35. Yule, "China Joe," 211; H. R. Shepard, "China Joe Is an Authority," *DAD*, February 20, 1912.

36. Kingston, *China Men*, 162. See also Neubauer, "Ties to the Past," 29–30.

37. The story of the driving-out is told by Diane Smith of the Atlin Historical Society, quoted in Chow, *Chasing Their Dreams*, 42.

38. Chow, *Chasing Their Dreams*, 46. China Joe is identified as, "one Chinese cook, name unknown." Chow's story proceeds to tell the tale of this cook saving white miners during the winter freeze, so I assume this cook to be China Joe.

39. Chow, *Chasing Their Dreams*, 42–43; Borthwick, *Gold Hunters*, 253; Shaw, *Ramblings in California*, 21–22.

40. See Herbert, "'Life's Prizes,'" 354.

41. Pike, *Subarctic Forest*, 58.

42. Bailey, *Alaska and Its People*, 6.

43. Emmons, *Tlingit Indians*, 26. Zachary Jones also notes that the Shtax'héen Ḵwáan sometimes refer to themselves at the Shx'at Ḵwáan people. Jones, "Battlefield Alaska," 51, n21.

44. Emmons, *Tlingit Indians*, 26. The suffix "héen" means "river," so the English "Stikine River" is redundant.

45. Thornton, *Being and Place*, 102.

46. See Goldschmidt and Haas, *Haa Aaní*, 73–74. For a map of Shtax'héen Ḵwáan territory see Goldschmidt and Haas, *Haa Aaní*, appendix C, chart 11: "Wrangell Territory," unnumbered.

47. Zachary Jones, "Battlefield Alaska"; Colyer, *Bombardment of Wrangel*; Emmons, *Tlingit Indians*, 334–35. Jones's article provides an important historical reassessment of colonial narratives through engagement with Tlingit sources of this conflict to show a U.S. military and government policy of violent reprisal for what is viewed as transgression, in willful disregard for Tlingit laws and understandings of reciprocity.

48. Service, "Spell of the Yukon," in *Spell of the Yukon*, 13.

49. Kelly, *Treadwell Gold*. The Treadwell mine would be followed in the early 1900s by the Alaska Gastineau (Perseverance) and Alaska Juneau gold mines.

50. Barry Rodrigue, "A Draft History of Southeast Alaska," Alaska Labor Unions and Social Activism Collection, MS 100, Box 1, ASL; Stone and Stone, *Hard Rock Gold*, 10.

51. Hinckley, "Prospectors, Profits," 63–65; "Driving Chinese Away," *NYT*, August 15, 1886; "Mob Law in Alaska," *NYT*, August 24, 1886.

52. This account, similar to the opening scene of this chapter, is a composite of an oft-repeated story. Some aspects are recorded almost verbatim. Playwright Brett Dillingham describes the mob as drunk and "bristling with weapons." He also describes the old-timers saying, "You are not taking him; he is one of us." See Ann Chandonnet, "China Joe: Baker, Prospector, and Benefactor Was 'One of Us,'" *JE*, August 15, 2003. Likewise, Ed Beattie in 1949 describes the appearance of the prospectors: "From every vantage point—doorways, windows, behind logs, and stumps—riflemen appeared, each ready to lay down his life if necessary in defense of China Joe." See Beattie, "China Joe," 26. Of course, it should be noted that these authors are constructing their own speculative versions of this event.

53. Yule, "China Joe," 212.

54. Beattie, "China Joe," 26.

55. "Juneau's One Chinaman Celebrates," *Alaska Searchlight*, February 6, 1897.

56. Ann Chandonnet, "China Joe: Baker, Prospector, and Benefactor Was 'One of Us,'" *JE*, August 15, 2003.

57. Almost all of the published accounts of China Joe's tale use some combination of these three adjectives to describe him, especially in his later life.

58. Yule, "China Joe," 211.

59. Beattie, "China Joe," 27.

60. R. N. DeArmond, *Founding of Juneau*, 146.

61. *Alaska Journal*, May 6, 1893.

62. Newspaper accounts immediately following his death report that his visitors the night before his death included Jim Young (or Yong) who was employed by a local judge, a man identified simply as "Sing" who was a cook for the governor, and a third unidentified Chinese caller. See "China Joe Is Found Dead in His Old Home," *Alaska Daily Empire*, May 18, 1917; "China Joe Dies of Heart Failure," *DAD*, May 19, 1917.

63. In thinking through lynching as a specific form of terrorizing violence and colonial control visited on Native bodies and peoples, I am in conversation with Native and Indige-

nous studies scholarship on lynching as well as government-sanctioned hangings. See Keith Thor Carlson, "Lynching of Louie Sam"; Cothran, *Remembering the Modoc War*, 8–26; Stark, "Criminal Empire." Carlson's examination of the lynching of a fifteen-year-old Stó:lō youth in 1884, in particular, posits lynching and vigilante violence as a U.S. expression and attempt to establish settler social order.

64. Mbembe, "Necropolitics."

65. Morgensen, "Biopolitics of Settler Colonialism," 54 (emphasis in original).

66. Pierrepont, *Fifth Avenue to Alaska*, 206.

67. The description of the altercation and details of the deaths are taken from the following sources: Pierrepont, *Fifth Avenue to Alaska*, 206–16; Murphy, "Frontier Incidents," 24–25; "Troublesome Alaska Indians," *NYT*, September 9, 1883.

68. Douglass, "Lynch Law"; Wells, *Southern Horrors*; Wells, *A Red Record*.

69. Scholarly works that challenge this historical elision include Gonzales-Day, *Lynching in the West*, and Pfeifer, *Lynching beyond Dixie*.

70. Dray, *Lynching of Black Americans*, vii.

71. Gonzales-Day, *Lynching in the West*. Gonzales-Day records lynchings of Latinx of Mexican and Latin American descent, American Indians, Chinese, and African Americans. Jean Pfaelzer states that of more than 300 lynchings in California between 1849 and 1902, nearly two-thirds were of Asians. Pfaelzer, *Driven Out*, 54.

72. Gonzales-Day, *Lynching in the West*, 6, 42.

73. Pierrepont, *Fifth Avenue to Alaska*, 193.

74. Nancy Furlow (Tlingit, Deisheetaan clan) examines the historical, cultural, and psychological aspects of the destruction of Angoon by the U.S. Navy, in conversation with the Tlingit concepts of ownership, balance, and reciprocity. See Furlow, "Angoon Remembers." For a discussion of the Kake War, see Zachary Jones, "'Search for and Destroy.'" Jones points out that "war" is a misnomer, given that the army launched a unilateral military attack that met with no Tlingit resistance.

75. Pierrepont, *Fifth Avenue to Alaska*, 193–94.

76. W. H. Pierce, *Thirteen Years*, 37. Pierce's comments echo that of an Oregon Territory sheriff who attempted to purchase Modoc leader Captain Jack's body after his public hanging at Fort Klamath in 1873. As Boyd Cothran discusses in his study of the Modoc War, the sheriff wished to display Jack's body as a deterrent to Native resistance. His bid was ultimately unsuccessful, but Captain Jack's body (and those of the five Modoc men hung with him) still met a grisly fate: the heads of the Modoc men were severed and preserved, becoming part of the Smithsonian's "People of the United States" collection for eight decades. As Cothran argues, representations and memorabilia (pieces of the hanging rope and locks of the dead men's hair were sold as souvenirs) of the Modoc War ultimately worked to redeem U.S. colonial violence in the construction of American innocence. See Cothran, *Remembering the Modoc War*, 8–26.

77. Stark, "Criminal Empire."

78. Organic Act of 1884.

79. Formulating the lynching and driving-out in Juneau as "spectacle" builds from scholarship on the lynching of Black Americans and depictions of slavery. See Wood, *Lynching and Spectacle*; Goldsby, *A Spectacular Secret*; Markovitz, *Legacies of Lynching*; Hartman, *Scenes of Subjection*. Though neither the lynching nor the driving-out operated in a larger

economy of visual culture, as did the southern lynching of Blacks, they nonetheless were narratively represented in the press and, moreover, were large public spectacles that made a lasting impact on the local community.

80. Shah, *Stranger Intimacy*, 36.

81. Seventeen Chinese were lynched (including one woman) and two others were knifed to death on the night of October 24, 1871. For a detailed accounting, see Pfaelzer, *Driven Out*, 47–79.

82. See Wood, *Lynching and Spectacle*, 5–14; Goldsby, *Spectacular Secret*, 23–27.

83. Mbembe, "Necropolitics," 40 (emphasis in original).

84. Morgensen, "Biopolitics of Settler Colonialism," 52.

85. Grinëv, "Distribution of Alcohol"; Nella Lee, "Impossible Mission"; Lain, "Russian America's Colonial Society."

86. Ehrlander, "Dry Vote"; DeLorme, "Liquor Smuggling."

87. Mawani, *Colonial Proximities*, 125.

88. Pierrepont, *Fifth Avenue to Alaska*, 214.

89. Knapp, *Annual Report*, 4.

90. Pierrepont, *Fifth Avenue to Alaska*, 206.

91. Worl, "First Murder in Juneau." The quotations in this section are quoted directly from Cecilia Kunz's story in Rosita Worl's paper. The central elements in the story, including the mistaken identity of the Kaagwaantaan arrested, Kaakayeik taking his own life, and the payment of the L'eeneidí to the Kaagwaantaan were also conveyed to me by Cecilia's son, Ed Kunz Jr. (Edward Kunz Jr., conversations). Cecilia Kunz walked into the woods (passed away) in 2004.

92. Hong and Ferguson, *Strange Affinities*, 1.

93. I-Chun Che, "China Joe: Man of the Golden Rule," *JE*, October 10, 2004.

94. Yule, "China Joe," 212.

95. Ann Chandonnet, "China Joe: Baker, Prospector, and Benefactor Was 'One of Us,'" *JE*, August 15, 2003.

96. Ann Chandonnet, "China Joe: Baker, Prospector, and Benefactor Was 'One of Us.'"

97. Cecilia Kunz, interview.

98. Hong and Ferguson, *Strange Affinities*, 17.

99. Even in the 2020 summer season, when most cruise ship travel in Alaska was suspended because of the coronavirus pandemic, the walking tour was advertised to Juneau visitors.

100. Juneau-Douglas City Museum Website; Cruise Port Insider website.

101. Lowe, *Intimacies of Four Continents*, 3.

Chapter Three

1. Organic Act of 1912.

2. Lowe, "Intimacies," 203.

3. Lowe, *Intimacies of Four Continents*, 17–18.

4. Ngai, *Impossible Subjects*.

5. It should be noted that I'm conceptualizing "men" and "women" not as biologically determined, but socially constructed, and, even more specifically, how these gendered (and

racialized) categories become constituted as classes within the extractive salmon canning economy. Therefore, I keep these broad categorizations in place to denote the economic structure even as it becomes evident that some of those in the classed category of Asian men may not have considered themselves male.

6. Roppel, "Salting Salmon"; Moser, *Salmon Fisheries*, 62.

7. For more on Tlingit social organization see Thornton, *Being and Place*, 36–67. For more on at.óow, see Dauenhauer and Dauenhauer, *Haa Shuká*, 24–29.

8. Goldschmidt and Haas, *Haa Aaní*; a map detailing Indigenous use and ownership of the Ketchikan area is located on pages 204–5.

9. Beynon, "Tsimshians of Metlakatla"; Neylan, "'Choose Your Flag'"; Dangeli, "Bringing to Light," 265–66.

10. Hinckley, "Canoe Rocks," 270–71.

11. Dauenhauer, "Some Slices of Salmon," in *Life Woven with Song*, 3.

12. Barnett, "Gateway to Getaway."

13. Kiffer, "Catching a Can."

14. For Tlingit opposition to Chinese workers, see Hinckley, "Prospectors, Profits," 62–63; Wyatt, "Wage Earners," 44.

15. Woodman, *Picturesque Alaska*, 116.

16. Alaska Packers Association Records, MS 9, Box 1, ASL.

17. Bashford, "Frontier Town."

18. George Yanagimachi, interview.

19. Bancroft, *History of Alaska*.

20. Bancroft, 662.

21. See, for example, Swineford, *Alaska, Its History*; Wickersham, *Old Yukon*. One notable exception to the historic elision of Asian migrant workers is Ted Hinckley's *The Americanization of Alaska*. Hinckley includes both Chinese cannery workers and Chinese miners in his monograph. His work is limited, however, because of his naturalizing depictions of Asian workers as "passive, extremely diligent orientals," denying their subjectivity as well as capacity for labor organizing, and eliding the possibility for social relations with other communities (127).

22. Gruening, *State of Alaska*, 65.

23. Day's theorization is influenced by Marxist historian and political economist Moishe Postone. See Postone, *Time*.

24. Haycox, *Alaska*.

25. Hinkley, "Review"; Morse, "Review." In his more critical review, historian Claus-M. Naske's largest critique is not of Haycox's historical undertaking but Naske takes issue with Haycox's central argument that Alaska is a colony. See Naske, "Review."

26. Haycox describes the cannery labor force as "mostly Chinese, later Filipino" (*Alaska*, 193) and a following passage explains that the "labor in a large cannery consisted of 100 to 150 white fishermen and 150 to 200 mostly Filipino cannery workers" (*Alaska*, 241).

27. Haycox, *Alaska*, 192 and 193. The second quotation comes from a description offered by territorial governor Alfred P. Swineford, an assessment with which Haycox agrees.

28. Day, *Alien Capital*, 16.

29. Alaska newspapers *Alaska Daily Empire* and *Ketchikan Miner* for the year 1913 make no mention of Local 283 or its activities. At the same time, lacunae in the archival record

surround 1913 and cannery labor. Alaska Packers Association ledgers for 1914, for instance, demonstrate a shift in the ethnic composition of the workforce reflected by the categorical count of laborers. As mentioned in text, starting in the 1910s, the "Oriental Contract" is divided into categorizations of "Chi," "Jap," and "Misc." In 1914, however, these categories change to "Chi," "Mexican," "Filipino," and "Misc." A designation for Japanese workers is noticeably absent. See Alaska Packers Association Records, MS 9, Box 1, ASL. Another indication of labor organizing on the part of cannery workers is expressed in the government's annual report on Alaska fisheries from 1913. Citing difficulties in recruiting Chinese laborers, canneries shifted to a workforce of a "miscellaneous collection of Mexicans and Japanese, Filipinos and other Orientals, who are not as tractable and dependable as the Chinese." The report cautions "constant vigilance" for the "labor troubles that mean heavy loss to the salmon packer" and proposes "importing white girls" from the Pacific Northwest who are preferable to both Native laborers and immigrant workers of color. See Evermann, *Alaska Fisheries*, 94–95.

30. Yoneda "Japanese Labor," 150–58.

31. Ichioka, "Introduction," xi–xvii. Yoneda was a member of the International Longshoremen's and Warehousemen's Union (ILWU) and the elected union official of the San Francisco Alaska Cannery Workers Union Local 5, a CIO (Congress of Industrial Organizations) union.

32. Yoneda, "Japanese Labor," 153.

33. Yoneda, *Zai-Bei Nihonjin*, 65–66. My thanks to Yuichiro Onishi for his translation from Japanese to English.

34. Omatsu, "Racism or Solidarity?" 34–35.

35. Robert Lee, "Hidden World," 276.

36. Takaki, *Strangers*, 317; Shah, *Stranger Intimacy*.

37. Friday, *Asian American Labor*, 88–89.

38. Haycox, *Alaska*, 243. One clear exception within Alaska history is Wyatt's "Alaskan Indian Wage Earners." Wyatt states that Native cannery labor started in the late nineteenth century and lasted well into the twentieth, and is well documented in towns such as Klawock, Sitka, Kasaan, and Loring.

39. See Dauenhauer and Dauenhauer, *Haa Shuká*; Dauenhauer and Dauenhauer, *Haa Tuwunáagu Yís*; Dauenhauer and Dauenhauer, *Haa K̲usteeyí*. Most of the examples in this section are from the life stories in *Haa K̲usteeyí*. Another important source is the diary of William Wanamaker, less for its details of cannery work than for his recording of the yearly departure and return of his wife and children to and from the Hawk Inlet Cannery, from 1928 through the 1930s. Wanamaker (1889–1944) was a Tlingit of the Kiks.ádi clan and a member of the Alaska Native Brotherhood (ANB) and the union Juneau Mine Workers Association. See William S. Wanamaker Collection, MS 047, Box 1, Item 1, SHI.

40. Thornton, *Being and Place*, 124.

41. Amy K̲ooteen Marvin oral history in Dauenhauer and Dauenhauer, *Haa K̲usteeyí*, 467.

42. Jennie Jeeník White oral history in Dauenhauer and Dauenhauer, *Haa K̲usteeyí*, 605; Frank Taakw K'wát'i Johnson oral history in Dauenhauer and Dauenhauer, *Haa K̲usteeyí*, 311.

43. Some of these cannery jobs shifted with increased mechanization. For example, fillers began to run the machine that sliced and diced fish into cans. The most notable mecha-

nization was a fish butchering machine developed in 1909 to replace Chinese cannery workers and dubbed the "Iron Chink," a stark reminder of the racialized category of cannery work transmitted through epithet. See Day, *Alien Capital*, 191–98; Mawani, *Colonial Proximities*, 49–51.

44. Knack and Littlefield, "Native American Labor," 3.

45. Coulthard, *Red Skin, White Masks*.

46. Jessie Daax'wudaak̲ Starr Dalton oral history in Dauenhauer and Dauenhauer, *Haa K̲usteeyí*, 151–63. Similar labor practices are widespread in oral histories; see Austin Daanawáak̲ Hammond oral history in Dauenhauer and Dauenhauer, *Haa K̲usteeyí*, 207–50; Sally Shx̲aastí Hopkins oral history in Dauenhauer and Dauenhauer, *Haa K̲usteeyí*, 269–78; Emma Seigeigéi Marks oral history in Dauenhauer and Dauenhauer, *Haa K̲usteeyí*, 378–406; Jim K̲uháanx' Marks and Jennie K̲ultuyáx̲ Sée Marks oral history in Dauenhauer and Dauenhauer, *Haa K̲usteeyí*, 407–51; Doris Volzke oral history in Smith and Harrington, *I Never Did Mind*, 91–95.

47. Norrgard, *Seasons of Change*; Raibmon, *Authentic Indians*; O'Neill, *Navajo Way*; Bauer, *Migrant Workers*.

48. Bhattacharya, "Mapping Social Reproduction Theory"; Ferguson, "Children, Childhood, and Capitalism."

49. Karuka specifically engages the theorization of Dakota scholar and novelist Ella Deloria, Paiute author Sarah Winnemucca, and Ojibwe environmentalist and activist Winona LaDuke. See Karuka, *Empire's Tracks*, 20–37.

50. Dauenhauer and Dauenhauer, *Haa K̲usteeyí*, x; Thornton, *Being and Place*, 117.

51. Sally Shx̲aastí Hopkins oral history in Dauenhauer and Dauenhauer, *Haa K̲usteeyí*, 272.

52. Susie Kaasgéiy James oral history in Dauenhauer and Dauenhauer, *Haa K̲usteeyí*, 285–87.

53. Audra Simpson, "State Is a Man"; Leanne Betasamosake Simpson, *As We Have Always Done*.

54. "New Local in Ketchikan Alaska," *IW*, February 27, 1913. The *Industrial Worker* suspended publication after September 1913 and was not resumed until 1916 because of internecine disagreements between the editor and publisher. By September, however, the cannery season would be ending or had already ended. This sharing of space between the IWW and the Socialist Party appears quite common, as notes from the Juneau Socialist Party in 1912 indicate that Ketchikan's socialists were renting their hall to IWW members in exchange for work. Socialist Party (Alaska), Manuscript Collection 4-7-2, Box 7, Folders 2-1 to 2-4, ASL.

55. Glenn Omatsu, "Racism or Solidarity?" 33.

56. The opening lines to the Preamble to the IWW Constitution. The first paragraph of the preamble reads, "The working class and the employing class have nothing in common. There can be no peace so long as hunger and want are found among millions of working people and the few, who make up the employing class, have all the good things in life." The preamble is included in almost all histories and memoirs of the IWW and its members. The preamble was adopted by the IWW on the sixth day of its founding meeting, July 3, 1905. The entire preamble, along with the attendees' discussion preceding adoption can be found in Industrial Workers of the World, *Founding Convention*, 219–48.

57. Examples abound, such as, "The world of the Wobblies was one realized in its best moments by solidarity across race, ethnic, gender and nationality lines," in Buhle and Schulman, *Wobblies!*, 3; similarly, "The IWW welcomed Chinese, Japanese, Filipino and other Asian workers to its ranks, once more setting a new standard of solidarity for organized labor," in Bird, Georgakas, and Shaffer, *Solidarity Forever*, 140. Similar sentiments can be found in IWW histories such as Brissenden, *The IWW*; Foner, *Industrial Workers*; Dubofsky, *We Shall Be All*.

58. Industrial Workers of the World, *Founding Convention*. From the names of speakers and union representatives, it appears that the one identifiable person of color at the convention was Lucy Parsons, noted American anarchist and labor organizer of mixed Black, Native, and Mexican descent.

59. Within the organization's first year, the IWW reported that its representatives visited the Seattle-based Japanese newspaper *Hokubei jiji* (*The North American Times*) to invite Japanese workers to a mass meeting. See *IW*, July 1906.

60. Survey of Race Relations Collection, Box 24, Item 16, Hoover Institute Archives, Stanford University.

61. Hall, *Harvest Wobblies*, 58; "Testimonial Meeting on the Oriental," Survey of Race Relations Collection, Box 24, Item 16, Hoover Institute Archives, Stanford University.

62. *IW*, September 19, 1919, qtd. in Foner, *Industrial Workers*, 127.

63. Haywood, *Drops of Blood*, 2.

64. I am not the first historian to trace this act of retaliatory violence. In correspondence related to his research on Alaska socialist and anarchist movements, Barry Rodrigue also starts from the presupposition that the dragging occurred in 1913. Finding no supporting documentation in the Alaska history archives he consulted, he additionally searched Ketchikan papers from 1912 to 1921 with no results. See Roderick (Rodrigue), Barry Hadfield, Alaska Labor Unions and Social Activism Collection, MS 100, Box 1, Folder II-1, ASL.

65. *IW* editorial, April 3, 1913; "The Yellow Peril," *IW*, May 15, 1913; "The Japanese, the Land, and Labor," *IW*, May 29, 1913; "Better Clean His Glasses," *IW*, June 12, 1913.

66. Thompson, *The I.W.W.*, 66–67; Archie Green, *Wobblies, Pile Butts*, 194; Renshaw, *Wobblies*, 1; Leier, "Racial Prejudice," 164.

67. Downing, *Nation*, September 5, 1923, 242.

68. Buhle and Schulman, *Wobblies!*, 5.

69. Buhle and Schulman, 7, 52.

70. Bird, Georgakas, and Shaffer, *Solidarity Forever*, 143. Even in the case of Little, a member of the IWW General Executive Board and known for his role in multiple strikes and free speech fights, and who was ultimately lynched in Montana, historians frequently mention his Cherokee ancestry without any elaboration of tribal enrollment or connection to Cherokee people.

71. Huhndorf, *Going Native*; Philip Deloria, *Indians in Unexpected Places*.

72. Haywood biographer Peter Carlson utilizes a creative example to demonstrate how Haywood was viewed as larger than life, showing that Haywood was often described as a "giant" who stood "well over six feet" or "almost seven feet" when Haywood stood, in reality, five feet, eleven inches. See Carlson, *Roughneck*, 16.

73. The only Asian workers named in Haywood's memoir are a Chinese cook and his personal assistant Taro Yoshihara, but, even then, Yoshihara is mentioned only once

because he was arrested with Haywood during an FBI raid, and no detail is given of who Yoshihara is or his relationship to Haywood. Yoshihara joined the IWW as a merchant seaman, participated in more than a dozen IWW strikes, and was working daily with Haywood by the time he moved to IWW headquarters in Chicago. See Haywood, *Haywood's Book*, 22 and 303; and Chaplin, *Wobbly*, 214.

74. Haywood, *Haywood's Book*, 26.
75. Dauenhauer, *Life Woven with Song*, 57.
76. Cardiff, "Dauenhauer's *Life Woven with Song*," 65–73.
77. Dauenhauer, *Life Woven with Song*, 63–64.
78. Dauenhauer, 42. Nora Marks Dauenhauer walked into the woods in 2017.
79. Dauenhauer, *Life Woven with Song*, 63.
80. Friday, *Asian American Labor*, 88.
81. Moser, *Salmon Fisheries*, qtd. in Friday, *Asian American Labor*, 88–89.
82. Dauenhauer, *Life Woven with Song*, 63–64.
83. Dauenhauer, 63.
84. Dauenhauer, 11.
85. In addition to the coho heads and tails eaten raw, Dauenhauer details another Tlingit practice of using the entire fish when saving salmon heads to ferment in a beach pit, using the natural rhythm of the tides to rinse and salt the fish heads to make the food k'ink'. See Dauenhauer, *Life Woven with Song*, 12–13.
86. Dauenhauer, 44.
87. Holm, *Northwest Coast Indian Art*, xxi.
88. Dauenhauer, *Life Woven with Song*, 42.
89. Dauenhauer, 63, 64.
90. Dauenhauer, *The Droning Shaman*, 11–16.
91. Russell, "Tools of Self Definition," 44.
92. Dauenhauer, *Life Woven with Song*, 64.
93. See Jackson, *Alaska, and Missions*; and Young, *Mushing Parson*.
94. Bailey, *Alaska and Its People*, 44. For a superb critical analysis of the representation of Alaska Native women as prostitutes, see Campbell, *In Darkest Alaska*, 120–36.
95. I intentionally write "possible" prostitution—even though numerous historical accounts of Alaska Native sex workers exist, it is likely that some of these accounts are mistaken descriptions of Native gestures to kinship alliances through unions with Native women. See Boas, *Social Organization*, 358–59.
96. Miller, "Perfect Mistress"; Miller, *Kodiak Kreol*.
97. Thrush, *Native Seattle*, 111.
98. Dauenhauer, *Life Woven with Song*, 42.
99. Leanne Betasamosake Simpson, *As We Have Always Done*, 116.
100. Rifkin, "Erotics of Sovereignty," 173. In framing an "Indigenous structure of feeling," Rifkin alludes to Raymond Williams' conceptualization of structures of feeling and Rifkin's theorization can be thought of in juxtaposition to the affective settler common sense discussed in chapter 1. See Raymond Williams, *Marxism and Literature*.
101. Dauenhauer, *Life Woven with Song*, 64.
102. Bascara, *Model-Minority Imperialism*; Isaac, *American Tropics*.

103. Masson and Guimary, "Asian Labor Contractors"; Friday, *Asian American Labor*; Guimary, *Marumina Trabaho*.
104. Yoneda, *Ganbatte*, 86.
105. Boag, *Re-Dressing*, 6–7.
106. Shah, *Stranger Intimacy*.
107. Shah, 40.
108. De Jesús, "Rereading History."
109. Bulosan, *America*, 101, 103.
110. Bulosan, 101.
111. Bulosan, 103.
112. Rachel Lee, *Asian American Literature*, 18.
113. Bulosan, *America*, 102.
114. Bolanz, "My Trap Line," 49.
115. Bulosan, *America*, 102.
116. Finley, "Decolonizing the Queer"; Morgensen, *Spaces between Us*.

Chapter Four

1. Sources for this segment include Margaret Thomas, *Picture Man*, 79–80; Margaret Thomas, "Kayamori a Spy?," 53–54; Caroline Powell, conversation; Byron Mallott, conversation. Caroline Powell (Tlingit of the Kwaashk'i K̲wáan clan) was among those who found the photographs. She enlisted the help of her brother, Bryon Mallott, who worked to get the photos printed, including the eventual success with the Alaska State Library. Mallott, also known by his Tlingit name, Dux̲ da neik̲, and Eyak name, K'oo del ta', was a former mayor of Yakutat, mayor of Juneau, CEO of the Sealaska Corporation, and the lieutenant governor of Alaska until his resignation in 2018. He walked into the woods in 2020. In this passage, I refer to Yakutat as both a "village" and a "town" deliberately, to signal its small population, rural nature, and historical Native presence, as well as its involvement in national and global commerce, including a nationally and internationally diverse workforce, as well as mirroring many residents' reference to Yakutat as "town."

2. Though Kayamori has been identified as "Fhoki Kayamori" in various scholarship and sources, Fhoki is not a Japanese name. Margaret Thomas has confirmed with Kayamori's family in Japan that his given name was Seiki, of which Shoki is an alternate pronunciation of the same Japanese characters. I refer to Kayamori's given name as Shoki as I believe that was his preference. Margaret Thomas, *Picture Man*, ix.

3. R. C. Vogel letter to J. Edgar Hoover, December 7, 1940. Seiki (Shoki, Fhoki) Kayamori Collection, PCA 55, ASL.

4. My research centers primarily on the original 694 photographs printed in 1977 for the Alaska State Library and the city of Yakutat. Since that time, 28 additional photographs were donated to the Sealaska Heritage Institute, and the Alaska State Library made prints of 220 additional photographs, and I do include these photographs in my analysis. Seiki (Shoki, Fhoki) Kayamori Collection, PCA 55, ASL; Seiki Kayamori Photograph Collection, PO 072, SHI; Kayamori Photograph Collection, Yakutat City Hall.

5. Veracini, *Settler Colonialism*, 3 (emphasis in original).

6. Rayna Green, "Rosebuds"; Moosang, *First Son*; Mimura, "Frank Matsura's Photography"; Francis, *Creative Subversions*, 59–94.

7. Turner, *Ritual Process*.

8. Lowe, *Immigrant Acts*; Ngai, *Impossible Subjects*; Sang Hyun Lee, *Liminal Place*.

9. Ngai, *Impossible Subjects*, 13.

10. Bow, *Partly Colored*; Jung, *Coolies and Cane*; Claire Jean Kim, *Bitter Fruit*.

11. Bow, *Partly Colored*, 11 (emphasis in original).

12. Mawani, *Colonial Proximities*.

13. Bruyneel, *Third Space*, xvii. Bruyneel is working from postcolonial scholar Homi Bhabha's formulation of third space. See Bhabha, *Location of Culture*.

14. Stephen Haycox, *Alaska*, 257–72; Cloe, "Legacy of War."

15. Jodi Kim, "Settler Modernity's Spatial Exceptions"; Jodi Kim, "Settler Modernity, Debt Imperialism."

16. Sources for this segment include descriptions of the cannery workers' journey by Donald Guimary and Yakutat fisherman Oscar Frank Sr.'s memory that Kayamori worked as a cooker at the cannery. See Guimary, *Marumina Trabaho*; Thomas, "Kayamori a Spy?," 50–51. The multiracial demographics of migrant cannery workers is discussed in chapter 3—I reiterate them here to connect Kayamori to the multiracial migrant waves of cannery workers while also signaling the choice of some of these transient workers to settle.

17. Shoki Kayamori Alien Registration Form, December 8, 1940, Form Number 5749551, U.S. Department of Homeland Security.

18. *Thirteenth Census of the United States*, Microfilm T624, Records of the Bureau of the Census, Record Group 29.

19. U.S. Bureau of the Census, *Thirteenth Census*, 1129, 1133.

20. Wedding photograph of Sheldon and Annie James. Seiki (Shoki, Fhoki) Kayamori Collection, P55-514, ASL. The date of December 1913 is attributed to Yakutat resident Raymond Sensmeier. Kayamori Photograph Collection, Yakutat City Hall. Raymond Sensmeier, interview.

21. Thomas, "Kayamori a Spy?," 49.

22. I offer this assessment to highlight the multiracial aspect of Alaska documented in Kayamori's photos, realizing the problematic nature of identifying markers of ethnicity and race, which are always fraught with limitations and guesswork, including that of the author. In the photo of Lon Wun Gee's café, the proprietor and men have been directly identified in the photo. Lon Wun Gee was Chinese, and those sitting at the counter (L–R), Dick Albert, George Bremner, Sam Henniger, and Richard Reese were Alaska Natives from Yakutat. Seiki Kayamori Photograph Collection, P55-007. See *Fifteenth Census of the United States*, Microfilm T626, 1B, Records of the Bureau of the Census, Record Group 29.

23. Trask, *Native Daughter*; Fujikane, "Introduction," in *Asian Settler Colonialism*.

24. Byrd et al., "Predatory Value."

25. Don Bremner, interview.

26. Regarding "subsistence" through Tlingit language and worldview is reflected in the shift of title in the third edition of *The Subsistence Lifeway of the Tlingit People* to *Haa At_xaayí Haa K_usteeyíx Sitee*. See Newton and Moss, *Haa At_xaayí*. For Indigenous versus settler governmental understandings of subsistence, see Voluck, "First Peoples."

27. Thornton, *Being and Place*, 116–18.

28. Ting, "Bachelor Society"; Eng, *Racial Castration*; Lowe, *Intimacies of Four Continents*.

29. Gmelch, *Tlingit Encounter*, 69–84.

30. Lang, *Making Wawa*, 40–42. I stress that this was the vocabulary and meaning ascribed by colonial men involved in the fur trade; additional understandings and motivations for sexual relations may have been known by Native communities or Native women themselves.

31. Hansen, Needham, and Nichols, "Pornography," 204. In making this connection, I want to be clear that I offer no negative judgment on the Native women who posed for these types of photos, nor do I wish to question their choices within a colonial economy.

32. Case and Draper Collection, PCA 39, ASL; Winter and Pond Collection, PCA 87, ASL; Wyatt, *Alaskan Portrait*. Since my initial research on Kayamori's photographs, a subsequently printed photograph in the Alaska State Library Historical Collection has caused me to reassess my original evaluation. One photograph of an unidentified woman (ASL-P55-700) stands in stark contrast to the rest of Kayamori's body of work. In the photo, a Native woman sits on a wood chair with a blanket pinned behind as a backdrop. Her hair is down and she wears a loose undershirt, with one shoulder suggestively bared. Kayamori biographer Margaret Thomas offers that, because this image is so atypical of Kayamori's photographs, it may have been commissioned. See Margaret Thomas, *Picture Man*, 98–100.

33. Gmelch, *Tlingit Encounter*, 169–71.

34. Thunderbird House Exhibit, Alaska State Museum; Dauenhauer and Dauenhauer, *Haa Ḵusteeyí*, 389.

35. Lorraine D. Adams, interview; Bert Adams Sr., interview.

36. Don Bremner, interview.

37. Thank you to Angelica Lawson for pointing out the connection between Kayamori's photographs and Tlingit visual culture. For scholarship on Tlingit visual culture, see Boas, "Decorative Art"; Holm, *Northwest Coast Indian Art*; Jonaitis, *Northern Tlingit*.

38. The sources for this segment are oral histories provided in Frederica de Laguna's *Under Mount Saint Elias*, as told by Harry K. Bremner (231–32), Maggie Harry (235–36), Sarah Williams (237), Katy Dixon Isaac, and Violet Sensmeier (238–39).

39. Curtis, *North American Indian*.

40. Gidley, "Pictorialist Elements."

41. Carol J. Williams, *Framing the West*, 28–29.

42. Gmelch, *Tlingit Encounter*, 86.

43. Seiki (Shoki, Fhoki) Kayamori Collection, photos P55-001, P55-22, P55-100, P55-193, P55-463, P55-524, ASL.

44. De Laguna, *Under Mount Saint Elias*.

45. De Laguna, 1000.

46. Briggs and Bauman, "Franz Boas, George Hunt."

47. It should be noted that other resident Alaskan photographers with close connections to Native communities, such as Winter and Pond, E. W. Merrill, and Vincent Soboleff, also photographed Native subjects wearing a combination of Native and Western dress. See Wyatt, *Alaskan Portrait*, 35–36; Kan, *Russian American Photographer*, 70–71, 74–77, 84–87;

Gmelch, "Elbridge Warren Merrill." Kayamori's photograph remains unique in capturing a Tlingit dance indoors in a European-American-style house.

48. Lyman, *Vanishing Race*, 85–86, 106.

49. Lorraine D. Adams, interview; Bert Adams Sr., interview. Bert Adams Sr. is a Tlingit elder of the Boulder House and a noted author and artist who writes under his Tlingit names Kadashan and Naats'keek. Lorraine Adams was a Tlingit elder of the Frog House, the clan mother of the L'uknax̱.ádi, and a master Lingít speaker and educator. She walked into the woods in 2018.

50. Drucker, *Native Brotherhoods*, 41–44; Mitchell, *Sold American*, 193; Dauenhauer and Dauenhauer, *Haa Ḵusteeyí*, 83–96.

51. Case and Voluck, *Alaska Natives*, 24, 63–65.

52. Raibmon, *Authentic Indians*, 196.

53. Bruyneel, *Third Space*, 65.

54. On Soboleff, see Case and Voluck, *Alaska Natives*, 358. On nested sovereignty, see Audra Simpson, *Mohawk Interruptus*, 11–12. Not only a leader in the ANB, Rev. Dr. Soboleff led one of the first racially mixed congregations in Alaska and helped to create the first Alaska Native Studies program, at the University of Alaska Fairbanks. He walked into the woods in 2011.

55. W. B. Adams, qtd. in Mitchell, *Sold American*, 196.

56. For more on the ANB's role in land claim struggles, see Metcalfe, *A Dangerous Idea*.

57. Don Bremner, interview.

58. Byrd, *Transit of Empire*, 52–53.

59. Margaret Thomas, "Attack Prompted Suicide of Yakutat Photographer," *JE*, December 6, 1991; Margaret Thomas, "Kayamori a Spy?"; Inouye, "For Immediate Sale"; Shoki Kayamori Death Certificate, Territory of Alaska, 1942, Alaska Bureau of Vital Statistics.

60. Fern Chandonnet, "Introduction," in *Alaska at War*, ix.

61. Demmert, "W.W.II."; Anderstrom et al., *Invasion!*

62. Nellie Lorde and Lena Farkas, qtd. in Dennis and Yamamoto, "People and the War," 20–21.

63. MaryAnn Paquette, qtd. in Demmert, "W.W.II.," 41.

64. Dennis and Yamamoto, "People and the War," 21. Farkas belonged to the K'inéix̱ Kwáan clan, Dís Hít (Moon House). Fluent in Lingít, she was a noted language instructor. She walked into the woods in 2017.

65. Dennis and Yamamoto, "People and the War," 22.

66. Demmert, "W.W.II."; Dennis and Yamamoto, "People and the War."

67. Inouye, "For Immediate Sale."

68. Special Agent of the Juneau / Field Division R.C. Vogel letter to FBI Director J. Edgar Hoover, December 7, 1940, Seiki (Shoki, Fhoki) Kayamori Collection, PCA 55, ASL; U.S. Army Brigadier General Sherman Miles letter to FBI Director J. Edgar Hoover, December 13, 1941, Seiki (Shoki, Fhoki) Kayamori Collection, PCA 55, ASL.

69. Margaret Thomas, "Kayamori a Spy?," 53.

70. Inouye, "For Immediate Sale," 260. Elaine Abraham would go on to become the first Tlingit registered nurse and the first woman and Alaska Native to hold a senior administrative position at the University of Alaska, helping to establish several community colleges in Native communities. She also co-founded the Alaska Native Language Center. Abraham

was Naa Tláa (clan mother) of the K'inéix̱ Kwáan from the Tsísk'w Hít (Owl House). She walked into the woods in 2016.

71. Margaret Thomas, "Kayamori a Spy?"; Shoki Kayamori Death Certificate, Territory of Alaska, 1942, Alaska Bureau of Vital Statistics.

72. Margaret Thomas, "Kayamori a Spy?"

73. Wayne Axelson, qtd. in Margaret Thomas, "Kayamori a Spy?," 52.

74. Don Bremner, interview.

75. R. C. Vogel letter to J. Edgar Hoover, December 7, 1940, Seiki (Shoki, Fhoki) Kayamori Collection, PCA 55, ASL.

76. Caroline Chung Simpson, *Absent Presence*.

77. Gordon, *Ghostly Matters*, 19.

78. Lorraine D. Adams, interview; Bert Adams Sr., interview.

79. Inouye, "For Immediate Sale," 262.

80. Reedy-Maschner, *Aleut Identities*, 52–53.

81. Estlack, *Aleut Internments*, 114–15.

82. Commission on Wartime Relocation and Internment of Civilians, *Personal Justice Denied*, 324.

83. For Hubbard's quotations on the Unangax̂, see Hubbard, *Cradle of the Storms*, 26–28. For Hubbard's racial and linguistic assessment of the Iñupiat, the source is Caprice Murray Scarborough, "The Legacy of the 'Glacier Priest': Bernard R. Hubbard, S.J.," Santa Clara University, Department of Anthropology and Sociology, Anthropology Research Manuscript Collection, 2001, 17.

84. Driscoll, *War Discovers Alaska*, 33.

85. Kohlhoff, *Wind Was a River*, 55.

86. Tuck and Yang, "Decolonization," 18.

87. Irene Makarin recalls this incident as the first time U.S. military detained Unangax̂ men from Biorka on suspicion of being Japanese, implying it was a repeated occurrence. See Hudson and Mason, *Lost Villages*, 222.

88. Kirtland and Coffin, *Relocation and Internment*, 12–15.

89. Furlow, "Angoon Remembers"; Worl, "Tlingit Law."

90. De Laguna, *Tlingit Community*; Kan, *Russian American Photographer*; Mobley, *Aleut Relocation Camps*.

91. Kirtland and Coffin, *Relocation and Internment*, 37–63; Kohlhoff, *Wind Was a River*, 87–107; Aleutian Pribilof Islands Association, *Alaska Aleut Evacuation*.

92. Kohlhoff, *Wind Was a River*, 114, 120, 128. The mortality for Unangax̂ from the village of Attu, imprisoned by the Japanese on Hokkaido, was even higher—approximately 44 percent died during World War II, mostly from starvation and malnutrition. See Golodoff, *Attu Boy*; Kohlhoff, *Wind Was a River*, 180.

93. Aleutian Pribilof Islands Association, *Alaska Aleut Evacuation*. Estlack, *Aleut Internments*, 160.

94. Kirtland and Coffin, *Relocation and Internment*, 101–2.

95. Miller, *Kodiak Kreol*, 11–27.

96. Aleutian Pribilof Islands Association, *Alaska Aleut Evacuation*.

97. Golodoff, *Attu Boy*; Hudson and Mason, *Lost Villages*.

98. Public Law 100–383, 903.

99. Public Law 100–383, 903–4.
100. Public Law 100–383, 904.
101. Coulthard, *Red Skin, White Masks*, 105–29; Le, *Unsettled Solidarities*, 59–94.
102. Furlow, "Angoon Remembers."
103. Shigematsu and Camacho, "Introduction," in *Militarized Currents*, xv–xlvii.
104. Camacho, *Sacred Men*, 31–33.

105. Driscoll, *War Discovers Alaska*, 321. Juliet Nebolon also uses "settler militarism" to theorize the simultaneous settler colonialism and militarism that marks public health regimes during World War II martial law in Hawaiʻi. Though Nebolon is concerned with the biopolitical and racialized disciplining of Kānaka Maoli (Native Hawaiians) and Asian settlers in Hawaiʻi, I note her conceptualization to implicitly mark the transition of both Alaska and Hawaiʻi to military defense economies during and after World War II to reflect their connection in the Cold War constructed Asia-Pacific through settler militarism. See Nebolon, "Straight from the Heart."

106. Whitehead, *Completing the Union*, 32, 185.

107. Jodi Kim, "Settler Modernity's Spatial Exceptions"; Jodi Kim, "Settler Modernity, Debt Imperialism."

108. On transpacific critique, see Yoneyama, "Decolonial Genealogy," and Espiritu, "Critical Refugee Studies."

109. John Bremner Sr., qtd. in Margaret Thomas, "Kayamori a Spy?," 53.

110. Don Bremner, interview.

Epilogue

1. Empty Chair Project website; Grummett, *Quiet Defiance*.
2. Hayes, *Blonde Indian*, 34.
3. Hayes, "Waiting Room," 23.
4. Wanamaker's Tlingit name is Tsaaw Eesh, and he is a member of the Kaagwaantaan or Wolf clan. He is the former board chair of Goldbelt, Juneau's Alaska Native corporation, as well as a former Juneau Assembly member.
5. Randy Wanamaker and Connie Lundy's biography of Kiichi (Henry) Akagi in Grummett, *Quiet Defiance*, 103–6.
6. Empty Chair Project website, August 30, 2012, entry; Alice Hikido, "In the Same Boat."

Bibliography

Archival Records and Museum Collections

Alaska Bureau of Vital Statistics, Juneau, Alaska
Alaska State Library Historical Collections, Juneau, Alaska
   Alaska Packers Association Records, Manuscript Collection 9
   Case and Draper Collection, Photograph Collection 39
   "China Joe" Papers, Manuscript Collection 217
   Early Prints of Alaska, Photograph Collection 297
   Roderick (Rodrigue), Barry Hadfield, Alaska Labor Unions and Social Activism Research, Bulk 1980s, Manuscript Collection 100
   Seiki (Shoki, Fhoki) Kayamori Collection, Photograph Collection 55
   Socialist Party (Alaska), Manuscript Collection 4-7-2
   Winter and Pond Collection, Photograph Collection 87
Alaska State Museum, Juneau, Alaska
   Thunderbird House Exhibit, Permanent Collection
Hoover Institute Archives, Stanford University, Stanford, California
   Survey of Race Relations Collection
National Archives and Records Administration, Washington, D.C.
   Records of the Bureau of the Census, Record Group 29
Santa Clara University Archives and Special Collections, Santa Clara, California
   Anthropology Research Manuscript Collection
U.S. Department of Homeland Security, U.S. Citizenship and Immigration Services Genealogy Program, Washington, D.C.
William L. Paul Sr. Archives, Sealaska Heritage Institute, Juneau, Alaska
   William S. Wanamaker Collection, MS/047
   Seiki Kayamori Photograph Collection, PO/072
Yakutat City Hall, Yakutat, Alaska
   Kayamori Photograph Collection

Interviews

Adams, Bert, Sr. Interview with author. June 2, 2011.
Adams, Lorraine D. Interview with author. June 2, 2011.
Bremner, Don. Interview with author. May 31, 2011.
Hikido, Alice Tanaka. "In the Same Boat." *California of the Past* Digital Storytelling Project, City of San Leandro Library. https://www.youtube.com/watch?time_continue=27&v=c91_F56A4ZQ&feature=emb_logo.
Howard, Morgan. Interview with author. February 28, 2013.

Kunz, Cecilia. Interview. November 17, 1995. University of Alaska Fairbanks Oral History Program, Oral History Archive 2010-06.
Kunz, Edward, Jr. Conversations with author. October 8 and October 10, 2019.
Mallott, Byron. Conversation with author. December 26, 2012.
Powell, Caroline. Conversation with author. June 1, 2011.
Ramos, George. Interview with author. May 31, 2011.
Sensmeier, Raymond. Interview with author. June 2, 2011.
Simard, James. Interview with author. May 23, 2011.
Worl, Rico. Interview with author. May 25, 2011.
Yanagimachi, George. Interviewed by Ron Inouye. October 14, 1991. Alaska Japanese Pioneers Research Project. University of Alaska Fairbanks Oral History Program, Oral History Archive 92-06-19.

Newspapers and Magazines

Alaska Daily Empire
Alaska Journal
Alaska Searchlight
Alaska Sourdough
Daily Alaska Dispatch
Industrial Worker
Juneau Empire
Ketchikan Miner
Nation
New York Times
Seattle Post Intelligencer

Government Documents

Bailey, George W. *Alaska and Its People: Giving Statistics as to the Numbers, Location, Pursuits, and Social Condition of the Inhabitants; The Climate, Productions, and General Resources of the Country and of The Commerce, Ocean Currents, Etc.* Washington: Government Printing Office, 1880.
Boas, Franz. *The Social Organization and the Secret Societies of the Kwakiutl Indians.* Washington: Government Printing Office, 1897.
Colyer, Vincent. *Bombardment of Wrangel, Alaska: Report of the Secretary of the Interior and Letter to the President.* 41st Cong., 2nd Sess., Ex. Doc. No. 67 and 68. Washington: Government Printing Office, 1870.
Commission on the Wartime Relocation and Internment of Civilians. *Personal Justice Denied: Report of the Commission on Wartime Relocation and Internment of Civilians.* Washington: Government Printing Office, 1992.
De Laguna, Frederica. *The Story of a Tlingit Community: A Problem in the Relationship between Archeological, Ethnological, and Historical Methods.* Smithsonian Institution Bureau of Ethnology Bulletin 172. Washington: Government Printing Office, 1960.
Drucker, Philip. *The Native Brotherhoods: Modern Intertribal Organizations on the Northwest Coast.* Washington: Government Printing Office, 1958.
Evermann, Barton Warren. *Alaska Fisheries and Fur Industries, 1913.* Washington: Government Printing Office, 1914.
Golodoff, Nick. *Attu Boy.* Edited by Rachel Mason. Anchorage: National Park Service, Alaska Regional Office, Department of the Interior, 2012.

Hudson, Ray, and Rachel Mason. *Lost Villages of the Eastern Aleutians: Biorka, Kashega, Makushin*. Washington: Government Printing Office, 2014.
Knapp, Lyman E. *Annual Report of the Governor of Alaska for the Fiscal Year Ended June 30, 1890*. Washington: Government Printing Office, 1890.
Mobley, Charles M. *World War II Aleut Relocation Camps in Southeast Alaska*. Anchorage: National Park Service, Alaska Region, 2012.
Moser, Jefferson F. *The Salmon and Salmon Fisheries of Alaska: Report of the Alaska Salmon Investigations of the U.S. Fish Commission Steamer* Albatross *in 1900 and 1901*. Washington: Government Printing Office, 1902.
Newton, Richard G., and Madonna L. Moss. *Haa Atx̱aayí Haa K̲usteeyí Sitee, Our Food Is Our Tlingit Way of Life*. Juneau: Department of Agriculture, Forest Service, 2005.
Sumner, Charles. *Speech of Hon. Charles Sumner of Massachusetts on the Cession of Russian America to the United States*. Washington: Congressional Globe Office, 1867.
U.S. Bureau of the Census. *Thirteenth Census of the United States: 1910 Population*. Washington: Government Printing Office, 1913.
———. *Fourteenth Census of the United States*. Vol. 3. *Population 1920, Composition and Characteristics of the Population by States*. Washington: Government Printing Office, 1922.
———. *Fifteenth Census of the United States, 1930. Population Volume I, Number and Distribution of Inhabitants; Total Population for States, Counties, and Townships or Other Minor Civil Divisions; for Urban and Rural Areas; and for Cities and Other Unincorporated Places*. Washington: Government Printing Office, 1931.
U.S. Congress. House. "Indian Commissioner's Annual Report." 41st Congress, 2d Session, 1869, Executive Document 1, Part 3, 975–1058.
———. "Conditions of the Inhabitants of Alaska." 42nd Congress, 2nd Session, 1872, Executive Document 197, 3–4.
U.S. Department of the Interior, Census Office. *Report of Population and Resources of Alaska at the Eleventh Census: 1890*. Washington: Government Printing Office, 1893.

Government Statutes

Organic Act of 1884, May 17, 1884, Section 8, 23 Stat. 24.
Organic Act of 1912, August 24, 1912, 37 Stat. 512.
Public Law 100–383, August 10, 1988, 102 Stat. 903.
Treaty of Cession, June 20, 1867, 15 Stat. 539.

Websites and Film

Aleutian Pribilof Islands Association, dir. *Alaska Aleut Evacuation: The Untold War Story*. Girdwood, Alaska: Gaff Rigged Productions, 1992. DVD, 59 min.
Empty Chair Project. http://emptychairproject.wordpress.com/. Accessed March 12, 2020.
Kiffer, Dave. "Catching a Can in Ketchikan: A History of the 'Salmon Capital of the World.'" Stories in the News, Ketchikan, Alaska, website. September 23, 2009. http://www.sitnews.us/Kiffer/SalmonCapital/092309_ketchikan.html.

"Lee Hing, or 'China Joe.'" Lit Site Alaska website. University of Alaska Anchorage. http://www.litsitealaska.org/index.cfm?section=digital-archives&page=People-of-the-North&cat=Heroes-and-Scoundrels&viewpost=2&ContentId=2719. Accessed March 9, 2020.

Tlingit Language Dictionary on Lingít Yoo X̱'atángi website. May 13, 2020. https://tlingitlanguage.com/resources/dictionary-2/.

"Walking Tour of Juneau/Downtown Juneau Walking Tour." Cruise Port Insider. http://www.cruiseportinsider.com/juex71.html#.Ufakv-uE7tI. Accessed March 9, 2020.

"Walking Tours." Juneau-Douglas City Museum. https://beta.juneau.org/library/museum/walking-tours. Accessed March 9, 2020.

Dissertations and Unpublished Papers

Anderstrom, Eric, Aaron Bonnand, Yvonne Demmert, Leah Dennis, Rob Eklund, Melenda Lekanof, Rochelle Lekanof, and Allison Yamamoto. *Invasion! World War II Comes to Yakutat*. Yakutat: Sawmill Cove, 1994. Booklet made by Yakutat High School's 11/12 grade research class, taught by Sheila Bonnand.

Arnett, Jessica Leslie. "Between Empires and Frontiers: Alaska Native Sovereignty and U.S. Settler Imperialism." PhD diss., University of Minnesota, 2018.

Barnett, William C. "From Gateway to Getaway: Labor, Leisure, and Environment in American Maritime Cities." PhD diss., University of Wisconsin–Madison, 2005.

Casaday, Lauren Wilde. "Labor Unrest and the Labor Movement in the Salmon Industry of the Pacific Coast." PhD diss., University of California, Berkeley, 1938.

Demmert, Corbin. "W.W. II." In *Painting a Portrait: The Colors of Yakutat*, 38–42. Yakutat: Sawmill Cove, 1994.

Demmert, Corbin, Chinook Deveraux, James Eklund, Amber Elton, Amy Hills, Samantha Ross, and Mary Angel Ryman. *Painting a Portrait: The Colors of Yakutat*. Yakutat: Sawmill Cove, 1994. Booklet made by Yakutat High School's 11/12 grade research class, taught by Sheila Bonnand.

Dennis, Leah, and Allison Yamamoto. "People and the War." In *Invasion! World War II Comes to Yakutat*, 18–24. Yakutat: Sawmill Cove, 1996.

Fugikawa, Laura Sachiko. "Domestic Containment: Japanese Americans, Native Americans, and the Cultural Politics of Relocation." PhD diss., University of Southern California, 2011.

Haywood, William. *With Drops of Blood the History of the Industrial Workers of the World Has Been Written*. Chicago: Industrial Workers of the World, 1919. Pamphlet.

Worl, Rosita. "The First Murder in Juneau: The L'eeneidí Payment to the Kaagwaantaan. As Told by Cecilia Kunz to Rosita Worl." Unpublished paper, 1990.

———. "Tlingit Law, American Justice, and the Destruction of Tlingit Villages." Excerpt of speech. http://www.sealaskaheritage.org/sites/default/files/ExcerptRositaWorl Speech.pdf. Accessed May 16, 2020.

Books, Essays, and Articles

Anderson, Benedict. *Imagined Communities: Reflections on the Origin and Spread of Nationalism*. Rev. ed. London: Verso, 2006.

Atwood, Evangeline, and Lew Williams Jr. *Bent Pins to Chains: Alaska and Its Newspapers*. Bloomington, IN: Xlibris, 2006.
Azuma, Eiichiro. *Between Two Empires: Race, History, and Transnationalism in Japanese America*. Oxford: Oxford University Press, 2005.
Baker, George E., ed. *The Works of William H. Seward*. Vol. 4. Boston: Houghton Mifflin, 1884.
Bancroft, Hubert Howe. *History of Alaska, 1730–1885*. New York: Antiquarian Press, 1959.
Barr, Juliana. "Geographies of Power: Mapping Indian Borders in the 'Borderlands' of the Early Southwest." *William and Mary Quarterly* 68, no. 1 (January 2011): 5–46.
Bascara, Victor. *Model-Minority Imperialism*. Minneapolis: University of Minnesota Press, 2006.
Bashford, James. "Frontier Town." *Alaska Sportsman* 14, no. 3 (March 1948): 12–13, 39–40.
Bauer, William J., Jr. *We Were All Like Migrant Workers Here: Work, Community, and Memory on California's Round Valley Reservation: 1850–1941*. Chapel Hill: University of North Carolina Press, 2009.
Beattie, Ed. "China Joe." *Alaska Sportsman* 15, no. 9 (September 1949): 18–19, 24–27.
Beynon, William. "The Tsimshians of Metlakatla, Alaska." *American Anthropologist* 43, no. 1 (Jan–Mar 1941): 83–88.
Bhabha, Homi. *The Location of Culture*. London: Routledge, 1994.
Bhattacharya, Tithi. "Introduction: Mapping Social Reproduction Theory." In *Social Reproduction Theory: Remapping Class, Recentering Oppression*, edited by Tithi Bhattacharya, 1–20. London: Pluto Press, 2017.
Bird, Stewart, Dan Georgakas, and Deborah Shaffer, eds. *Solidarity Forever: An Oral History of the IWW*. Chicago: Lake View Press, 1985.
Boag, Peter. *Re-Dressing America's Frontier Past*. Berkeley: University of California Press, 2011.
Boas, Franz. "The Decorative Art of the Indians of the North Pacific Coast." *Bulletin of the American Museum of Natural History* 9 (1897): 123–76.
———. *The Ethnography of Franz Boas: Letters and Diaries of Franz Boas Written on the Northwest Coast from 1886 to 1931*. Edited by Ronald Rohner. Translated by Hedy Parker. Chicago: University of Chicago Press, 1969.
Bolanz, Maria. "Memories of My Trap Line." In *The Alaska Native Reader: History, Culture, Politics*, edited by Maria Shaa Tláa Williams, 49–55. Durham, NC: Duke University Press, 2009.
Borthwick, J. D. *The Gold Hunters*. Cleveland, OH: International Fiction Library, 1917.
Bow, Leslie. *Partly Colored: Asian Americans and Racial Anomaly in the Segregated South*. New York: New York University Press, 2010.
Bradford, Sarah. *Scenes in the Life of Harriet Tubman*. Auburn, NY: W. J. Moses, 1869.
———. *Harriet Tubman: Moses of Her People*. New York: George R. Lockwood, 1886.
Breinig, Jeane T'áawxíaa. "Alaskan Haida Stories of Language Growth and Regeneration." *American Indian Quarterly* 30, nos. 1/2 (Winter/Spring 2006): 110–18.
———. "In Honor of Nastáo: Kasaan Haida Elders Look to the Future." *Studies in American Indian Literatures* 25, no. 1 (Spring 2013): 53–67.
Briggs, Charles L., and Richard Bauman. "'The Foundation of All Future Researches': Franz Boas, George Hunt, Native American Texts and the Construction of Modernity." *American Quarterly* 51, no. 3 (1999): 479–528.

Brinton, Daniel G. *Races and Peoples: Lectures on the Sciences of Ethnography*. New York: N.D.C. Hodges, 1890.

———. *Essays of an Americanist*. Philadelphia: David McKay, 1980.

Brissenden, Paul Frederick. *The I.W.W.: A Study of American Syndicalism*. New York: Columbia University, 1919.

Bruyneel, Kevin. *The Third Space of Sovereignty: The Postcolonial Politics of U.S.-Indigenous Relations*. Minneapolis: University of Minnesota Press, 2007.

Buchholdt, Thelma. *Filipinos in Alaska, 1788–1959*. Anchorage, AK: Aboriginal Press, 1996.

Buhle, Paul, and Nicole Schulman, eds. *Wobblies!: A Graphic History of the Industrial Workers of the World*. London: Verso, 2005.

Bulosan, Carlos. *America Is in the Heart*. Rev. ed. Seattle: University of Washington Press, 1978.

Buteau, Frank. "My Experiences in the World." In *Sourdough Sagas: The Journals, Memoirs, Tales, and Recollections of the Earliest Alaskan Gold Miners, 1833–1923*, edited by Herbert L. Heller, 93–118. Cleveland, OH: World Publishing Company, 1967.

Buttenwieser, Sarah Werthan. Review of *Blonde Indian: An Alaska Native Memoir*, by Ernestine Hayes. *Fourth Genre: Explorations in Nonfiction* 10, no. 1 (Spring 2008): 180–82.

Byrd, Jodi A. *The Transit of Empire: Indigenous Critiques of Colonialism*. Minneapolis: University of Minnesota Press, 2011.

Byrd, Jodi A., Alyosha Goldstein, Jodi Melamed, and Chandan Reddy. "Predatory Value: Economies of Dispossession and Disturbed Relationalities." *Social Text* 36, no. 2 (June 2018): 1–39.

Camacho, Keith L. *Sacred Men: Law, Torture, and Retribution in Guam*. Durham, NC: Duke University Press, 2019.

Campbell, Robert. *In Darkest Alaska: Travel and Empire along the Inside Passage*. Philadelphia: University of Pennsylvania Press, 2007.

Cardiff, Gladys. "Nora Marks Dauenhauer's *Life Woven with Song*." *Studies in American Indian Literatures* 16, no. 2 (2004): 65–73.

Carlson, Keith Thor. "The Lynching of Louie Sam." *BC Studies* 109 (Spring 1996): 63–79.

Carlson, Peter. *Roughneck: The Life and Times of Big Bill Haywood*. New York: W.W. Norton, 1983.

Carpenter, Cari M., and K. Hyoejin Yoon, eds. "Asian/Native Encounters." Special issue, *College Literature* 41, no. 1 (Winter 2014).

Case, David S., and David A. Voluck. *Alaska Natives and American Laws*. 3rd ed. Fairbanks: University of Alaska Press, 2012.

Chan, Sucheng. *Asian Americans: An Interpretive History*. Boston: Twayne, 1991.

Chandonnet, Fern, ed. *Alaska at War, 1941–1945: The Forgotten War Remembered*. Fairbanks: University of Alaska Press, 2008.

Chaplin, Ralph. *Wobbly: The Rough-and-Tumble Story of an American Radical*. Chicago: University of Chicago Press, 1948.

Che, I-Chun. "Lonesome Land: In 1886, China Joe Became the Only Chinese Person in All of Juneau, Alaska." *Hyphen* 6 (Summer 2005). https://hyphenmagazine.com/magazine/issue-6-makeover-summer-2005/lonesome-land. Accessed March 12, 2020.

Chong, Sylvia Shin Huey. *The Oriental Obscene: Violence and Racial Fantasies in the Vietnam Era*. Durham, NC: Duke University Press, 2011.

———. "Orientalism." In *Keywords for Asian American Studies*, edited by Cathy J. Schlund-Vials, Linda Trinh Võ, and K. Scott Wong, 182–85. New York: New York University Press, 2015.

Chow, Lily. *Chasing Their Dreams: Chinese Settlement in the Northwest Region of British Columbia*. Prince George, BC: Caitlin Press, 2000.

Choy, Catherine Ceniza. *Empire of Care: Nursing and Migration in Filipino American History*. Durham, NC: Duke University Press, 2003.

Clinton, Catherine. *Harriet Tubman: The Road to Freedom*. Boston: Little, Brown, 2004.

Cloe, John Haile. "The Legacy of War." In *Alaska at War, 1941–1945: The Forgotten War Remembered*, edited by Fern Chandonnet, 393–98. Fairbanks: University of Alaska Press, 2008.

Collis, Septima. *A Woman's Trip to Alaska*. New York: Cassell, 1890.

Cothran, Boyd. *Remembering the Modoc War: Redemptive Violence and the Making of American Innocence*. Chapel Hill: University of North Carolina Press, 2014.

Coulthard, Glen Sean. *Red Skin, White Masks: Rejecting the Colonial Politics of Recognition*. Minneapolis: University of Minnesota Press, 2014.

Cruikshank, Julie. "Images of Society in Klondike Gold Rush Narratives: Skookum Jim and the Discovery of Gold." *Ethnohistory* 39, no. 1 (Winter 1992): 20–41.

———. *Do Glaciers Listen? Local Knowledge, Colonial Encounters, and Social Imagination*. Vancouver: University of British Columbia Press; Seattle: University of Washington Press, 2005.

Curtis, Edward S. *The North American Indian*. Seattle: E.S. Curtis; Cambridge, MA: The University Press, 1907–1930.

Dall, William Healy. *Alaska and Its Resources*. Boston: Lee and Shepard, 1870.

Dangeli, Mique'l Icesis. "Bringing to Light a Counternarrative of Our History: B. A. Haldane, Nineteenth-Century Tsimshian Photographer." In *Sharing Our Knowledge: The Tlingit and Their Coastal Neighbors*, edited by Sergei Kan, 265–93. Lincoln: University of Nebraska Press, 2015.

Dauenhauer, Nora Marks. *The Droning Shaman*. Haines, AK: Black Current Press, 1988.

———. *Life Woven with Song*. Tucson: University of Arizona Press, 2000.

Dauenhauer, Nora Marks, and Richard Dauenhauer, eds. *Haa Shuká, Our Ancestors: Tlingit Oral Narratives*. Seattle: University of Washington Press; Juneau, AK: Sealaska Heritage Foundation, 1987.

———. *Haa Tuwunáagu Yís, for Healing Our Spirit: Tlingit Oratory*. Seattle: University of Washington Press; Juneau, AK: Sealaska Heritage Foundation, 1990.

———. *Haa Ḵusteeyí, Our Culture: Tlingit Life Stories*. Seattle: University of Washington Press; Juneau, AK: Sealaska Heritage Foundation 1994.

Day, Iyko. "Alien Intimacies: The Coloniality of Japanese Internment in Australia, Canada, and the U.S." *Amerasia Journal* 36, no. 2 (2010): 107–24.

———. *Alien Capital: Asian Racialization and the Logic of Settler Colonial Capitalism*. Durham, NC: Duke University Press, 2016.

De Acosta, José, Jane E. Mangan, Walter Mignolo, and Frances M. López-Morillas. *Natural and Moral History of the Indies*. Durham, NC: Duke University Press, 2002.

DeArmond, Dale. *Juneau: A Book of Woodcuts*. Anchorage: Alaska Northwest Publishing Company, 1973.
DeArmond, R. N. *The Founding of Juneau*. Juneau, AK: Gastineau Channel Centennial Association, 1980. First published 1967 by Color Press (College Place, Wash.).
De Jesús, Melinda L. "Rereading History, Rewriting Desire: Reclaiming Queerness in Carlos Bulosan's *America Is in the Heart* and Bienvenido Santos' *Scent of Apples*." *Journal of Asian American Studies* 5, no. 2 (2002): 91–111.
De Laguna, Frederica. *Under Mount Saint Elias: The History and Culture of the Yakutat Tlingit*. Washington, DC: Smithsonian Institution Press, 1972.
Deloria, Philip J. *Indians in Unexpected Places*. Lawrence: University Press of Kansas, 2004.
Deloria, Vine, Jr. *God Is Red: A Native View of Religion*. Golden, CO: Fulcrum, 1994.
———. *Red Earth, White Lies: Native Americans and the Myth of Scientific Fact*. Golden, CO: Fulcrum, 1997.
DeLorme, Roland L. "Liquor Smuggling in Alaska, 1867–1899." *Pacific Northwest Quarterly* 77, no. 4 (October 1975): 145–52.
Dillehay, Tom D., Carlos Ocampo, José Saavedra, Andre Oliveira Sawakuchi, Rodrigo M. Vega, Mario Pino, Michael B. Collins, et al. "New Archaeological Evidence for an Early Human Presence at Monte Verde, Chile." *PLOS One* 10, no. 12 (November 2015). https://doi.org/10.1371/journal.pone.0141923.
Dilworth, Leah. *Imagining Indians in the Southwest: Persistent Visions of a Primitive Past*. Washington: Smithsonian Institution, 1997.
Douglass, Frederick. "Lynch Law in the South." *North American Review* (July 1892): 17–24.
Dray, Philip. *At the Hand of Persons Unknown: The Lynching of Black Americans*. New York: Random House, 2002.
Driscoll, Joseph. *War Discovers Alaska*. Philadelphia: J.B. Lippincott, 1943.
Dubofsky, Melvin. *We Shall Be All: A History of the Industrial Workers of the World*. Chicago: Quadrangle Books, 1969.
Ehrlander, Mary F. "The Paradox of Alaska's 1916 Alcohol Referendum: A Dry Vote within a Frontier Alcohol Culture." *Pacific Northwest Quarterly* 102, no. 1 (Winter 2010/2011): 29–42.
Emmons, George Thornton. *The Tlingit Indians*. Edited by Frederica de Laguna. Seattle: University of Washington Press; New York: American Museum of Natural History, 1991.
Eng, David. *Racial Castration: Managing Masculinity in Asian America*. Durham, NC: Duke University Press, 2001.
Espiritu, Yến Lê. "Critical Refugee Studies and Native Pacific Studies: A Transpacific Critique." *American Quarterly* 69, no. 3 (September 2017): 483–90.
Estlack, Russell W. *The Aleut Internments of World War II*. Jefferson, NC: McFarland, 2014.
Fabian, Johannes. *Time and the Other: How Anthropology Makes Its Object*. New York: Columbia University Press, 1983.
Fajardo, Kale Bantigue. *Filipino Crosscurrents: Oceanographies of Seafaring, Masculinities, and Globalization*. Minneapolis: University of Minnesota Press, 2011.
Ferguson, Susan. "Children, Childhood, and Capitalism: A Social Reproduction Perspective." In *Social Reproduction Theory: Remapping Class, Recentering Oppression*, edited by Tithi Bhattacharya, 112–30. London: Pluto Press, 2017.

Finck, Henry Theophilus. *The Pacific Coast Scenic Tour: From Southern California to Alaska, the Canadian Pacific Railway, Yellowstone Park, and the Grand Canyon.* New York: Charles Scribner, 1891.
Finley, Chris. "Decolonizing the Queer Native Body (and Recovering the Native Bull-Dyke): Bringing 'Sexy Back' and Out of Native Studies' Closet." In *Queer Indigenous Studies: Critical Interventions in Theory, Politics, and Literature,* edited by Qwo-Li Driskill, Chris Finley, Brian Joseph Gilley, and Scott Lauria Morgensen, 31–42. Tucson: University of Arizona Press, 2011.
Fitzhugh, William W. "Yamal to Greenland: Global Connections in Circumpolar Archaeology." In *Archaeology: The Widening Debate,* edited by Barry Cunliffe, Wendy Davies, and Colin Renfrew, 91–144. Oxford: Oxford University Press, 2002.
Foner, Philip S. *The Industrial Workers of the World, 1905–1917.* Vol. 4. History of the Labor Movement in the United States. New York: International Publishers, 1965.
Foucault, Michel. *The Order of Things: An Archaeology of the Human Sciences.* Rev. ed. New York: Vintage Books, 1994.
Francis, Margot. *Creative Subversions: Whiteness, Indigeneity, and the National Imaginary.* Vancouver: University of British Columbia Press, 2011.
Friday, Chris. *Organizing Asian American Labor: The Pacific Coast Canned Salmon Industry, 1870–1942.* Philadelphia: Temple University Press, 1994.
Fujikane, Candace. "Introduction: Asian Settler Colonialism in the U.S. Colony of Hawai'i." In *Asian Settler Colonialism: From Local Governance to the Habits of Everyday Life in Hawai'i,* edited by Candace Fujikane and Jonathan Y. Okamura, 1–42. Honolulu: University of Hawai'i Press, 2008.
Fujikane, Candace, and Jonathan Y. Okamura, eds. *Asian Settler Colonialism: From Local Governance to the Habits of Everyday Life in Hawai'i.* Honolulu: University of Hawai'i Press, 2008.
Furlow, Nancy. "Angoon Remembers: The Religious Significance of Balance and Reciprocity." In *The Alaska Native Reader: History, Culture, Politics,* edited by Maria Shaa Tláa Williams, 144–50. Durham, NC: Duke University Press, 2009.
Gercken, Becca. Review of *Blonde Indian: An Alaska Native Memoir,* by Ernestine Hayes. *Studies in American Indian Literatures* 21, no. 2 (Summer 2009): 78–81.
Gidley, Mick. "Pictorialist Elements in Edward S. Curtis' Photographic Representation of American Indians." *Yearbook of English Studies* 24 (1994): 180–92.
Gmelch, Sharon Bohn. "Elbridge Warren Merrill: The Tlingit of Alaska, 1899–1929." *History of Photography* 19, no. 2 (1995): 159–72.
———. *The Tlingit Encounter with Photography.* Philadelphia: University of Pennsylvania Museum of Archaeology and Anthropology, 2008.
Goeman, Mishuana. *Mark My Words: Native Women Mapping Our Nations.* Minneapolis: University of Minnesota Press, 2013.
Goldsby, Jacqueline. *A Spectacular Secret: Lynching in American Life and Literature.* Chicago: University of Chicago Press, 2006.
Goldschmidt, Walter R., and Theodore H. Haas. *Haa Aaní, Our Land: Tlingit and Haida Land Rights and Use.* Seattle: University of Washington Press; Juneau, AK: Sealaska Heritage Foundation, 1998.

Gonzales-Day, Ken. *Lynching in the West, 1850–1953*. Durham, NC: Duke University Press, 2006.
Gordon, Avery. *Ghostly Matters: Haunting and the Sociological Imagination*. 2nd ed. Minneapolis: University of Minnesota Press, 2008.
Gramsci, Antonio. *Selections from the Prison Notebooks*. Translated and edited by Quintin Hoare and Geoffrey Nowell Smith. New York: International, 1971.
Green, Archie. *Wobblies, Pile Butts, and Other Heroes: Laborlore Explorations*. Urbana: University of Illinois Press, 1993.
Green, Rayna. "Rosebuds of the Plateau: Frank Matsura and the Fainting Couch Aesthetic." In *Partial Recall: Photographs of Native North Americans*, edited by Lucy R. Lippard, 47–53. New York: New Press, 1992.
Grinëv, Andrei V. "The Distribution of Alcohol among the Natives of Russian America." *Arctic Anthropology* 47, no. 2 (2010): 69–79.
Gruening, Ernest. *The State of Alaska*. New York: Random House, 1954.
Grummett, Karleen. *Quiet Defiance: Alaska's Empty Chair Story*. Anchorage, AK: A.T. Publishing and Printing, 2016.
Guimary, Donald L. *Marumina Trabaho: A History of Labor in Alaska's Salmon Canning Industry*. Lincoln: iUniverse, Inc., 2006.
Hall, Greg. *Harvest Wobblies: The Industrial Workers of the World and Agricultural Laborers in the American West, 1905–1930*. Corvallis: Oregon State University Press, 2001.
Hallock, Charles. *Our New Alaska; Or, the Seward Purchase Vindicated*. New York: Forest and Stream, 1886.
Hansen, Christian, Catherine Needham, and Bill Nichols. "Pornography, Ethnography, and the Discourses of Power." In *Representing Reality: Issues and Concepts in Documentary*, edited by Bill Nichols, 201–28. Bloomington: Indiana University Press, 1991.
Harley, J. Brian. "Rereading the Maps of the Columbian Encounter." *Annals of the Association of American Geographers* 82, no. 3 (September 1992): 522–36.
Hartman, Saidiya. *Scenes of Subjection: Terror, Slavery, and Self-Making in Nineteenth-Century America*. Oxford: Oxford University Press, 1997.
Haven, Samuel F. *Archaeology of the United States, or Sketches, Historical and Bibliographical, of the Progress of Information and Opinion Respecting Vestiges of Antiquity in the United States*. Philadelphia: T.K. and P.G. Collins, 1855.
Haycox, Stephen. "'Races of a Questionable Ethnical Type': Origins of the Jurisdiction of the U.S. Bureau of Education in Alaska, 1867–1885." *Pacific Northwest Quarterly* 75, no. 4 (October 1984): 156–63.
———. *Alaska: An American Colony*. Seattle: University of Washington Press, 2002.
Hayes, Ernestine. *Blonde Indian: An Alaska Native Memoir*. Tucson: University of Arizona Press, 2006.
———. "Waiting Room." *Forum: The Magazine of the Alaska Humanities Forum* (Spring 2017): 23–24.
Haywood, William D. *Bill Haywood's Book: The Autobiography of William D. Haywood*. New York: International Publishers, 1929.
Herbert, Christopher. "'Life's Prizes Are by Labor Got': Risk, Reward, and White Manliness in the California Gold Rush." *Pacific Historical Review* 80, no. 3 (August 2011): 339–68.

Higginson, Ella. *Alaska: The Great Country*. New York: Macmillan Company, 1926.
Hikido, Alice Tanaka. "Shonosuke & Nobu Tanaka." In *Gastineau Channel Memories: 1880–1959*, edited by Pioneer Book Committee, 499–500. Juneau, AK: Pioneer Book Committee, 2001.
Hinckley, Ted C. "The Inside Passage: A Popular Gilded Age Tour." *Pacific Northwest Quarterly* 56, no. 2 (April 1965): 67–74.
———. "Prospectors, Profits, & Prejudice." *American West* 2 (Spring 1965): 58–65.
———. "The Canoe Rocks—We Do Not Know What Will Become of Us." *Western Historical Quarterly* 1, no. 3 (July 1970): 265–90.
———. *The Americanization of Alaska, 1867–1897*. Palo Alto: Pacific Books, 1972.
———. "William Henry Seward and His Sitka Address of August 12, 1869: Notes on the Heretofore Unpublished and Probably Correct Version." In *Alaska and Japan: Perspectives of Past and Present*, edited by Tsuguo Arai, 49–61. Anchorage: Alaska Methodist University Press, 1972.
———. Review of *Alaska: An American Colony*, by Stephen Haycox. *Western Historical Quarterly* 34, no. 3 (Autumn 2003): 378–79.
Holm, Bill. *Northwest Coast Indian Art: An Analysis of Form*. Seattle: University of Washington Press, 1965.
Hong, Grace Kyungwon, and Roderick A. Ferguson, eds. *Strange Affinities: The Gender and Sexual Politics of Comparative Racialization*. Durham, NC: Duke University Press, 2011.
hoʻomanawanui, kuʻualoha. "This Land Is Your Land, This Land Was My Land: Kanaka Maoli versus Settler Representations of ʻĀina in Contemporary Literature of Hawaiʻi." In *Asian Settler Colonialism: From Local Governance to the Habits of Everyday Life in Hawaiʻi*, edited by Candace Fujikane and Jonathan Y. Okamura, 116–54. Honolulu: University of Hawaiʻi Press, 2008.
Hubbard, Bernard R. *Cradle of the Storms*. New York: Dodd, Mead, 1935.
Huhndorf, Shari M. *Going Native: Indians in the American Cultural Imagination*. Ithaca, NY: Cornell University Press, 2001.
———. *Mapping the Americas: The Transnational Politics of Contemporary Native Culture*. Ithaca, NY: Cornell University Press, 2009.
Ichioka, Yuji. "Introduction." In *Ganbatte: Sixty-Year Struggle of a Kibei Worker*, by Karl G. Yoneda, xi–xvii. Los Angeles: Resource Development and Publications, Asian American Studies Center UCLA, 1983.
———. *The Issei: The World of the First Generation Japanese Immigrants, 1885–1924*. New York: The Free Press, 1988.
Industrial Workers of the World. *Founding Convention of the Industrial Workers of the World*. New York: Merit Publishers, 1969.
Ingersoll, Ernest. *Gold Fields of the Klondike: And the Wonders of Alaska*. Philadelphia: Edgewood, 1897.
Inouye, Ronald K. "For Immediate Sale: Tokyo Bathhouse—How World War II Affected Alaska's Japanese Civilians." In *Alaska at War, 1941–1945: The Forgotten War Remembered*, edited by Fern Chandonnet, 259–63. Fairbanks: University of Alaska Press, 2008.
Inouye, Ronald K., Carol Hoshiko, and Kazumi Hashiki. *Alaska's Japanese Pioneers: Faces, Voices, Stories: A Synopsis of Selected Oral History Transcripts*. Fairbanks: Alaska's Japanese Pioneers Research Project, 1994.

Irmscher, Christoph. *Louis Agassiz: Creator of American Science*. Boston: Houghton Mifflin Harcourt, 2013.

Isaac, Allan Punzalan. *American Tropics: Articulating Filipino America*. Minneapolis: University of Minnesota Press, 2006.

Ismail, Qadri. *Abiding by Sri Lanka: On Peace, Place, and Postcoloniality*. Minneapolis: University of Minnesota Press, 2005.

Jackson, Sheldon. *Alaska, and Missions on the North Pacific Coast*. New York: Dodd, Mead, & Company, 1880.

Jafri, Beenash. "Desire, Settler Colonialism, and the Racialized Cowboy." *American Indian Culture and Research Journal* 37, no. 2 (2013): 73–86.

Jonaitis, Aldona. *Art of the Northern Tlingit*. Seattle: University of Washington Press, 1986.

Jones, Livingston F. *A Study of the Thlingets of Alaska*. New York: Fleming H. Revell, 1914.

Jones, Zachary R. "'Search For and Destroy': U.S. Army Relations with Alaska's Tlingit Indians and the Kake War of 1869." *Ethnohistory* 60, no. 1 (Winter 2013): 1–26.

———. "Battlefield Alaska: The U.S. Army's 1869 Bombardment of the Tlingit Village of Khaachxhan.áak'w." *Alaska History* 34, no. 1 (Spring 2019): 32–55.

Jung, Moon-Ho. *Coolies and Cane: Race, Labor, and Sugar in the Age of Emancipation*. Baltimore: Johns Hopkins University Press, 2006.

Kan, Sergei. "'It's Only Half a Mile from Savagery to Civilization': American Tourists and Southeastern Alaska Natives in the Late 19th Century." In *Coming to Shore: Northwest Coast Ethnology, Traditions, and Visions*, edited by Marie Mauzé, Michael E. Harkin, and Sergei Kan, 201–20. Lincoln: University of Nebraska Press, 2004.

———. *A Russian American Photographer in Tlingit Country: Vincent Soboleff in Alaska*. Norman: University of Oklahoma Press, 2013.

Kaplan, Amy. *The Anarchy of Empire in the Making of U.S. Culture*. Cambridge, MA: Harvard University Press, 2002.

Karuka, Manu. *Empire's Tracks: Indigenous Nations, Chinese Workers, and the Transcontinental Railroad*. Oakland: University of California Press, 2019.

Kauanui, J. Kēhaulani. *Hawaiian Blood: Colonialism and the Politics of Sovereignty and Indigeneity*. Durham, NC: Duke University Press, 2008.

Kelly, Sheila. *Treadwell Gold: An Alaska Saga of Riches and Ruin*. Fairbanks: University of Alaska Press, 2010.

Kim, Claire Jean. *Bitter Fruit: The Politics of Black-Korean Conflict in New York City*. New Haven, CT: Yale University Press, 2003.

Kim, Jodi. *Ends of Empire: Asian American Critique and the Cold War*. Minneapolis: University of Minnesota Press, 2010.

———. "Settler Modernity's Spatial Exceptions: The US POW Camp, Metapolitical Authority, and Ha Jin's *War Trash*." *American Quarterly* 69, no. 3 (September 2017): 569–87.

———. "Settler Modernity, Debt Imperialism, and the Necropolitics of the Promise." *Social Text* 36, no. 2 (June 2018): 41–61.

Kingston, Maxine Hong. *China Men*. New York: Alfred A. Knopf, 1980.

Kirtland, John C., and David F. Coffin Jr. *The Relocation and Internment of the Aleuts During World War II*. Anchorage, AK: Aleutian/Pribilof Association, 1981.

Knack, Martha C., and Alice Littlefield. "Native American Labor: Retrieving History, Rethinking Theory." In *Native Americans and Wage Labor: Ethnohistorical Perspectives*, edited by Alice Littlefield and Martha C. Knack, 3–44. Norman: University of Oklahoma Press, 1996.

Kohlhoff, Dean. *When the Wind Was a River: Aleut Evacuation in World War II*. Seattle: University of Washington Press, 1995.

Lai, Larissa. "Epistemologies of Respect: A Poetics of Asian/Indigenous Relation." In *Critical Collaborations: Indigeneity, Diaspora, and Ecology in Canadian Literary Studies*, edited by Smaro Kamboureli and Christl Verduyn, 99–126. Waterloo, ON: Wilfrid Laurier University Press, 2014.

Lai, Paul, and Lindsey Clair Smith, eds. "Alternative Contact: Indigeneity, Globalism, and American Studies." Special issue, *American Quarterly* 62, no. 3 (September 2010).

Lain, B. D. "The Decline of Russian America's Colonial Society." *Western Historical Quarterly* 7, no. 2 (April 1976): 143–53.

Lang, George. *Making Wawa: The Genesis of Chinook Jargon*. Vancouver: University of British Columbia Press, 2008.

Langdon, Steve J. *The Native People of Alaska: Traditional Living in a Northern Land*. Anchorage, AK: Greatland Graphics, 2002.

Larson, Kate Clifford. *Bound for the Promised Land: Harriet Tubman, Portrait of an American Hero*. New York: Ballantine, 2003.

Lawrence, Bonita, and Enakshi Dua. "Decolonizing Antiracism." *Social Justice* 32, no. 4 (2005): 120–43.

Le, Quynh Nhu. *Unsettled Solidarities: Asian and Indigenous Cross-Representations in the Américas*. Philadelphia: Temple University Press, 2019.

Lee, Erika. *At America's Gates: Chinese Immigration during the Exclusion Era, 1882–1943*. Chapel Hill: University of North Carolina Press, 2005.

Lee, Nella. "Impossible Mission: A History of the Legal Control of Native Drinking in Alaska." *Wicazo Sa Review* 12, no. 2 (Autumn 1997): 95–109.

Lee, Rachel C. *The Americas of Asian American Literature: Gendered Fictions of Nation and Transnation*. Princeton, NJ: Princeton University Press, 1999.

Lee, Robert G. "The Hidden World of Asian Immigrant Radicalism." In *The Immigrant Left in the United States*, edited by Paul Buhle and Dan Georgakas, 256–87. Albany: State University of New York Press, 1996.

———. *Orientals: Asian Americans in Popular Culture*. Philadelphia: Temple University Press, 1999.

Lee, Sang Hyun. *From a Liminal Place: An Asian American Theology*. Minneapolis, MN: Fortress Press, 2010.

Leier, Mark. "'We Must Do Away with Racial Prejudice and Imaginary Boundary Lines': British Columbia Wobblies before the First World War." In *Wobblies of the World: A Global History of the I.W.W.*, edited by Peter Cole, David Struthers, and Kenyon Zimmer, 155–67. London: Pluto Press, 2017.

Leonard, Beth Ginondidoy, Jeane Táaw Xíwaa Breinig, Lenora Ac'aralek Carpluk, Sharon Chilux Lind, and Maria Shaa Tláa Williams, eds. *Transforming the University: Alaska Native Studies in the 21st Century*. Minneapolis, MN: Two Harbors, 2014.

Leong, Karen J., and Myla Vicenti Carpio, eds. "Carceral States: Converging Indigenous and Asian Experiences in the Americas." Special issue, *Amerasia Journal* 42, no. 1 (2016).

Levi, Steven C. *Boom and Bust in the Alaska Goldfields*. Westport, CT: Praeger, 2008.

Lo, Marie. "Model Minorities, Models of Resistance: Native Figures in Asian Canadian Literature." *Canadian Literature* 196 (2008): 96–112.

London, Jack. "To Build a Fire." *Century Magazine* 76 (August 1908): 525–34.

———. *Call of the Wild*. Mineola, NY: Dover, 1990. First published 1903 by Macmillan (New York).

Lorde, Audre. *Zami: A New Spelling of My Name*. Watertown, MA: Persephone Press, 1982.

Lowe, Lisa. *Immigrant Acts: On Asian American Cultural Politics*. Durham, NC: Duke University Press, 1996.

———. "The Intimacies of Four Continents." In *Haunted by Empire: Geographies of Intimacy in North American History*, edited by Ann Laura Stoler, 191–212. Durham, NC: Duke University Press, 2006.

———. *The Intimacies of Four Continents*. Durham, NC: Duke University Press, 2015.

Lye, Colleen. *America's Asia: Racial Form and American Literature, 1893–1945*. Princeton, NJ: Princeton University Press, 2005.

Lyman, Christopher M. *The Vanishing Race and Other Illusions: Photographs of Indians by Edward S. Curtis*. New York: Pantheon Books, 1982.

Markovitz, Jonathan. *Legacies of Lynching: Racial Violence and Memory*. Minneapolis: University of Minnesota Press, 2004.

Masson, Jack, and Donald Guimary. "Asian Labor Contractors in the Alaskan Canned Salmon Industry." *Labor History* 22, no. 3 (1981): 377–97.

Mawani, Renisa. *Colonial Proximities: Crossracial Encounters and Juridical Truths in British Columbia, 1871–1921*. Vancouver: University of British Columbia Press, 2009.

Mbembe, Achille. "Necropolitics." *Public Culture* 15, no. 1 (Winter 2003): 11–40.

McClintock, Anne. *Imperial Leather: Race, Gender, and Sexuality in the Imperial Conquest*. New York: Routledge, 1995.

McClintock, James I. *White Logic: Jack London's Short Stories*. Grand Rapids, MI: Wolf House Books, 1975.

Medak-Saltzman, Danika, and Antonio T. Tiongson Jr., eds. "Racial Comparativism Reconsidered." Special issue, *Critical Ethnic Studies* 1, no. 2 (Spring 2015).

Metcalfe, Peter. *A Dangerous Idea: The Alaska Native Brotherhood and the Struggle for Indigenous Rights*. Fairbanks: University of Alaska Press, 2014.

Miller, Gwenn A. "'The Perfect Mistress of Russian Economy': Sighting the Intimate on a Colonial Alaskan Terrain, 1784–1821." In *Haunted by Empire: Geographies of Intimacy in North American History*, edited by Ann Laura Stoler, 297–324. Durham, NC: Duke University Press, 2006.

———. *Kodiak Kreol: Communities of Empire in Early Russian America*. Ithaca, NY: Cornell University Press, 2010.

Mimura, Glen A. "A Dying West? Reimagining the Frontier in Frank Matsura's Photography, 1903–1913." *American Quarterly* 62, no. 3 (September 2010): 687–716.

Mitchell, Donald Craig. *Sold American: The Story of Alaska Natives and Their Land, 1867–1959*. Hanover, CT: University Press of New England, 1997.

Moosang, Faith. *First Son: Portraits by C.D. Hoy*. Vancouver, BC: Presentation House Gallery and Arsenal Pulp Press, 1999.
Morgensen, Scott Lauria. "The Biopolitics of Settler Colonialism: Right Here, Right Now." *Settler Colonial Studies* 1, no. 1 (2011): 52–76.
———. *Spaces between Us*. Minneapolis: University of Minnesota Press, 2011.
Morse, Kathryn. "Review: *Alaska: An American Colony*." *Oregon Historical Quarterly* 104, no. 1 (Spring 2003): 128–29.
Muir, John. *Travels in Alaska*. Boston: Houghton Mifflin, 1915.
———. *John of the Mountains: The Unpublished Journals of John Muir*. Edited by Linnie March Wolfe. Madison: University of Wisconsin Press, 1979.
Murphy, D. A. "Frontier Incidents at Juneau." In *Sourdough Sagas: The Journals, Memoirs, Tales, and Recollections of the Earliest Alaskan Gold Miners, 1833–1923*, edited by Herbert L. Heller, 25–27. Cleveland, OH: World Publishing Company, 1967.
Naske, Claus-M. "Review: *Alaska: An American Colony*." *Pacific Northwest Quarterly* 95, no. 1 (Winter 2003/2004): 42–43.
Naske, Claus-M., and Herman E. Slotnick. *Alaska: A History of the 49th State*. Norman: University of Oklahoma Press, 1979.
Nebolon, Juliet. "'Life Given Straight from the Heart': Settler Militarism, Biopolitics, and Public Health in Hawai'i during World War II." *American Quarterly* 69, no. 1 (March 2017): 23–45.
Neubauer, Carol E. "Developing Ties to the Past: Photography and Other Sources of Information in Maxine Hong Kingston's China Men." *MELUS* 10, no. 4 (Winter 1983): 17–36.
Neylan, Susan. "'Choose Your Flag': Perspectives on the Tsimshian Migration from Metlakatla, British Columbia to New Metlakatla, Alaska, 1887." In *New Histories of Old: Changing Perspectives on Canada's Native Pasts*, edited by Ted Binnema and Susan Neylan, 196–219. Vancouver: University of British Columbia Press, 2007.
Ngai, Mae N. *Impossible Subjects: Illegal Aliens and the Making of Modern America*. Princeton, NJ: Princeton University Press, 2004.
Norrgard, Chantal. *Seasons of Change: Labor, Treaty Rights, and Ojibwe Nationhood*. Chapel Hill: University of North Carolina Press, 2014.
O'Brien, Jean M. *Firsting and Lasting: Writing Indians Out of Existence in New England*. Minneapolis: University of Minnesota Press, 2010.
Omatsu, Glenn. "Racism or Solidarity? Unions and Asian Immigrant Workers." *Radical Teacher* 46 (1995): 33–37.
O'Neill, Colleen. *Working the Navajo Way: Labor and Culture in the Twentieth Century*. Lawrence: University Press of Kansas, 2005.
Paolino, Ernest N. *The Foundation of American Empire: William Henry Seward and U.S. Foreign Policy*. Ithaca, NY: Cornell University Press, 1973.
Patel, Shaista. "Complicating the Tale of 'Two Indians': Mapping 'South Asian' Complicity in White Settler Colonialism along the Axis of Caste and Anti-Blackness." *Theory & Event* 19, no. 4 (2016). https://www.muse.jhu.edu/article/633278.
Pfaelzer, Jean. *Driven Out: The Forgotten War against Chinese Americans*. New York: Random House, 2007.

Pfeifer, Michael J., ed. *Lynching beyond Dixie: American Mob Violence outside the South.* Urbana: University of Illinois Press, 2013.

Piatote, Beth H. *Domestic Subjects: Gender, Citizenship, and Law in Native American Literature.* New Haven, CT: Yale University Press, 2013.

Pierce, W. H. *Thirteen Years of Travel and Exploration in Alaska, 1877–1889.* Anchorage: Alaska Northwest Publishing, 1977. First published 1890 by Journal Publishing (Lawrence, Kansas).

Pierrepont, Edward. *Fifth Avenue to Alaska.* New York: G.P. Putnam's Sons, 1884.

Pike, Warburton. *Through the Subarctic Forest: A Record of a Canoe Journey from Fort Wrangel to the Pelly Lakes and down the Yukon River to the Bering Sea.* London: Edward Arnold, 1896.

Postone, Moishe. *Time, Labor, and Social Domination: A Reinterpretation of Marx's Critical Theory.* Cambridge, UK: Cambridge University Press, 1993.

Potter, Jean. *Alaska under Arms.* New York: Macmillan Company, 1942.

Pratt, Mary Louise. *Imperial Eyes: Travel Writing and Transculturation.* 2nd ed. New York: Routledge, 2007.

Raibmon, Paige. *Authentic Indians: Episodes of Encounter from the Late-Nineteenth-Century Northwest Coast.* Durham, NC: Duke University Press, 2005.

Reedy-Maschner, Katherine L. *Aleut Identities: Tradition and Modernity in an Indigenous Fishery.* Montreal: McGill–Queen's University Press, 2010.

Renshaw, Patrick. *The Wobblies: The Story of the I.W.W. and Syndicalism in the United States.* Rev. ed. Chicago: Ivan R. Dee, 1999.

Rickard, T. A. *Through the Yukon and Alaska.* San Francisco: Mining and Scientific Press, 1909.

Rifkin, Mark. "The Erotics of Sovereignty." In *Queer Indigenous Studies*, edited by Qwo-Li Driskill, Chris Finley, Brian Joseph Gilley, and Scott Lauria Morgensen, 172–89. Tucson: University of Arizona Press, 2011.

———. *Settler Common Sense: Queerness and Everyday Colonialism in the American Renaissance.* Minneapolis: University of Minnesota Press, 2014.

———. *Beyond Settler Time: Temporal Sovereignty and Indigenous Self-Determination.* Durham, NC: Duke University Press, 2017.

Robinson, Cedric. *Black Marxism: The Making of the Black Radical Tradition.* Chapel Hill: University of North Carolina Press, 1983.

Roppel, Patricia. "Salting Salmon at Boca de Quadra." *Alaska Southeaster* (December 1998): 10–11.

Russell, Caskey. "Tools of Self Definition: Nora Marks Dauenhauer's 'How to Make Good Baked Salmon.'" *Studies in American Indian Literatures* 16, no. 3 (Fall 2004): 29–46.

Said, Edward. *Orientalism.* New York: Vintage Books, 1978.

Saranillio, Dean Itsuji. "Why Asian Settler Colonialism Matters: A Thought Piece on Critiques, Debates, and Indigenous Difference." *Settler Colonial Studies* 3, nos. 3/4 (2013): 280–94.

———. *Unsustainable Empire: Alternative Histories of Hawai'i Statehood.* Durham, NC: Duke University Press, 2018.

Scidmore, Eliza. *Alaska, Its Southern Coast and the Sitkan Archipelago.* Boston: D. Lothrop, 1885.

Service, Robert. *The Spell of the Yukon and Other Verses*. New York: Barse and Hopkins, 1907.
Seward, William H. *Immigrant White Free Labor, or Imported Black African Slave Labor*. Washington, DC: Buell and Blanchard, 1857.
———. *Our North American States, Speeches of William H. Seward in Alaska, Vancouver's [Island], and Oregon, August 1869*. Washington, DC: Philip and Solomons, 1869.
Shah, Nayan. *Stranger Intimacy: Contesting Race, Sexuality, and the Law in the North American West*. Berkeley: University of California Press, 2011.
Shaw, Pringle. *Ramblings in California*. Toronto: James Bain, 1857.
Shigematsu, Setsu, and Keith Camacho, eds. *Militarized Currents: Toward a Decolonized Future in Asia and the Pacific*. Minneapolis: University of Minnesota Press, 2010.
Silva, Noenoe K. *Aloha Betrayed: Native Hawaiian Resistance to American Colonialism*. Durham, NC: Duke University Press, 2004.
Simpson, Audra. *Mohawk Interruptus: Political Life across the Borders of Settler States*. Durham, NC: Duke University Press, 2014.
———. "The State Is a Man: Theresa Spence, Loretta Saunders, and the Gender of Settler Sovereignty." *Theory & Event* 19, no. 4 (2016). https:www.muse.jhu.edu/article/633280.
Simpson, Caroline Chung. *An Absent Presence: Japanese Americans in Postwar American Culture, 1945–1960*. Durham, NC: Duke University Press, 2002.
Simpson, Leanne Betasamosake. *As We Have Always Done: Indigenous Freedom through Radical Resistance*. Minneapolis: University of Minnesota Press, 2017.
Simpson, Sherry. *Juneau*. Anchorage: Alaska Geographic Society, 1990.
Smith, Mary C., and Louise Brinck Harrington, eds. *I Never Did Mind the Rain: A Collection of Oral Histories from Southern Southeast Alaska*. Ketchikan, AK: Friends of Ketchikan Library, 1995.
Stark, Heidi Kiiwetinepinesiik. "Criminal Empire: The Making of the Savage in a Lawless Land." *Theory & Event* 19, no. 4 (Fall 2016). https://muse.jhu.edu/article/633282.
Steeves, Paulette. "Decolonizing the Past and Present of the Western Hemisphere (The Americas)." *Archaeologies* 11, no. 1 (2015): 42–69.
Stoler, Ann Laura. *Carnal Knowledge and Imperial Power: Race and the Intimate in Colonial Rule*. Berkeley: University of California Press, 2002.
———. "Intimidations of Empire: Predicaments of the Tactile and Unseen." In *Haunted by Empire: Geographies of Intimacy in North American History*, edited by Ann Laura Stoler, 1–22. Durham, NC: Duke University Press, 2006.
Stone, David, and Brenda Stone. *Hard Rock Gold: The Story of the Great Mines That Were the Heartbeat of Juneau*. Juneau, AK: City and Borough of Juneau, Juneau Centennial Committee, 1980.
Swineford, A. P. *Alaska, Its History, Climate, and Natural Resources*. Chicago: Rand McNally, 1898.
Takaki, Ronald. *Strangers from a Different Shore: A History of Asian Americans*. New York: Little, Brown, and Company, 1998.
Taylor, Charles M., Jr. *Touring Alaska and the Yellowstone*. Philadelphia: George W. Jacobs, 1901.
Tchen, John Kuo Wei. *New York before Chinatown: Orientalism and the Shaping of American Culture, 1776–1882*. Baltimore: Johns Hopkins University Press, 1999.

Thomas, David Hurst. *Skull Wars: Kennewick Man, Archaeology, and the Battle for Native American Identity*. New York: Basic Books, 2001.

Thomas, Margaret. "Was Kayamori a Spy?" *Alaska* (November 1995): 48–54.

———. *Picture Man: The Legacy of Southeast Alaska Photographer Shoki Kayamori*. Fairbanks: University of Alaska Press, 2015.

Thompson, Fred. *The I.W.W., Its First Fifty Years (1905–1955)*. Chicago: Industrial Workers of the World, 1955.

Thornton, Thomas S. *Being and Place among the Tlingit*. Seattle: University of Washington Press; Juneau, AK: Sealaska Heritage Institute, 2008.

Thrush, Coll. *Native Seattle: Histories from the Crossing-Over Place*. Seattle: University of Washington Press, 2007.

Ting, Jennifer. "Bachelor Society: Deviant Heterosexuality and Asian American Historiography." In *Privileging Positions: The Sites of Asian American Studies*, edited by Gary Okihiro et al., 271–79. Pullman: Washington State University Press, 1995.

Tiongson, Antonio T., Jr. "Asian American Studies, Comparative Racialization, and Settler Colonial Critique." *Journal of Asian American Studies* 22, no. 3 (October 2019): 419–43.

Trask, Haunani-Kay. *From a Native Daughter: Colonialism and Sovereignty in Hawai'i*. Honolulu: University of Hawai'i Press, 1999.

Tuck, Eve. "ANCSA as X-Mark: Surface and Subsurface Claims of the Alaska Native Claims Settlement Act." In *Transforming the University: Alaska Native Studies in the 21st Century*, edited by Beth Ginondidoy Leonard et al., 240–72. Minneapolis, MN: Two Harbors, 2014.

Tuck, Eve, and K. Wayne Yang. "Decolonization Is Not a Metaphor." *Decolonization: Indigeneity, Education, and Society* 1, no. 1 (2012): 1–40.

Turner, Victor W. *Ritual Process: Structure and Anti-Structure*. Ithaca, NY: Cornell University Press, 1969.

Upadhyay, Nishant. "Making of 'Model' South Asians on the Tar Sands: Intersections of Race, Caste, and Indigeneity." *Critical Ethnic Studies* 5, nos. 1/2 (Spring/Fall 2019): 152–73.

Veracini, Lorenzo. *Settler Colonialism: A Theoretical Overview*. Basingstoke, UK: Palgrave Macmillan, 2010.

Vimalassery, Manu, Juliana Hu Pegues, and Alyosha Goldstein. "On Colonial Unknowing." *Theory & Event*, no. 4 (Fall 2016). https://www.muse.jhu.edu/article/633283.

Vizenor, Gerald. *Manifest Manners: Narratives on Postindian Survivance*. Lincoln: University of Nebraska Press, 1999.

Voluck, David Avraham. "First Peoples of the Tongass: Law and Traditional Subsistence Way of Life." In *The Book of the Tongass*, edited by Carolyn Servid and Donald Snow, 89–118. Minneapolis, MN: Milkweed Editions, 1999.

Wardman, George. *A Trip to Alaska: A Narrative of What Was Seen and Heard during a Summer Cruise in Alaskan Waters*. San Francisco: Samuel Carson, 1884.

Wells, Ida B. *Southern Horrors: Lynch Law in All Its Phases*. New York: New York Age Print, 1892.

———. *A Red Record: Tabulated Statistics and Alleged Causes of Lynchings in the United States, 1892–1893–1894*. Chicago, 1895.

Whitehead, John S. *Completing the Union: Alaska, Hawai'i, and the Battle for Statehood.* Albuquerque: University of New Mexico Press, 2004.
Wickersham, James. *Old Yukon: Tales-Trails-and Trials.* Washington, DC: Washington Law Book, 1938.
Williams, Carol J. *Framing the West: Race, Gender, and the Photographic Frontier in the Pacific Northwest.* Oxford: Oxford University Press, 2003.
Williams, Maria Shaa Tláa. "Alaska and Its People: An Introduction." In *The Alaska Native Reader: History, Culture, Politics,* edited by Maria Shaa Tláa Williams, 1–11. Durham, NC: Duke University Press, 2009.
Williams, Maria Shaa Tláa, ed. *The Alaska Native Reader: History, Culture, Politics.* Durham, NC: Duke University Press, 2009.
Williams, Raymond. *Marxism and Literature.* Oxford: Oxford University Press, 1977.
Wolfe, Patrick. *Settler Colonialism and the Transformation of Anthropology: The Politics and Poetics of an Ethnographic Event.* London: Cassell, 1999.
———. "Settler Colonialism and the Elimination of the Native." *Journal of Genocide Research* 8, no. 4 (December 2006): 387–409.
Wong, Rita. "Decolonizasian: Reading Asian and First Nations Relations in Literature." *Canadian Literature* 199 (2008): 158–80.
Wood, Amy Louise. *Lynching and Spectacle: Witnessing Racial Violence in America, 1890–1940.* Chapel Hill: University of North Carolina Press, 2009.
Woodman, Abby Johnson. *Picturesque Alaska: A Journal of a Tour among the Mountains, Seas and Islands of the Northwest, from San Francisco to Sitka.* Boston: Houghton Mifflin, 1890.
Wu, Frank. *Yellow: Race in America beyond Black and White.* Rev. ed. New York: Basic Books, 2003.
Wyatt, Victoria. "Alaskan Indian Wage Earners in the 19th Century." *Pacific Northwest Quarterly* 78, nos. 1/2 (1978): 43–49.
———. *Images from the Inside Passage: An Alaskan Portrait by Winter & Pond.* Seattle: University of Washington Press; Juneau: Alaska State Library, 1989.
Yaw, Leslie W. *Sixty Years in Alaska.* Caldwell, IA: Caxton Printers and Sheldon Jackson College Press, 1985.
Yoneda, Karu [Karl]. *Zai-Bei Nihonjin rodosha no rekishi [History of Japanese laborers in America].* Tokyo: Shin Nihon Shuppansha, 1967.
———. "One Hundred Years of Japanese Labor in the U.S.A." In *Roots: An Asian American Reader,* edited by Amy Tachiki et al., 150–58. Los Angeles: University of California, Los Angeles, 1971.
———. *Ganbatte: Sixty-Year Struggle of a Kibei Worker.* Los Angeles: University of California, Los Angeles, Asian American Studies Center, 1983.
Yoneyama, Lisa. "Toward a Decolonial Genealogy of the Transpacific." *American Quarterly* 69, no. 3 (September 2017): 471–82.
Young, S. Hall. *Hall Young of Alaska: "The Mushing Parson."* New York: Fleming H. Revell, 1927.
Yu, Henry. "Global Migrants and the New Pacific Canada." *International Journal* 64, no. 4 (Autumn 2009): 1011–26.
Yule, Emma Sarepta. "China Joe." *Pacific Monthly* 24, no. 2 (August 1910): 211–13.

Index

Page numbers in *italics* refer to illustrations.

Abo, Mary Tanaka, 155
abolition, 27–28
Abraham, Elaine Chuu Shah, 142, 181n70
absence, 2–3, 23, 84, 90–91, 94–95
Acosta, José de, 24
Adams, Bert, Sr., 137, 181n49
Adams, Lorraine, 137, 144, 181n49
African slave trade, 11, 27–28, 163n24
Agassiz, Louis, 25, 164n21, 166–67n78
Akagi, Kiichi "Henry," 158
Akagi, William, 158
Alaska: as "Last Frontier," 2, 16, 49, 51; liminality of, 14, 113; militarization of, 140–41; purchase of, 2–3, 5, 14–15, 25, 27–28; Russian occupation of, 15; in social and cultural imagination, 2; statehood movement in, 9–10
Alaska Act of 1900, 55
Alaska Native(s): racialized as Asian, 5–6, 21–22; cultural groups of, 3–4, *4*; exceptionalism, 22, 29, 42, 49; languages spoken by, 3; legal status of, 5; orientalism and, 132; studies, 4, 94, 161n5, 181n54; Sumner on, 25–27; as term, xv–xvi. *See also* colonialism; Indigenous; labor; racialization; Tlingit; Unangax̂
Alaska Native Brotherhood (ANB), 125, 137–39, 141
Alaska Native Sisterhood (ANS), 81, 125, 137–38
Albert, Dick, *126*, 179n22
alcohol, 44–45, 75–77, 141
Aleut, 26, 144; as term, xvi
Aleutian Islands, 140–41, 144–45
America Is in the Heart (Bulosan), 84, 111–16

American Civil Liberties Act of 1988, 150
American Federation of Labor, 100
American Indians, 6, 31–32, 102–4. *See also* First Nation peoples
American Indian studies, 4
Americanization of Alaska, The (Hinckley), 173n21
ANB. *See* Alaska Native Brotherhood (ANB)
Anderson, Benedict, 55, 57, 60
ANS. *See* Alaska Native Sisterhood (ANS)
anthropology, 25, 41–42, 120, 135–36
Arnett, Jessica Leslie, 15
Asian: Alaska Natives racialized as, 5–6, 21–22; immigrants, 6, 14, 32, 38–39, 42, 53, 61–63, 66–67, 74, 89, 99; sexuality, 111–12; as term, xv. *See also* Chinese immigrants
Asian American(s): as labor force, 163n29; as liminal figures, 121; as term, xv. *See also* Chinese immigrants; Filipinx; Japanese Americans
Asian American studies, 6–7, 91–94, 107, 111, 120–21
Asian Canadian studies, 7
Asianness, 31–32, 35, 37, 39, 42–43, 48–49, 132
"Asia-Pacific," 123
Asiatic: as term, xv
assimilation, 22–23, 37, 72–73, 76–77, 122, 132
authenticity, 13, 34, 101, 165n45

Bailey, George, 63–64
Bancroft, Herbert Howe, 88–89
Bartlett, E. L., 145

Beattie, Ed, 170n52
Bering Land Bridge theory, 14, 20, 40–43, 156, 164n5, 164n22, 166n78
Bhabha, Homi, 29–30, 40
Bhattacharya, Tithi, 115
bilingualism, 38
biomythography, 51, 168n5
biopower, 70, 73
Black Americans, 71, 163n29, 171n79. *See also* slavery
Blonde Indian (Hayes), 23, 44–48, 158
Blue Scholars, 83
boarding schools, 19, 22–24, 36, 44–45, 134
Boas, Franz, 40–42, 137, 166n78
bootlegging, 75–76
Bow, Leslie, 121
"boys," 111–16
Brady, John G., 36
Brathwaite, Kamau, 10
Bremner, Don, 126–27, 129, 142–43
Bremner, George, 126, 179n22
Bremner, Harry K., 135
Bremner, John, Sr., 126
Brinton, Daniel Garrison, 166n78
Bruyneel, Kevin, 12–13, 122, 138
Buckner, Simon B., 151
Bulosan, Carlos, 84, 104, 111–16
Byrd, Jodi, 10–11, 15, 21, 31, 126, 139, 163n24

Callaham, Arthur B., 58
Call of the Wild (London), 58
Camacho, Keith, 151
Campbell, Robert, 35, 164n10
Canada, 7–8, 61–64, 66, 73, 120, 132, 164n5. *See also* First Nation peoples
canneries: absence and, 90–91; Alaska Natives in, 87–89; alcohol and, 76; Chinese laborers in, 87–88; Ketchikan, 85–88; in literature, 111–16; mechanization in, 174n43; in poetry, 104–5; tourism and, 32, 38–39, 42; unionization in, 83, 92, 98–104; whites in, 88; women in, 94–95, 105–9
capitalism, 11–12; absentee, 94; China Joe and, 53; colonial, 11, 39, 85, 89, 98, 106, 163n29; mimesis and, 29; print, 55–57; racial, 9–11, 17, 84, 108, 116, 146, 158
Cardiff, Gladys, 104
Carlson, Peter, 176n72
Carmack, George, 168n6
Case, William Howard, 128
chaos, 10
Chemawa Indian School, 23
Cherokee, 163n24
Chickasaw, 163n24
China Joe, 56; as baker, 55, 80; capitalism and, 53; colonialism and, 53–54, 65–66; disciplinary functions of, 63; as female, 68; gold rush and, 50–51, 53–54; identity of, 60–61; longevity of, as folktale, 81–82; making of, 54–61; orientalism and, 53; pedagogical function of, 59, 67; print culture and, 55–59; racialization and, 63, 68; violence and, 53, 68–69; as white, 68
China Men (Kingston), 51, 168n5
Chinese Exclusion Act, 57
Chinese, 6, 32, 38–39, 42, 53, 61–63, 66–67, 74, 89, 99
Chinook jargon, 20, 163n3
Choctaw, 163n24
Chong, Sylvia Shin Huey, 13
citizenship, 31, 37, 48, 72, 99, 119–20, 137, 154
Citizenship Act of 1924, 5, 137
Collis, Septima, 19–20, 22, 37
colonial accumulation, 85, 95–96, 116
colonialism: and Alaskan purchase, 2–3; arrivant, 10–12, 111, 113, 163n24; capitalism and, 39, 89, 98, 106; China Joe and, 53–54, 65–66; as cloaked process, 7; community and, 57; franchise, 148; mimicry and, 29–30; misogyny and, 114; place names and, 64; racialization and, 5–6, 12; settler colonialism *vs.*, 15; settler orientalism and, 36; sexuality and, 111–12; space-time, 12–16, 157; tourism and, 32. *See also* settler colonialism
colonialization, 24–29
Colyer, Vincent, 29–30, 165n39
Cook, James, 8
Cothran, Boyd, 171n76

Coulthard, Glen Sean, 85, 95–96, 151
Creek, 163n24
criminalization, 76, 112
Cruikshank, Julie, 35, 168n6
Curtis, Edward Sheriff, 132, 134, 137

Dall, William Healy, 33–34, 166n49
Dalton, George, 96–97
Darwin, Charles, 24
Dauenhauer, Nora Marks, 84, 87, 104–11, 177n83
Day, Iyko, 11–12, 85, 90–91, 163n29
death-world, 70, 75
dehumanization, 41, 74
De Jesús, Melinda, 112–13, 115
de Laguna, Frederica, 135
Deloria, Ella, 175n49
Deloria, Philip, 102
Deloria, Vine, Jr., 12
de Stoeckl, Eduard, 27
Dillingham, Brett, 170n52
disappearance, 13–14, 23, 40, 43, 75, 132, 156
discipline, 13, 36, 40, 48, 54, 63
Douglass, Frederick, 28
Downing, Mortimer, 101
Draper, Horace, 128
Dray, Philip, 71
Dua, Enakshi, 8
Dushkin, Dora, 150

Edwards, Sig, 141
elimination, 22–23, 46, 98
Ellis, Emma, 129, *130*, 139
Ellis, Jack, 129, *130*, 139
emancipation, 24–29
empiricism, 33–34
Empty Chair Project, 155–59
erasure, 69, 84, 91
Eskimo, as term, xv
ethnography, 25, 40–41, 48, 94, 129, 135–37
exceptionalism, xvi, 22, 28–29, 42, 49, 63, 68–69, 82, 132, 143

Fabian, Johannes, 24, 34
Fajardo, Kale Bantigue, 161n6

Farkas, Lena Achkwéi, 141
feminism, 24, 46–47, 109, 113, 115–16
Ferguson, Roderick, 80, 115
Ferguson, Susan, 97
fiction, in gold rush period, 52–53. *See also* literature
fictive kinship, 21–22, 104, 156
Filipinx: in *Blonde Indian*, 44–45; immigrants, 6; as term, xvi–xvii; workers, 42, 88, 92, 173n26. *See also* Bulosan, Carlos
Finck, Henry T., 33
Finley, Chris, 115–16
First Nation peoples: gold rush and, 51, 63, 66; studies, 7. *See also* Canada
Fish and Wildlife Service (FWS), 145, 148–49
"Five Civilized Tribes," 163n24
Foner, Philip, 100
Foucault, Michel, 24, 70
Frank, Oscar, Sr., 179n16
Friday, Chris, 94
Fujikane, Candace, 9
Furlow, Nancy, 151, 171n74
fur trade, 9, 26–27, 75, 149, 163n3, 165n23, 180n30
FWS. *See* Fish and Wildlife Service (FWS)

Geary Act, 57, 60, 69, 169n21
Gee, Lon Wun, *126*, 179n22
Geinax Éesh, 55
Ghost Dance movement, 103
Glave, Edward James, 35
Gmelch, Sharon Bohn, 128
Goeman, Mishuana, 46
gold rush, 50–81; China Joe and, 50–51, 53–54; Chinese labor and, 66–67; colonialism and, 52–54; effects of, 51; fiction and, 52–53; industrialization of, 66; Klondike, 51–52, 168n6; start of, 54–55; violence and, 53, 68–74, 76–79, 172n81; whites and, 63
Gonzales-Day, Ken, 72
Gordon, Avery, 143
Gramsci, Antonio, 34
Gruening, Ernest, 89–90

haa ḵusteeyí, 97, 127
Haida, 26, 29, 33, 35, 86, 137
haksuba, 10
Harriman, Edward Henry, 131–32
Harris, Richard, 54, 77, 168n16
Hawaiʻi, 3, 7–10, 27, 125, 162n6, 162n21, 183n105
Hawaiian studies, 9
Haycox, Stephen, 90–91, 94, 173n26
Hayes, Ernestine, 23–24, 44–48, 158
Haywood, William "Big Bill," 102–3, 176n72–176n73
hegemony, 10, 12, 29, 34, 46, 62, 140
Henniger, Sam, 126, 179n22
heteronormativity, 22, 91, 115
heteropatriarchy, 5, 22, 47–48, 110, 116
Hikido, Alice Tanaka, 159
Hinckley, Ted, 173n21
History of Alaska, 1730–1885 (Bancroft), 88–89
hoʻomanawanui, kuʻualoha, 9
homoeroticism, 112–13, 115
homosexuality, 111–16
homosociality, 53–54, 63, 68, 93, 98, 108, 112–13, 115
Hong, Grace Kyungwon, 80
"hooch," 76
Hope, Ishmael, 83
Hopkins, Amy, 97
Hopkins, Sally Shx̱aastí, 97
Hoy, C. D., 120
Hubbard, Bernard, 145
Huhndorf, Shari, 2–3, 15, 102
hypervisibility, 10, 14

immigration: Asian, to Alaska, 6, 14; Chinese, 6, 32, 38–39, 42, 53, 61–63, 66–67, 74, 89, 99; gold rush and, 42; labor and, 32, 39–40, 42, 89; liminality and, 120–21. *See also* gold rush
imperialism, 2–3, 14–15, 97, 151; abolition and, 28; in Philippines, 111; time and, 24–25
Indianness, 21, 31–32
Indigenous: Asianness and, 39, 42–43, 48; assimilation, 23; in *Blonde Indian*, 46; citizenship, 31; feminism, 24, 109, 115–16; food practices, 106; Jesup North Pacific Expedition and, 41; labor, 89–90, 95–98, 114; lynching and, 72; place names and, 64; racialization, 28; sovereignty, 22, 125; studies, 107, 122; Sumner and, 25–26; as term, xv
individualism, 22, 52, 90, 102
Industrial Workers of the World (IWW), 83, 92–93, 98–104, 175n54, 175n56, 176n57
internment, 1, 122, 143–44, 150, 155, 157–58
intimacy, 11, 22, 53, 57, 68, 79–80, 84, 113–14, 134
Iñupiaq (Iñupiat), xvi, 3, 145, 164n5
Irmscher, Christoph, 164n21
Ismail, Qadri, 34
IWW. *See* Industrial Workers of the World (IWW)

Jackson, Billy, 136, *136*, 138
Jackson, Sheldon, 36, 42, 132
James, Susie Kaasgéiy, 98
Japanese: immigrants, 6; in Hawaiʻi, 162n21; internment of, 1, 143, 155, 157–58; investigations of, 142–43; racialization, 39; workers, 83, 88, 92, 99–100, 111, 173–74n29, 176n59
Jesup North Pacific Expedition, 41–42
Jones, Livingston, 33–34
Jones, Zachary, 169n43
Juneau, Joe, 54, 77, 168n16
Juneau High School, 155

Kamehameha I, 8
Kan, Sergei, 164n10
Kanaka Maoli (Kānaka Maoli), 9, 162n19, 183n105
Karuka, Manu, 15, 175n49
Kauanui, J. Kēhaulani, 162n6
Ḵawa.ée, 55
Kayamori, Shoki, 118–31, *126*, *128*, *130*, *133*, 133–44, *136*, 152–54, *153*, 178n2, 179n16, 179n22, 180n32
Ketchikan, 85–88
Killisnoo, 146–48, 151, 158

Kim, Jodi, 122, 152
Kingston, Maxine Hong, 51, 168n5
Kitka, Herman, 94–95
Klondike Gold Rush, 51–52, 168n6
Knack, Martha, 95
"Koloschians," 25–26
Kunz, Cecilia Kintoow, 78, 80–81, 168n16, 172n91
Kunz, Edward, Jr., 172n91

labor: Chinese, 32, 39–40, 42, 57, 61–63, 66–67; family and, 110; Indigenous, 89–90, 95–98, 114; racialization and, 26, 30, 38–40, 42–43, 100; racism and, 99; sexuality and, 109–10; unions, 83, 90, 92; women and, 93–98, 107–9, 113–15. *See also* canneries; gold rush
LaDuke, Winona, 175n49
languages: bilingualism, 38; China Joe and, 58–59; diversity of, in Alaska, 3; orthography used with, xvi
Latinx, xvi–xvii, 171n71
Lawrence, Bonita, 8
Lawson, Angelica, 180n37
Le, Quynh Nhu, 151, 166n55
Lee, Erika, 169n21
Lee, Rachel, 113–14
Lee, Robert G., 92
Life Woven with Song (Dauenhauer), 104, 177n83
liminality, 14, 113, 119–22, 124, 143
Linnaeus, Carl, 24
liquor, 75–77
literature, 52, 111–16
Little, Frank, 101–2, 176n70
Littlefield, Alice, 95
Local 283, 83, 92–94, 100, 111, 173n26
"logic of elimination," 22–23
London, Jack, 52, 58, 167n1, 168n12
Lon Wun Gee Café, 125, *126*
Lorde, Audre, 168n5
Lowe, Lisa, 11, 84, 113–14
Lye, Colleen, 168n12
lynching, 54, 70–74, 77–78, 82, 170n63, 171n79, 172n81

Makarin, Irene, 182n87
male sex workers, 111–16
Mallott, Byron, 178n1
Marvin, Amy Ḵooteen, 95
Marx, Karl, 95, 97
Marxism, 95–96
masculinity, 27, 51–53, 63, 68–69, 77–78
Matsura, Frank, 120
Mawani, Renisa, 8, 76
Mbembe, Achille, 70, 75
men: in sex work, 111–16. *See also* masculinity
Merrill, E. W., 180n47
Merriman, E. C., 71, 147
Messerschmidt, Gustav, 80
militarism, 139–52
Miller, Frances, 27, 165n27
Miller, Gwen, 27, 149
mimesis, 29, 40
mimicry, 29–30, 40
misogyny, 114, 146
modernity, 13, 34, 43, 45, 70, 73–75, 77, 94–95, 108, 116–17, 122, 136, 143, 157, 159, 165n45
Mongol(ian), 20, 29, 33, 37; as term, xv
Morgensen, Scott, 70, 116
Muir, John, 19, 33, 40, 132
multiculturalism, 9–10, 18, 101, 113, 125–26

naming, of places, 64
Naske, Claus-M., 173n25
Native: as term, xv
Nebolon, Juliet, 183n105
necropolitics, 69–79
Ngai, Mae, 120
Nishnaabeg, Michi Saagig, 98
North American Indian, The (Curtis), 132
"North by Northwest" (Blue Scholars), 83
Northwest Passage, 8

O'Brien, Jean, 13
Office of Indian Affairs (OIA), 5, 30–31, 145, 150
OIA. *See* Office of Indian Affairs (OIA)

Okamura, Jonathan, 9
Omatsu, Glenn, 92, 99
"One Hundred Years of Japanese Labor in the USA" (Yoneda), 92
On the Origin of Species (Darwin), 24
Organic Act, 73, 84, 88
"(dis)Orient" (Stevens), 19
Oriental, 21, 88; as term, xv
orientalism, 6, 13; Alaska Natives and, 132; commercial, 36; mimicry and, 40; patrician, 35–36; settler, 36; tourism and, 32–33. *See also* settler orientalism
Orientalism (Said), 19
orthography, xvi, 161n2

Pacific Monthly (magazine), 59
Panama Canal, 3
Paquette, MaryAnn, 125, 142
Parsons, Lucy, 101, 176n58
paternalism, 26, 57, 145
Pearl Harbor, 1, 142
Philippines, 3, 27, 111
photography: of Curtis, 132, 134; of Kayamori, 118–20, *119*, 121–31, *126*, *128*, *130*, *133*, 133–35, *136*, 136–37, *139*
Piatote, Beth, 22, 37
Pierce, W. H., 171n76
Pierrepont, Edward, 70–71, 78
Pierrepont, Edwards, 70
Pike, Warburton, 62
Pilz, George, 54–55
place names, 46, 64
"Poem for Jim Nagatáak'w (Jak̲wteen), A" (Dauenhauer), 104
poetry, 104–11
polygenism, 25
Pond, E. Percy, 129, 180n47
pornography, 180n31
Powell, Caroline, 178n1
Pribilof Islands, 15
print culture, 55–59
prohibition, 75–77
promiscuity, 84–85

queer sociality, 112

racial capitalism, 9–11, 17, 84, 108, 116, 146, 158
racialization, 5–6; alcohol and, 75–76; capitalism and, 11–12; China Joe and, 63, 68; ethnography and, 40–41; government and, 21–22, 30, 48; imperialism and, 14; Indianness and, 31–32; Kayamori and, 124–25; labor and, 26, 30, 38–40, 42–43; liminality and, 122; orientalism and, 145, 156; Seward and, 28–29; time and, 91; tourism and, 33–35, 38–39; of Alaska Native women, 105, 113
racism: Japanese internment and, 150; labor and, 99–100; orientalism and, 13; scientific, 24, 166–67n78
Raibmon, Paige, 38, 137, 165n45
Reese, Richard, 126, 179n22
Reiquam, Peter, 155
relocations, 1, 26, 143–44, 146–51
Rennie, Dick, 71
Rifkin, Mark, 34–35, 110, 166n55, 177n100
Robinson, Cedric, 11
Rodrigue, Barry, 176n64
romantic anticapitalism, 78, 85, 90–91, 93, 99, 102, 103, 107, 116
Roots: An Asian American Reader (anthology), 92
rope, 77–78
Russell, Caskey, 108
Russia, 15, 26–27, 65, 124, 144, 148. *See also* fur trade
Said, Edward, 19, 21
salmon, 86–87. *See also* canneries
"Salmon Egg Puller—$2.15 an Hour" (Dauenhauer), 104–11
salvage anthropology, 135–36
Saranillio, Dean, 9
schools, 19, 22–24, 36–38, 44–45, 59, 133–34, 155
scientific racism, 24, 166–67n78
Seattle, 168n9
segregation, 45, 80
Seminole, 163n24
Service, Robert, 52, 65
settler colonialism: and Alaskan purchase, 2–3; arrivant colonialism and, 10–11, 111,

163n24; Asian America and, 7; in *Blonde Indian*, 46–48; capitalism and, 11, 85, 96, 107–8, 116; Chinese labor and, 40; colonialism *vs.*, 15; defined, 7; elimination and, 22–23, 98; family and, 37–38; gold rush and, 51, 60; in Hawai'i, 9–10, 125; heteronormative, 112; imperialism and, 140, 159; intimacy and, 53; Kayamori and, 119–24, 134, 139; militarism and, 151–52; necropolitics of, 69–79; racialization and, 6, 12; settler imperialism and, 15; sex work and, 115; sovereignty and, 122; space-time colonialism and, 157. *See also* colonialism
settler (colonial) space, xv, 13–15, 21, 43, 46, 48, 69, 73–75, 81, 117, 121, 124, 157
settler (colonial) time, 12–15, 18, 43, 46, 73–75, 77–78, 91, 95, 116, 122–123, 136, 138, 157
settler orientalism: Alaska purchase and, 20; in *Blonde Indian*, 23–24; China Joe and, 53; racialization and, 35, 37, 53, 82, 145, 156. *See also* orientalism
Seward, William H., 2–3, 27–29
sexuality, 84–85, 109–16
sexual violence, 109
sex work, 109–16, 177n95
Shah, Nayan, 73–74, 112
Sheep Creek Mary, 55
Shtax'héen Ḵwáan, 64, 169n43
Silva, Noenoe K., xvi, 161n6
Simpson, Audra, 98
Simpson, Caroline Chung, 143
Simpson, George, 165n26
Simpson, Leanne Betasamosake, 110
Simpson, Peter, 138
Sitka Industrial and Training School, 19, 36–37, 134
Sitka Mission School, 36
"Siwash," 20
slavery, 11, 27–28, 163n24, 171n79
Soboleff, Vincent, 180n47, 181n54
Soboleff, Walter, 138
social Darwinism, 20, 37
Socialist Party of California, 100
solidarity, 54, 80–81, 93, 98–104, 113, 176n57

sovereignty: elimination of Indigenous, 22; erotics of, 110; imperialism and, 151; Indigenous, 22, 125; multiculturalism and, 125; third space of, 122, 131–39
space-time colonialism, 12–16, 54, 77–78, 122, 145, 152, 157
spatial exclusion, 13
Stark, Heidi Kiiwetinepinesiik, 73
Starr Dalton, Jessie, 96
statehood movements, 9–10, 122
stereotypes, 128–29, 132, 168n12
Stevens, James Thomas, 19
subsistence, 126–27, 179n26
Sugpiaq (Sugpiat), 26, 33, 147; as term, xvi
Sumner, Charles, 25–27, 164n22–164n23, 165n26
surveillance, 40, 47, 57, 107, 111–12, 117, 122, 141
survivance, 23, 164n15
Swedish Mission Covenant of America, 133
Swineford, Alfred P., 39, 58
Systema Naturae (Linnaeus), 24

Takaki, Ronald, 93
"Talking with Nora" (Hope), 83
Tanaka, John, 155, 158–59
Tanaka, Nobu, 158
Tanaka, Shonosuke, 158
Tchen, John Kuo Wei, 35–36
terminology, xv–xvii
Thomas, Margaret, 180n32
Thomas, Mary, 127, 128, 129–30
Thornton, Thomas, 64
Thrush, Coll, 110
time: imperialism and, 24–25; linear, 12; racialization and, 91; settler colonial, 13–15, 18, 91, 95, 116, 123; spatialized, 24–25
Teel' Tlein 147
Tlingit, 26–27, 29, 33, 55, 64–65, 86, 121, 137, 146–47; as term, xvi, 161n2
Tlingit renaissance, 108
"To Build a Fire" (London), 52, 167n1
Tongass Packing Company, 85–86
tourism, 22, 32–39, 47, 51, 164n10
Trask, Haunani-Kay, 9

Travels in Alaska (Muir), 19
travel writing, 32
Treadwell, John, 66–67, 81
Treadwell mine, 66
treaties, 4–5, 162n6
Treaty of Cession, 5, 72
Tsimshian, 26, 33, 86
Tubman, Harriet, 28
Tuck, Eve, 11, 146
Twitchell, X̱'unei Lance, xvi

Unangax̂, xvi, 1, 15, 26, 29, 33, 122, 144–51, 182n87, 182n92
Under Mount Saint Elias: The History and Culture of the Yakutat Tlingit (de Laguna), 135
unions, 83, 90, 92–94, 98–104
University of Alaska, 181n70

Veracini, Lorenzo, 120
violence: China Joe and, 53, 68–69; colonial, 57, 170n63; dehumanization and, 74; gold rush and, 53, 68–74, 76–79, 172n81; lynching, 54, 70–74, 77–78, 82, 170n63, 171n79, 172n81; of militarism, 139–52; sexual, 109
Vizenor Gerald, 23, 164n10

Walker, Francis A., 5–6, 30–31
Wanamaker, Randy, 158
Wanamaker, William, 174n39, 183n4
Wawa, 163n3
Weed, Thurlow, 27
white masculinity, 51–53, 63, 77–78
whiteness: Asianness and, 30; China Joe and, 68, 78; and hegemony, 62

whites: in canneries, 88; gold rush and, 63; heroism and, 49, 58–59, 63, 90; as majority, 15; as tourists, 36, 39
white supremacy, 22, 38, 112, 129
Williams, Carol, 132
Williams, Maria Shaa Tláa, 2, 6
Williams, Raymond, 34, 177n100
Winnemucca, Sarah, 175n49
Winter, Lloyd, 129, 180n47
"Wobblies," 100–101, 176n57
Wolfe, Patrick, 22–23, 57, 75
Woman's Trip to Alaska, A (Collis), 19
women: labor and, 93–98, 105–9, 113–15; photography of, 127, 127–28, 128–29; pornography and, 180n31; racialization of, 105, 113; in sex work, 109–10; as tourists, 22, 36–37. *See also* feminism
Woodman, Abby Johnson, 33, 42
Worl, Rosita K̲aaháni, 78, 172n91
World War II, 1, 15, 122, 139–52, 182n92, 183n105
Wyatt, Victoria, 174n38

xenophobia, 69, 90

Yaakwaan, Jake, 78
Yakutat, 118–19, *119*, 121–25, 134–35, 137, 140, 178n1, 178n4
Yanagimachi, George, 88
Yang, K. Wayne, 11, 146
Yeesganaalx̱, 81
Yoneda, Karl, 92, 111, 113, 174n31
Yoshihara, Taro, 176n73
Young, S. Hall, 43
Yule, Emma Sarepta, 59
Yup'ik (Yupiit), xv, 3, 164n5

Printed in the USA
CPSIA information can be obtained
at www.ICGtesting.com
LVHW040612270924
792249LV00002B/148